Family Finance

An easy to read guide to
solving your money problems

Colm Rapple

With many thanks to the efficient subs Nuala and Simone and all who have helped over the years with information and advice.

ISBN 0 95300423 6
ISSN 0790-9683

Published by SQUIRREL PRESS

Cover designed by KAREN DOYLE

Printed and bound in Ireland
by βETAPRINT, Dublin.

By The Same Author
Your Guide to Pensions, Squirrel Press
Start Your Own Business, Ward River Press
Living with the Recession, Ward River Press

Contents

Checklists

Checklists for a new millennium

1

Tax changes have been coming fast and furious over recent years at the same time as the financial environment has been undergoing a rapid transformation. Income tax allowances have been mostly standard rated and will be replaced from April 2001 with tax credits. Income tax rates have been cut and the standard rate band widened and individualised in the case of two-income married couples. The inheritance tax rules have been eased and the family home exempt from the tax in certain circumstances. The financial environment is changing in many other ways. Having fallen to historical lows in the wake of our entry to Euroland interest rates are moving up again. House prices continue to soar although the rate of increase is slowing down. Incomes have been rising well ahead of inflation and the improving trends seem set to continue into the new Millennium.

Making the best use of the extra money requires some consideration and the right decisions. You can save tax by making the best possible use of allowances and reliefs. All it requires is a bit of knowledge and some planning. The end result can be very worthwhile. The drop in interest rates is good news for borrowers but it is more important than ever for savers to look for the best rates. There is plenty of scope for saving money in other areas too. Increased competition in the financial services sector is bringing prices down for those willing to shop around. All of these changes in the financial environment and in the budget, have implications for personal finance decisions. Past decisions need to be reviewed and altered if necessary in the light of the new circumstances. The following checklists may be used as a guide referring you to more detailed information elsewhere in the book.

Savings and investments

Low interest rates are a mixed blessing — good for the borrower but not good for the saver. Competitive pressures pushed up deposit rates late in 1999 and there is a wide range of investment funds that can yield higher returns. It is possible to have the capital guaranteed. It's a time for shopping around. There can be a significant difference in the potential returns so it pays to take a little time to consider the options.

Details can be found as follows:

Managing your budget

Simply managing your money between paydays has tended to become more complicated and more expensive. Banks are tending to charge more for some services but an increasingly diverse range of money transfer facilities for paying bills are becoming available.

Details of the options are given in **chapter two:**

Tax

It is surprising how many people do not even bother to check their certificate of tax free allowances, let alone look for legitimate ways of reducing their tax bill. The taxman can make mistakes on the certificate of tax free allowances but most errors are the fault of the tax payer himself. With all the changes currently taking place it is more important than ever to check. People often fail to claim all the allowances to which they are entitled. For the PAYE payer whose allowances are increasing — higher medical insurance premiums, medical expenses, rent in some circumstances or higher mortgage interest as a result of moving house — any delay in claiming the additional allowances is simply money lost. Tax reliefs can be backdated when you claim them but in the meanwhile you will have been out of pocket. Each successive budget brings changes in the tax code which may warrant some action. New taxes are imposed, old concessions closed off and new concessions introduced. There are plenty of old concessions still around, of course. Even PAYE taxpayers can take part of their income out of the income tax net by putting money into a pension fund, making use of proft sharing schemes, or by investing in a company under the Business Expansion Scheme. For more information see:

Life assurance

It's important to review your life assurance from time to time making sure that you have adequate cover. Pure life cover, the type which only pays out if the insured person dies within a fixed term of years, is relatively cheap. But the dearest company may charge you over twice the premium you'd pay to the cheapest company for exactly the same cover. So you do need to shop around or get someone to shop around for you. You may also want to consider insurance-linked saving plans as a vehicle for long term saving. Do not, however, get the two roles mixed up. And don't forget that there are two parents in most families whose lives may need to be covered by assurance. Life assurance as family protection is examined in **chapter four.** The topics covered include:

House insurance

The house insurance market has become more expensive but also more competitive over the past few years. So it pays to shop around. You could, just possibly, halve your insurance costs by changing companies. And check just what cover your policy provides: Does it cover the present day values of your house and contents; just what does the fine print exclude. Policies differ greatly in both cover and price. It makes sense to shop around well before the premium is due and also to update your cover with regard to the current value of the house and contents.

See **chapter nine** for an outline of what the basic policy normally covers:

Borrowing

Increased competition in the market brought mortgage rates down during 1999 while some other rates were tending upwards. Borrowing can still be expensive but competition means that its a good time to review your borrowings. Apart from shopping around to get the cheapest rate on fresh loans, there may be some advantage in switching your existing borrowings.

Remember that the lenders want your custom. They are not doing you a favour. It is the other way around. Without your custom, they wouldn't make any profits.

The options are looked at in **chapter five.**

Wills

If you are over eighteen and have not made a will, it is time to do so. It is downright irresponsible for a married man or woman with children not to have a will drawn up. Indeed, both spouses should have wills drawn up. If you have made a will, check it to see that it still reflects your wishes. Circumstances change. Is the executor you named still willing and able to act? Have you thought of the possible tax implications? The inheritance tax rules have changed but its still there. There are ways of reducing future liability to inheritance taxes. Wills are covered in **chapter seven.**

Pension rights

It is never too early to start planning for your retirement. If you are self-employed you need to make your own provisions. The rules governing pension contributions that provide now allow much greater flexibility in what can be done with the pension fund. If you are in a company scheme you are not precluded from looking for improvements or, at least, making extra voluntary contributions yourself in order to secure higher benefits. But you need to take stock of where you are and where you want to be. Within generous limits, contributions to pension funds are allowable in full for tax relief.

Social welfare

The social welfare code is constantly changing. You could be entitled to some assistance. Unless you claim your entitlements you are unlikely to get them:

Self-employed

A growing number of people are now self-employed either by choice or necessity. They face the same range of personal finance problems as anyone else except they can be even more complicated and more time consuming. The tax changes in the December 1999 budget may have made it worthwhile employing a spouse. Most of the items covered in later chapters relate as much to the self-employed as anyone else but there are sections dealing specifically with their particular concerns. The following signposts some of them:

Tax on self-employed income — **page 242.**

PRSI — **page 182.**

Motoring expenses — **page 247.**

Civil service motoring expenses — **page 314.**

Rental income — **page 246.**

Pensions — **page 178.**

Save tax by employing your child or your spouse — **page 266.**

Reducing inheritance tax liabilities — **page 268.**

Banking

Routine cash management 2.1

Most of the money which comes in each payday is spent before the next payday. Less and less of it is spent as cash. Increasingly money is being transferred either on paper or by computer from one account to another. This is true not only for the well-off. Many social welfare recipients can now have some of their bills paid directly by An Post from their weekly benefit payment. An Post does not charge for that service whereas most financial institutions do charge for handling your money and the charges have tended to rise.

But there is increased competition. The old traditional demarcation between banks, building societies and other financial institutions has broken down. Personal banking services are now provided by more than the high street banks. Indeed the definition of "high street bank" has been extended since two of the larger building societies, Irish Permanent and First Active gave up their mutual status and became banks in their own right and the remaining building societies have greatly expanded their range of services. Most of the institutions offering personal banking services provide fully fledged cheque book accounts while others offer banking facilities in a different way. They provide cash withdrawal services through ATMs and payment services by way of Laser Cards.

Introduced in 1996 the Laser card provides an electronic alternative to a cheque book. In all cases it is cheaper to use than a cheque. It is issued by all the larger banks and building societies and some don't charge for its use. There is more about the Laser card in chapter 2.2 which deals with plastic money.

Bank charges have become a bone of contention with many consumers but they are not the only factor to take into account

Avoid those unapproved overdrafts

Overdrawing your chequebook account without permission can be a very costly business, more so with some banks than with others. In all cases you will be charged a penal rate of interest on the overdrawn amount — perhaps six percentage points above the normal. On top of that you can be charged up to £3.50 per item. The cost can quickly mount up. Suppose you write one cheque which pushes you over the limit and then another three cheques, standing orders or direct debits are presented which push you further into the unapproved red you are charged an additional £3.50 per item — a total of £14.

The charges mentioned above are imposed when the bank actually honours the cheque, standing order or direct debit. But the bank may simply refuse to pay. In that case the person presenting the cheque for payment and the person who wrote it can end up paying other charges. The person who wrote the cheque — the drawer — loses some credibility, and maybe credit worthiness, too. The charges imposed are as follows:

Bank	Presenter	Drawer
AIB	£3.50	£5.00
Bank of Ireland	£2.60	£10.00
Irish Permanent Bank	£5.00	£5.00
Ulster Bank	£2.00	£10.00
National Irish Bank	£3.50	£3.50
TSB Bank	£3.50	£3.50
Tusa	£3.50	£3.50

So what can you do to avoid paying these charges? The best advice, of course, is not to overdraw your account at all. In that way you incur no penal charges and can qualify for free banking. But one of the advantages of a current account is that you can overdraw in times of need. To ensure that you have that flexibility make sure to negotiate an adequate overdraft permission. Check every now and then that it is still in place. If you think that you are going to exceed your permission, let the bank know in advance. Banks will normally be only too pleased to increase your overdraft permission. AIB and Ulster Bank charge £20 while Bank of Ireland charges £12 to approve an overdraft. The other banks make no standard charge although they may sometimes impose one.

when choosing a banking service. Cost is important but convenience is equally important. A few pennies saved in direct charges can easily be offset by inconvenience costs if, for instance, your bank or building society doesn't happen to have an ATM where you most need it.

So what is the best way to manage your money in the short term? There is no single choice suitable for all individuals. It depends on circumstances but most people need access to some method or methods of paying bills other than by cash. There are benefits in having wages paid directly into a financial institution provided there is ready access to your money through a good branch network, long opening hours, and/or cash dispensing machines. Access to short-term loans is also useful in meeting occasional heavy demands for money. Developing a track record with a financial institution which can provide longer term loans at competitive rates can also be a benefit. And you obviously want to do all that at the lowest possible cost. There are pluses and minuses for all the financial institutions. You need to weigh up the benefits and costs yourself. First you have to decide what you actually need. Let's consider some of the options and examine what's available.

Do you need a chequebook, for instance? Don't be too quick to answer yes! There are a growing number of alternative and cheaper ways of paying bills. And what else do you want the chequebook for? It used to be the case that only those with chequebooks had access to overdrafts and overdrafts are the most flexible form of loan and can be the cheapest. The interest rate is low and the flexibility keeps interest costs to the minimum in that you only borrow what you need as you need it. But there are now current accounts which provide access to overdrafts without a chequebook. The building societies, EBS and Irish Nationwide operate such accounts. Customers use ATM/Laser cards to withdraw cash and make payments.

So if you need access to an overdraft — and more about overdrafts below — you have a wide range of alternatives. You have to ask yourself which is best and one of the considerations has to be cost. Interest rates can vary and some lenders charge an arrangement fee. Allied Irish Banks, Bank of Ireland and Ulster Bank, for instance, charge for approving an overdraft permission. Bank of Ireland charges £12 and the other two charge £20. Another cost factor is that once you get an overdraft on your account you generally lose any entitlement you might have to free banking.

Those extra costs may be small enough if you make good use of an overdraft permission.

> There are cheaper ways of paying bills than through a bank account. There are a growing number of alternatives.

Current account charges — a comparison

Transaction	AIB	B of I[1]	NIB	Ulster	TSB	Irish Permanent	Tusa
Paper	24p	22p	24p	25p	23p	25p[2]	20p
Automated	17p	22p	15p	18p	12p[3]	15p[2]	15p
Standing order setup	£3.00	nil	£2.70	nil	£2.50	nil	nil
Standing order fee	12p	12p	15p	12p	18p	nil	15p
Cheque card	£3.00	nil	£5.00	£5.00	£3.50	nil	nil
Overdraft permission[4]	£20	£12	nil	£20[5]	nil	nil	nil
Quarterly fee	£3.75	nil	£3.75	£4.00	£3.00	£5 to £15[6]	nil

1. Customers can choose to pay a flat £9 per quarter and get up to 90 transactions free, thereafter paying 22p per transaction.
2. First 25 transactions free each quarter. 3. Only on TSB's own ATMs — 18p from other ATMs. 4. Other banks may charge for overdraft permissions on a discretionary basis but the charges are not included in their standard schedule. 5. £10 for renewal.
6. Depending on the type of account.

Qualifications for free banking

No transaction charges are applied where customers meet the following conditions:

AIB: A minimum credit balance of £100 is maintained in the account during the accounting period; retired, widowed and customers over 60 years of age; members of institutions for the blind; full time students who stay in credit.

B of I: All customers over 60 years of age; full time students and recent graduates with Ascent accounts.

National Irish: If the account is kept in credit for the full charging period.

Ulster: If the account is kept in credit for the full charging period.

Tusa: Account holders over 60, full-time students and, for the first eighteen months, account holders who have their salaries paid directly into the bank. It is necessary to apply for exemption from the charges.

TSB: Customers over 60 years of age; accounts which never go under £100 credit or have maintained an average balance of at least £300. Students may also qualify.

Another factor to consider in choosing your banking service is your possible future needs. If you think you might need a business loan in the future then it may be worthwhile building up a record with one of the larger banks and establishing a relationship with a bank manager.

Most personal bank customers need a relatively small range of services. Most like to have their wages paid directly into some safe depository from which they can draw cash readily when needed, arrange to pay regular and irregular bills, and maybe get interest on any surplus. All of those services can be obtained free outside the main banks. Indeed most building societies already provide them to holders of saving accounts.

While there are fewer of them now, the building societies have a growing network of ATM machines and their cards can be used on other ATM networks. You can make direct debits or standing orders from the account — all at no charge. And if you want to send a once-off payment you can get a third party cheque from the building society office — again at no cost. The EBS, also offers an alternative way of paying bills by phone. Once you arrange in advance for particular payments — the ESB, telephone or gas bills, for instance — you can arrange for the payment to be made from your account simply by dialling a freephone number. The Irish Permanent which is now a bank rather than a building society, offers four different types of cheque book accounts with access to overdrafts and interest paid on credit balances.

There are ways of paying bills at no cost. Sending a cheque off by post is a very expensive way of paying a bill, indeed. It can cost as much as 62p. That is made up of 25p to the bank, 7p to the government for the stamp duty on the cheque, and 30p for the stamp. And that's not including the price of the envelope.

Paying the same bill by credit card costs nothing for the actual transaction. That's assuming you have a credit card. There is an annual stamp duty of £15 while some issuers impose their own annual charges of between £8 and £10 – see the table on page 27. But if you have a credit card you have already incurred those costs and hopefully you get that money back by making use of as much free credit as possible. If you always pay your bill in full and on time you'll pay no interest.

You can pay your telephone or gas bill in any post office. So there are plenty of alternatives. But a current account has its advantages and it doesn't cost the earth. You can reduce the cost by careful management. By meeting certain criteria you can qualify for free banking. The banks claim that most customers do. But you won't qualify if you run up an overdraft. So don't get overdrawn except for a reasonable amount. Use as few direct debits and standing orders as possible. That gives you the flexibility to delay payments when the finances are tight. A bit of careful management can work wonders.

But let's have a look at the alternatives in detail.

Banks

The Bank of Ireland, Allied Irish Bank, National Irish and the Ulster Bank are known as the Associated Banks but they are not the only banks offering services to personal customers. There's also the ACCBank, TSB, Irish Permanent and the new joint venture between TSB and Superquinn known as Tusa. Apart from their role as holders of savings, they all provide a wide range of services in lending money and in transferring it from one person to another. Some provide a larger range of services than others but to some degree or another they all provide a depository for savings, a source of loans, and a mechanism for transferring money.

Most of them offer customers a range of options. The traditional division was between a simple deposit account and the current (or chequebook) account. But bank services are changing rapidly with increasing emphasis on the expanding network of 24 hour automatic teller machines (ATMs) and, in the case of AIB and Bank of Ireland, on the provision of round the clock internet and telephone services.

Plastic money in the form of credit cards, ATM and Laser cards is growing in importance and there is an expanding range of account types combining various elements of the old deposit and current accounts. A bank account gives you access to all of these services and it also offers loan facilities. But let us first look at the different types of accounts available. They all have their different uses, advantages and disadvantages.

Current Accounts

The operative word is "current". It is the ideal place to keep money which will be spent in the short-term. The holder of such an account is normally given a cheque book and can write cheques which are, in effect, money. A lasercard is an alterna-

Joint accounts and inheritance

There are many reasons for opening a joint bank, building society or Post Office account. People sharing living expenses may find it the easiest way to operate. Elderly people sometimes open joint accounts with a relative or friend to ease access to their money. They may give the other person the right to withdraw money but they can also maintain that right themselves. In this type of situation the intention may be that the money will automatically pass to the survivor. But that is not always the case.

Indeed up to fairly recently the opposite was more often the case. Where there was a joint account into which one of the joint owners had contributed the money, the other account holder did not automatically acquire sole ownership of the funds after the death of the other person.

This had been decided in a court case back in 1932 where it was decreed that the money in such an account should pass into the estate of the deceased person to be divided up in accordance with the terms of any will or, where there was no will, the division laid down by the courts or the Succession Act. It was considered that this was necessary to curtail fraud and that it was an attempt to avoid inheritance taxes.

The precedent created by this judgment was effectively overturned by a later Supreme Court in a ruling on a new case. It concerned an elderly woman who opened a joint account with a niece. She clearly wanted her niece to inherit the money after her death but also wished to retain sole access to the account during her own lifetime. Both aunt and niece were in the bank when the account was opened. Both signed the documentation. The account was made payable to the aunt or to the survivor. In other words only the aunt could withdraw money during her life time but it was her clear intention that after her death her niece should have access to the money.

After her death other claimants to her estate took a case against both the niece and the bank and a lower court found in their favour citing the 1932 case. That decision was appealed to the Supreme Court which found in favour of the niece. But the judgment does not give an automatic right of ownership to the survivor. There should be no problem, of course, where account holders have each contributed to the account but where only one has contributed, the other or others will gain ownership where there was a clear indication that this was the deceased person's intention.

So the advice is in a case like this to make the intention clear in writing. Money in a joint account escapes the two per cent Probate Tax in the event of death but it may still be liable to Capital Acquisitions Tax in the hands of the survivor — see page 263 for more details of inheritance tax and the transfer of assets on death.

Online banking – by phone and internet

Most banking services are now available over the phone or over the internet. AIB, Bank of Ireland, National Irish, TSB, Tusa and Ulster Bank all offer a basic range of telephone banking services including balance enquiries, payment of bills, and transfer of funds. It is also possible to order a chequebook or a statement over the phone. Some other financial institutions offer a more limit service. EBS, for instance, allows account holders to make payments to preselected companies over the phone.

The cost saving in doing your banking over the phone is in not having to visit your local branch. The charges are much the same as for other banking transactions and there is also the cost of the phone call – usually charged at the local rate once the call is made within Ireland. The benefits come by way of convenience. The service is available 24 hours a day either automatically using a touch tone phone or through a customer services operator.

In all cases you need a personal identification number (PIN) which you should never reveal to anyone. You also get a registration number. To use the service you are required to give your registration number and part of your PIN number, randomly selected. For instance you may be asked for the first, third and fifth digits of a six digit PIN number. The idea is that someone listening in will only get part of your PIN number and unless they listen in a few times they won't get it all. But there is obviously a security risk and care should be taken to ensure that people don't get the opportunity to assemble your full PIN number.

The banks advise you not to write your PIN number down but with a six-digit PIN number together with a registration number that advice is likely to be ignored. You can change your PIN number to one that is easier for you to remember but beware of picking something obvious like your birth date.

Only AIB and Bank of Ireland are currently offering banking over the internet. They both offer a range of services. You can check the balance on your account and details of recent transactions. You can view details of your standing orders, if any, and check if cheques have been paid. You can transfer funds between accounts that you have with the same bank and pay bills to nominated utilities such as ESB, Eircell, and Eircom. You can also access details of your credit card account for at least twelve months back. Normal transaction charges are applied.

The security considerations are the same as with telephone banking with the added need to ensure that you are connected to the right website on a secure line. Your web browser should confirm that you are on a secure line. As with telephone banking you are asked for some digits from your PIN number.

tive. Where cheque books are given it is given as well. The bank may also issue a Bankers' Card which guarantees that any cheque written by the holder, up to one hundred pounds in value, will be honoured even in certain countries abroad.

Normally, of course, the cheque is covered by funds which the current account holder has in the bank, but he may be given an overdraft permission, which allows him to borrow money over and above what he has in the bank by simply writing cheques as he needs the money. Overdrafts are one of the cheapest forms of loan in interest rate terms and they are also the most flexible available so it is worth having access to them. The interest is only charged on the amounts actually withdrawn and at the same rate as on term loans. Borrowing options are dealt with in detail in chapter 5.

A chequebook and an overdraft permission does provide a valuable degree of financial flexibility. With an overdraft you only pay interest on the amount you actually overdraw but operating a current account can cost you money over and above any interest you pay. In addition to the charges imposed by some banks for approving overdraft permissions there are also usually transaction charges although these may be waived if certain conditions are met.

Current accounts can be expensive to operate but they do give access to the cheapest possible loans.

If you do not qualify for free banking then you become liable for fixed quarterly maintenance charges and additional charges for every transaction made. Each paper transaction i.e. lodgement, cheque, withdrawal etc., costs at least twenty to twenty-six pence, depending on the bank. Writing a cheque costs more because of the additional Government stamp duty of 7p charged on each cheque. Even if you are eligible for free banking you still pay that stamp duty. You can avoid the stamp duty by using a Laser Card. This facility is included on your cheque or ATM card. For more on Laser Cards see chapter 2.2. They are an alternative to a cheque book but in most cases you are liable for a charge on each transaction. If you are doing a lot of shopping it would be cheaper to use your ATM to withdraw cash and use it for the transactions. That way you only incur one transaction charge. Alternatively you could use the cashback facility on the laser card to cut down on your transaction costs.

The table on page 16 gives details of current account charges. They are the charges which apply on current accounts held by personal customers. Higher charges generally apply to business accounts.

Deposit accounts

The distinction between a current and deposit account is far from clear cut. Originally a deposit account offered limited withdrawal facilities. They weren't designed to facilitate regular transactions. They were a place to save and keep money. But that's changed. Most banks now provide account holders with ATM cards so that the holder has 24 hour access to his or her money. They may also be provided with a Laser card which is, in effect, an electronic chequebook. The only remaining difference between this new form of deposit account and a current account is that there is no chequebook supplied. There may be transaction charges and, of course, the interest paid is not as good as on accounts with a longer notice of withdrawal. It is usually not possible to get an overdraft but some banks do offer overdraft facilities on non-chequebook accounts.

Building Societies

There are now only two independent building societies left – the EBS and the Irish Nationwide. The ICS is really a subsidiary of the Bank of Ireland. The societies have greatly enlarged their branch network in recent years and now have outlets in most large cities and towns. They also have their own ATM network. So for the bulk of the population there is little problem depositing funds or arranging withdrawals.

Both EBS and the Irish Nationwide provide account holders with Laser Cards. Both offer access to overdrafts at competitive interest rates and also provide other current account facilities such as standing orders and direct debits.

Building societies now offer almost as wide a range of services as the bigger banks.

But there is usually a hidden cost in opting for an account which provides ready access to your money. You have to accept a lower interest rate than you would get on longer term deposits. However, on ordinary demand accounts the interest rate is usually competitive with the big banks. Often it is a little higher. There is no difference in terms of tax.

Post Office Savings Bank

An Post schemes are, of course, government guaranteed so, in terms of security, they are second to none. It offers a number of different savings schemes, but in this chapter we will only consider the normal Post Office savings deposit account. This is the one most suited to the short-term saver who want to have speedy access to his or her money. There are other schemes aimed at regular savers or those with lump sums to invest either for growth or income. These are considered in the next chapter. As we mentioned, security is no problem and neither, indeed, is ease of access. The Post Office has about 1,400 branches throughout the country and they stay open six days a week and for longer hours than banks. There is no limit on withdrawals at the main post offices – there are about 1,000 of them known as Service Plus Post Offices. At smaller post offices the maximum withdrawal on demand is £500. Some form of identification is required.

As an adjunct to the normal Post Office deposit account there are schemes aimed at encouraging saving. Group schemes are organised in work places and schools, and there is a savings stamp scheme specially for children. There is also the Instalment Savings Scheme which is also dealt with in the next chapter. Here we are only concerned with money management and short term savings and An Post provides a good basic service. Interest on an ordinary post office savings account is credited on a daily basis. The interest rate is normally as good or better than that given by most of the banks on small deposits. Accounts can be opened in joint names with one or both signatures required for withdrawals. In addition to the ease of access it is possible to pay a range of household bills at the post office counter and buy postal orders or money orders. Some offices also provide a bureau de change service.

The Post Office does not lend money, so no matter how good your record of saving, you won't be able to get a loan if you need it.

Credit Unions

Credit unions are co-operative non profit making ventures established within a community covering perhaps a locality or a work place. Through that community all the members enjoy what is known as a "common bond". Their basic role is to encourage saving and provide loans but they are in the process of greatly expanding the range of financial services they provide. New laws which came into force on October 1, 1997 provided the framework for that expansion which is already underway.

There are over 500 credit unions in Ireland with about 2 million members and £2,800 million in savings. Before the new legislation members could hold no more than £6,000 in a share account. Additional savings were kept in deposit accounts. The limits on share accounts, deposits and the size of loans have been significantly increased. Members can now have savings of up to £50,000 subject to the amount being no more than 1 per cent of the Credit Union's total assets. Individual loans may not exceed 1.5 per cent of a credit union's assets although loans up to £30,000 are allowed even if they breach that 1.5 per cent rule.

In addition to being a home for savings and a source of loans many credit unions operate budget accounts which provide for the payment of regular bills. Members may also have access to group rate VHI premiums which offer a 10 per cent discount on individual rates and increasingly credit unions are providing a wider range of financial services. Most are members of the Irish League of Credit Unions which provides insurance services. A growing number of credit unions are issuing ATM cards to their members and many have or will have some or all of the following: chequebook accounts, credit cards, and facilities for direct payment of wages and social welfare benefits into credit union accounts.

The interest paid on deposits and the dividends paid on share accounts vary from credit union to credit union. But the rates are likely to be higher than bank rates during times of relatively low market interest rates as at present. No DIRT tax is stopped on the interest although it is considered to be taxable income and some have devised ways of paying tax free dividends in the form of bonuses. So members can be sure of getting a good deal in the knowledge that all 'profits' are either paid out in dividends or ploughed back into the credit union.

A major benefit, of course, is the access to loans at reasonable rates of interest compared particularly to the more expensive finance houses — see chapter five. Most credit unions charge the maximum rate of 12.6 per cent APR but some give subsequent discounts out of whatever surplus is generated. Loan protection insurance providing for the repayment of the loan in the event of death or permanent disablement is included. Limits may apply to the size of the loan and the cover is curtailed for the over 60s and not available for the over 70s.

Another built-in insurance provides for the payment of a benefit to a member's estate in the event of death. In the case of a member aged under 55 the benefit is equal to the amount on deposit or in shares at the time of death. The benefit is lower for those over 55 and not applicable in the case of the over 70s.

Credit unions are offering a wider range of services — sufficient in many cases to cover many people's money management needs. If the offices are close to your home or in your work place it is obviously easy to deposit or withdraw money, although normally a week's notice is required for withdrawals. It depends on the credit union although the law requires a minimum notice of 60 days in the case of shares and 21 days in the case of deposits. Individual credit unions may, by rule, impose longer periods of notice, so it can vary from union to union.

The security aspect also varies from one credit union to another. Depositors are insured against loss resulting from fraud on the part of officials, and there is a savings protection scheme which covers loans up to £10,000. The Irish League of Credit Unions also provides back-up funds and assistance to member credit unions should they run into difficulties. Credit union members also have the benefit of knowing that theirs is a self-help non-profit making organisation.

2.2 Plastic money — use sensibly

Plastic money is increasingly replacing cash. It's safer and more convenient and now comes in a wide range of different forms. There are credit cards, charge cards, debit cards, ATM cards and cheque guarantee cards. And that doesn't exhaust the possibilities. There is a range of variants within most of those categories. The definition of plastic money can even be extended to include prepaid phone cards and the prepaid cash cards that are already on trial in Ennis.

As the range of options has extended so has the competition and the need for the consumer to understand the pros and cons, the costs and benefits. These options can be downright confusing by times. All forms of plastic money can be used to advantage but, without care, they can all prove costly in one way or another. The first step towards avoiding the pitfalls is to understand how the types of card differ. There is money to be saved by knowing what you need and by shopping around.

Plastic money

Let's have a quick overview of the types of plastic money before looking at each in more detail.

- **Credit cards** such as Mastercard and Visa give you instant access to credit. You can make a purchase or pay a bill and not have to part with any cash for almost two months. You get a statement each month and can either pay off in full to avoid interest charges or spread the payments over a period, effectively taking a loan.

- **Charge cards** issued by American Express and Diners Club as well as by Mastercard and Visa, offer the same facilities as credit cards — usually with a wider range of extra benefits — but you are expected to pay the bill in full each month.

- **Debit cards** such as Laser Card operate like an electronic chequebook. They allow the holder to make payments from their own bank or building society account. The card is used to make payments just as a cheque would be.

- **Cheque guarantee cards and ATM or cash dispenser cards** are often lumped in on a Laser card and provide the holders with cash withdrawal and cheque guarantee facilities linked to their bank or building society accounts.

Credit Cards — the costs

Issuer	Card	Interest rate	Annual Charge	Interest charged from
ACCBank	Visa	18.5%	None	Statement
AIB	Mastercard and Visa	20.9%[1]	£10[2]	Purchase[3]
Bank of Ireland	Mastercard and Visa	20.8%	£8[4]	Purchase[3]
EBS	Visa	20.9%	None	Purchase[3]
First Active	Visa	20.8%	£8	Purchase[3]
Hibernian	Mastercard	17.9%	£8	Purchase[3]
Irish Permanent	Visa	19.9%	£8	Purchase[3]
MBNA	Visa	18.9%	None	Purchase[3]
National Irish	Mastercard and Visa	18.2%	None	Purchase[3]
TSB Bank	Visa	18.9%	None	Statement
Tusa	Visa	17.5%	None	Statement
Ulster Bank	Mastercard and Visa	22.6%	None	Purchase[3]

Notes: 1. AIB offers a lower rate on a non-standard card with no free credit period. 2. Waived in the first year and thereafter if there have been 50 transactions with the card during the preceding year. 3. When charged to account. 4. Waived if there have been 60 transactions with the card during the preceding year.

Those are the basic forms of plastic money. Within each type there can be a wide variation. For instance there are "Gold Card" variants of credit and charge cards for people who are genuinely high spenders or for those who just want to pretend that they are. Interest rates vary greatly as do the extra add-on benefits.

So let's have a look at each option in some more detail.

Mastercard and Visa

Mastercard and Visa are both credit cards and come in a wide range of guises. While they have a global acceptance they are operated at a local level by individual banks and financial institutions who apply their own variations. Some banks will issue both cards. Mastercard is issued by the Bank of Ireland, Ulster and National Irish Bank while Visa is issued by Allied Irish Banks, Bank of Ireland, National Irish, TSB Bank, Irish Permanent Bank, ACCBank, EBS Building Society, First Active, MBNA and Tusa.

There are also so-called 'affinity' cards in the names of various organisations, universities and charities. The interest rates on such cards is usually lower and the credit card companies make payments to the organisation involved on the basis of a small percentage of the amount transacted on the card.

Eircell, the mobile phone company, also issues its own Visa card.

You do not have to be a customer of the issuing bank to get one and, indeed, it is possible to have both, either from the same bank — where they issue both — or from different banks. They are true credit cards which enable the holder to spread the cost of purchases, or cash withdrawals, over a period of months. And, of course, both provide some free credit.

Mastercard and Visa cost very little to obtain. Some issuers make no charge other than the annual Government stamp duty of £15. Bank of Ireland and Irish Permanent Bank charge £8 a year while Allied Irish Banks impose a supplementary charge of £10 on some holders. The charge is waived in the first year and also in subsequent years provided the card is used more than fifty times during the preceding year. So the minimum cost of a card is £15 a year — the stamp duty — but it can be as high as £25. If used wisely, however, that is the total annual cost and it can be more than repaid in free credit or just plain convenience.

There are four basic types of credit cards: the standard card, the low interest card, the gold card and the affinity card. Not all issuers have a low interest card.

- **Standard card**: With the standard card the customer is billed for purchases and payments once a month and then usually has about 25 days to pay. If the account is paid in full during that

> Credit cards are a boon if used wisely. That means paying up in full and on time each month.

period, no interest charges are incurred. But if the full amount is not paid by the due date, interest is charged at the rather high rate — it can be over 20 per cent. The interest is backdated to either the date of the statement or, in some cases, back to the date at which the transaction was presented for payment by the seller — sometimes the actual date of the transaction but seldom more than a day or two later. So it makes sense to pay on time, allowing a few days for your payment to get through the system.

In most cases interest is charged on cash withdrawals immediately from the date of the withdrawal so it is an expensive way of getting cash.

Interest rates do vary greatly — some of the rates applicable at the end of 1999 are shown in the table on page 27. But the interest rate shouldn't worry you because ideally you should always pay off the bill in full each month and never incur interest charges.

- **Low interest card:** These cards can be a better option for someone who wants a credit card and seldom, if ever, intends paying off the bill in full when the statement comes in. Just like the standard card a monthly statement is issued but interest is always charged from the date of the transaction so that even if the bill is paid in full there are interest charges incurred. But the interest rate is lower than on the standard card.

- **Gold card:** A gold card operates in the same way as a standard card but the credit limit is usually higher. There may also be a higher annual fee although not all issuers charge a fee. Most credit cards provide some add-on travel insurance — gold cards provide extra cover and may also provide easy access to personal loans. Holders have to satisfy an income qualification so they are also viewed as a status symbol.

- **Affinity card:** These are standard or gold cards issued in the name of some organisation such as a university, professional body, or charity that is given a small percentage of the money transacted on the card. Interest rates may be slightly lower than on similar non-affinity cards.

Those are the basic options and the competition for customers is keen although it is obvious that many card holders don't bother to shop around otherwise interest rates would have converged more. But some people do check out the rates on offer and some credit card issuers compete on rates.

MBNA, a US bank which offers no banking services in Ireland other than credit card services entered the market with a lower rate than any of the other card issuers. And more recently Tusa, the joint venture between TSB and Superquinn has issued a Visa card with an interest rate of 17.5 per cent.

The gap between the cheapest and dearest is significant ranging in late 1999 from a low of just 17.5 per cent to a high of almost 23 per cent. These are annual percentage rates (APRs) and even 17.5 per cent is a very high interest rate It is best not to borrow on a credit card at all. A significant proportion of credit card users do manage to do just that. You should try to be one of them. But it is all too easy to incur charges even by simply making a late payment so it obviously makes sense to get the cheapest card in terms of interest.

There are other considerations. Some issuers charge for their cards and the annual charge is not the only cost item. Don't forget the interest rate and there can be other charges. MBNA imposes a charge of £12 if a repayment is missed by even one day. AIB imposes a late payment charge of £3. Ideally, of course, you shouldn't incur either interest or late payments charges – not if you manage the account correctly.

AIB does offer a credit card without any annual charge but the interest rate is higher and you are required to pay within ten days of the statement date if you are not to incur interest. It also issues a low interest card with a rate of only 12.9 per cent but without any free credit period so that the interest starts accruing from the date a purchase is charged to the account.

There are other costs besides interest and annual charges. Some companies also make a flat charge for late payments. As mentioned above, if the minimum payment is not made on time MBNA makes a flat charge of £12. The commission charges on foreign transactions also vary from company to company.

Another factor to bear in mind is the date at which interest starts clocking up. As mentioned above, interest is charged on most cards from the date on which the bill is presented for payment by the retailer or trader. That can be a good deal earlier than the actual statement date. But with ACCBank and TSB Bank the interest is backdated only to the date of the statement. That can also save you a little.

It is well worth having at least one credit card. It can be worthwhile getting both a Mastercard and Visa card alternating their use to get the longest possible period of free credit. This simply means using the card whose bill you last received.

Both Mastercard and Visa offer up to £30,000 in free travel insurance if you buy your ticket with the card; and there are special discounts. These are perks which are often forgotten — keep the leaflets sent with the card. Both are accepted worldwide — Mastercard being interchangeable with Access and Eurocard. It is also possible to use them to withdraw cash abroad. With Mastercard there is no charge if you put money into your account so that it is in credit and then draw it out as needed during a holiday.

Some card issuers don't make any charge for cash withdrawals at home and others waive the charge when the account is in credit. This free withdrawal could be usefully employed as a means of sending money to family members abroad or vice versa. The parents of a child studying in England, for instance, can get an extra card on their Visa or Mastercard account and give it to the child. The parents can lodge money into the account and the child can draw it out through a bank automatic teller machine in England. It is completely secure and there is no cost involved.

Do not be tempted to make a habit of postponing payment of the accounts beyond the due date. If you find yourself permanently in debt to the credit card company you could save money by getting a bank loan at a lower rate of interest and paying off the credit card. If you have built up a credit card debt already, or intend making a big purchase get a term loan from one of the big four banks, or from a credit union. Any of those options would be far cheaper than borrowing on the credit card.

If you just tend to forget paying off your credit card bill there is always the option of signing a direct debit form. That allows the credit card company to either take the full payment or a minimum payment from your account. So the payment is made automatically. It's a good idea if you intend making the full payment each time. Opting to make partial payments is, in effect, accepting that you are going to remain all the time in debt to the credit card company. And given the interest rates charged, that's not a good idea.

Charge cards

The front runners in this area are American Express and Diners Card although both Mastercard and Visa also issue charge cards. Charge cards have particular attractions for individuals who are high spenders or who do a fair amount of travel. Both Mastercard and Visa can be used at a far greater number of outlets worldwide but, if the quantity of outlets accepting charge cards is smaller, the quality may be slightly better and the big spender will possibly find his charge card accepted in most of the outlets he will want to frequent.

The charge cards have another advantage. It is possible to use them as super cheque guarantee cards to get cash from one's own account. As mentioned above, if you borrow cash on your Visa or Mastercard card you are immediately liable for interest at up to 25 per cent.

With the charge card the cash can come from your own bank account incurring no interest if there is a credit balance in your account and only the relevant bank rate if there is not. With American Express, for instance, the ordinary card holder can cash personal cheques for up to £500 at any office of American Express worldwide. Within Ireland seven days must elapse between each encashment — abroad the period is 21 days.

Like credit cards, the charge cards offer some free insurance cover when you buy your travel tickets with the card — a point sometimes forgotten by the holders. Indeed the charge cards are more generous in this regard. For instance, if you have charged the cost of a scheduled flight to your American Express card and it is delayed for four hours or more, you can claim up to £50 for meals, refreshments and hotel accommodation. There is also insurance for lost or delayed luggage. Charge cards are, however, not free. In addition to the £15 stamp duty there is an annual subscription — it depends on the card but an annual charge of £37.50 a year is fairly typical.

Both American Express and Diners Club provide cash withdrawal facilities too. In addition to its cheque guarantee facility American Express can be used at cash dispensers world-wide. Diners Club lets you draw up to the equivalent of $1,000 in local currency each week from its dispensers.

Charge cards can provide an increased spread of outlets which may be important to the international traveller but most individuals will get by with Mastercard and Visa. The charge cards do provide emergency access to cash which may be important to some and worth the extra expense.

For those who travel a lot, the extra cost of getting one or both charge cards is possibly small when set against the extra flexibility and security provided. But for most individuals, the cheaper credit cards should be sufficient.

Gold cards

These are just super credit or charge cards for high fliers. There is a wide range on offer. At the upper end the American Express Gold Card, for instance, provides access to an un-secured borrowing facility of at least £7,500 from the Bank of Ireland; cheque encashment of up to £300 a day from Bank of Ireland branches and up to £1,000 from any American Express office during any 21 day period. It costs £70 a year plus the standard £15 annual stamp duty.

There are other similar super cards of the credit card variety and other "gold" cards that are little more than dressed up standard cards. The more services offering the higher the annual fee.

If you are the type of person who might make use of the facilities offered, the cost is possibly insignificant. Alternatively, you may be willing to pay for the impression a Gold Card can create. But that's hardly worth the extra cost for most people.

Laser cards

The Laser card is a debit card — a new generation of plastic money. In essence it is an electronic chequebook with an endless number of cheques. It is issued by ten banks and building societies linked to their current accounts. In most cases that means a chequebook account but some of the building societies which issue Laser Cards don't have chequebooks. Laser is used by almost 700,000 people. It is accepted in more than 13,000 retail outlets countrywide.

You use a Laser card as you would a chequebook. Payments made with a Laser Card are debited to the holder's account in exactly the same way as a payment made by cheque or a withdrawal from an ATM. The money may come out of your account a bit quicker but transaction charges are lower — there's no 7p stamp duty for one thing — and the upper limit for single payments is £1,000. Cheque payments are often limited to a maximum of £100 because that's the limit of the cheque guarantee card.

Apart from that limit the same sort of rules apply to the use of Laser as apply to the use of a chequebook. You should have the money in your account or an overdraft permission. If you run up an unapproved overdraft you'll be liable for heavy charges. They were outlined in the previous section.

The shops accepting the card are charged about 15p per transaction by the operators of the system — that amount varies from shop to shop and from issuer to issuer. In most cases the customer is charged for the transaction too, but paying by cheque would cost more. With most of the banks the charge is similar to that imposed on a transaction at an ATM. Some of the building societies charge nothing, however — see the table on page 35. Where charges are applicable they are added to the customer's current account in the normal way. But they are also waived in the normal way if the customer qualifies for 'free banking'.

There is no cost in actually getting the card. The facility has been bundled with existing ATM and/or cheque guarantee cards.

The main advantage of having a Laser card is that you don't have to carry cash around. For those liable for bank charges Laser is cheaper than writing a cheque for single transactions. But someone out on a mini spending spree could save money by withdrawing cash from an ATM and using it for his or her various purchases. An ATM withdrawal only attracts a single charge while there would be a separate charge for each Laser transaction. In some outlets shoppers are able to draw out up to £75 in cash in addition to paying for their purchases.

The mechanics of using a Laser Card are similar to using a credit card. You present your card to the sales assistant who 'swipes' it through the till and gives you a receipt to sign. The money doesn't come out of your account immediately although that will eventually be the case, no doubt. At present, however, the process takes a couple of days so that there is time to make a deposit to keep yourself in credit. But you would have to act quickly and make the lodgement at your own branch.

Store cards

Some of these are operated by the stores themselves but most are now operated for them by finance houses. There are a number of different types of account. There are monthly accounts which are like charge cards. The amount due has to be paid each month and no interest is charged. It is obviously a worthwhile facility to have if you do a lot of shopping in one store or with the one group.

Then there are budget accounts. The store generally sets a maximum credit limit calculated as a multiple of the minimum monthly payment. It may be twenty times so that if you are prepared to pay £50 a month, the limit is set at £1,000. The interest rate is usually quite high — about the same as on a credit card.

Laser Cards — who charges what?

Issuer	Type of card	Transaction charge
ACCBank	3 in 1 (ATM, cheque guarantee and Laser)	20p
AIB	2 in 1 (cheque guarantee and Laser)	17p
Bank of Ireland	3 in 1 (ATM, cheque guarantee and Laser)	22p[1]
EBS Building Society	2 in 1 (ATM and Laser)	nil
Irish Nationwide	2 in 1 (ATM and Laser)	nil
Irish Permanent	3 in 1 (ATM, cheque guarantee and Laser)	15p[2]
National Irish Bank	3 in 1 (ATM, cheque guarantee and Laser)	17p
TSB	3 in 1 (ATM, cheque guarantee and Laser)	18p or 20p[3]
Tusa	6 in 1 (ATM, cheque guarantee, Laser, Super Club, telephone banking registration, and Eircom charge card)	15p
Ulster Bank	3 in 1 (ATM, cheque guarantee and Laser)	20p

Notes: 1. There is an option of paying a flat fee of £9 a quarter for up to 90 transactions. Additional transactions are charged at 22p. 2. Free with some accounts. 3.The 18p charge is applied to Regular Current Accounts and the 20p to Current Account Plus

The credit limit remains set so that the customer can continue to buy more goods as the amount due goes down.

There are other accounts which are like a Mastercard or Visa account. They are known as option accounts and allow the customer to pay off in full at the end of each month — incurring no interest — or else make a minimum repayment and incur the interest. There is usually no charge for getting a card — other than the interest.

Store cards encourage you to shop in that particular store or group and not to shop around for the best price. A budget account may be worthwhile to cover the cost of a major purchase but not if the money could be borrowed from one of the larger banks instead. An overdraft or term loan would cost far less in interest charged. The advice must be to generally steer clear of store cards. Mastercard or Visa would provide similar benefits in most cases without the drawback of confining you to shopping in one store.

There may be some exceptions. Monthly cards involve you in no cost and you can benefit from promotions which stores sometimes put on for card holders — special sales and pre-Christmas openings for instance. Both Clerys and the Brown Thomas Group issue cards that are true credit cards. They can be used in any outlet. The Esso charge card is another exception in so far as it provides a company with a better control of spending on motor fuel. Companies with a number of people on the road can benefit from getting an itemised monthly account with the VAT shown separately. A lot of reclaimable VAT can be lost if the accountant has to rely on drivers keeping "invoices".

Cheque guarantee cards

To make full use of a cheque-book account you need a cheque guarantee card. It will cost you about £2.50 and guarantees your cheques up to a value of £100 each. Without the card you may find it very hard to cash cheques except where you are very well known. But remember that cheques are an expensive way of paying bills. It is far cheaper to pay by credit card provided you don't run up interest charges. If you need cash it is cheaper to draw money out of a bank machine. The charges for automated transactions are generally much lower and there is no stamp duty.

Automatic teller cards

All the major banks and the building societies have their own ATM cards and they all use different names. With AIB it is Banklink while Bank of Ireland has PASS; Ulster Bank has Service Till and the National Irish card is known as Autobank. The building societies operate the Cashere network.

All of the bank systems are interlinked so it is possible to use your bank card on any of the other banks' machines. On the basis of the queues it seems that many people don't realise this.

It is, of course, necessary to have an account with one of the institutions concerned and to either have some money in it or else have permission to overdraw. The machine is simply an automated teller and the transactions are just computerised versions

Plastic Money — Some Rules

Do not draw money on your Visa or Mastercard Card except in an emergency or unless you have already put the money in. The charges can be high and interest may start accruing immediately.

The accounts of charge cards like American Express and Diners Club must be paid in full each month. Otherwise penal charges are imposed.

Store cards are best avoided since they discourage shopping around, encourage overspending, and some charge hefty rates of interest.

Do not keep constantly in debt to the credit card company. The interest rates are too high. There are much cheaper ways of borrowing.

Take care of your vouchers. Remember they contain both your credit card number and a copy of your signature and could be useful to a fraudster.

Never reveal your PIN to anyone even if they claim to be from the credit card company.

Never leave your cards in your car. And don't leave them in the pocket of your jacket on the back of a chair in a restaurant or even at work.

Keep a couple of separate notes of your credit card numbers and the phone numbers of the relevant companies so that you can act quickly if they are lost or stolen.

If you want to be sure of paying off your monthly statement in full and on time arrange to do it by direct debit.

Make sure to check the accounts. Did you hear about the petrol pump attendant who regularly ran two slips off some cards? The spare one was put through for a fictitious fill of petrol a few days later. Slips can be altered and cards can be put through an electronic swipe machine twice.

Do not forget that there are other benefits going with most cards, like travel insurance. Read the leaflets fully and know what you are entitled to.

If you are making a large purchase and have the cash, see what sort of a discount you can get by offering it as an alternative to the credit card. Remember that the shop has to pay the card company a commission of up to 6 per cent.

Buy only from reputable firms over the phone or on the internet.

of what was, and still is, done at the bank counter. Most of the machines operate on a round-the-clock basis providing the most flexible way of getting ready access to cash.

Getting the necessary funds to pay for a holiday is not the only problem which has to be faced in this area. If you are going abroad there is also the question of getting the best exchange rate for your Irish pounds and also the matter of how best to carry your spending money.

The introduction of the euro, a single currency for eleven European countries, is going to simplify matters a lot but not just yet. Exchange rates between the eleven participating currencies have been fixed since January 1, 1999. The countries involved are: Austria, Belgium, Denmark, Finland, France, Germany, Italy, Luxembourg, Portugal, Spain and, of course Ireland. There is now no exchange rate risk between them so the charges for converting money have correspondingly been reduced. But the individual currencies will still remain until 2002. Britain remains outside the eurozone, of course.

There'll be no euro coins or notes in general circulation before January 1, 2002. By the end of June that year the national currencies will have been replaced by the new single currency. It is now possible to open euro bank accounts and to have euro chequebooks and make euro payments. But the absence of notes and coins means that such payments will be confined mainly to inter-business transactions. Some larger stores may accept euro payments but they are in the minority although as January 1, 2002 comes nearer many more stores will undoubtedly start displaying prices in both euros and the local currency.

Eventually, there will be a single currency area covering eleven countries and exchange difficulties will be totally eliminated within that zone. But the problems are going to remain for another couple of years and like most money problems there is no single correct answer. There are four basic options — the best solution contains elements of each. The mix depends on individual choice and also on the holiday maker's destination. A Visa card is great in Paris but it is not likely to be much use in an out of the way Greek island. But let us first have a look at the broad options:

Euro notes and coins won't be in circulation until January 1, 2002.

Cash

Cash is the most readily acceptable form of money — not Irish cash, of course, but rather the local currency. Some other currencies, such as the US dollar, the D-mark or sterling are also widely accepted in many popular holiday resorts. And in some developing countries there may be advantages in having a recognisable currency like dollars or D-marks. But apart from that, there is not much sense in changing Irish money into anything but the local currency.

The simplest thing, of course, is to change all your holiday money into local cash before you leave Ireland. You can shop around for the best exchange rate and incur only one set of commission charges. The only drawback is the risk — and it is a major one. Cash is too easily lost. But it is advisable to have some local cash to take with you — if only for incidental expenses when you arrive and maybe to carry you though a weekend if you arrive on a Friday night or Saturday morning.

Travellers' cheques

Travellers' cheques can be bought in a wide range of currencies and there is some advantage in buying cheques denominated in the local currency of wherever you are going. Usually a commission of 1 per cent to 2 per cent is charged when the cheques are bought and a further commission may be charged when they are cashed. The commissions vary from place to place. Remember that the cost includes not only those commissions but also the exchange rates you get.

If your cheques are not in the local currency it is better to cash them in a bank — shops and hotels often give bad exchange rates particularly those that don't charge a commission. There should be no commission on cashing local currency cheques, at least in banks, but that is not always the case. Sometimes those cashing travellers' cheques charge a fixed commission on each transaction, so using them for small purchases can be very expensive. It is better to change them in bulk every now and then in a bank — weighing the risk of holding the extra cash against the cost of a multitude of transactions.

Credit cards

The credit cards, Mastercard and Visa, together with the charge cards, American Express and Diners, can all be used abroad. Not all outlets accept them, of course. So in many continental countries — and particularly in the more remote areas — they cannot to be relied on. But they are, at the very least, a very useful standby and in the more popular holiday resorts they may cover most requirements — although they would always need to be supplemented with some local cash.

The cost of purchases abroad are translated into Irish pounds at the exchange rate on the day the item is debited to the credit card account — usually a very competitive rate. But some of the gains from the better exchange rate are offset by a commission charge. Most banks charge 1.75 per cent although some only charge 1.5 per cent. The Ulster Bank charges 2 per cent and MBNA 2.75 per cent. Those charges are waived or reduced in the eurozone.

But in addition to the charges interest is often applied on any cash withdrawal from the day it is made. You can get around this in some cases by lodging money to your account in advance. Some issuers pay interest on credit balances. The amount you can withdraw abroad varies but it can be as low as the equivalent of $200 a day.

So it's better to see the cash withdrawal facility as a useful standby for use only in an emergency. It can be a good idea to have your credit limit increased before you go on holiday to cover extra expense and emergencies. If you use your card to book your hotel or car hire the full amount of the expected bill may be immediately reserved against your card sharply reducing the credit available.

Read the section on credit cards on page 26.

Don't keep your PIN number with your card. Remember you may be held responsible for its fraudulent use if you have not taken adequate care. It is possible to draw up to $2,000 a day from some ATMs abroad.

Travel Insurance

Travel insurance can provide a real benefit in the form of peace of mind even if you never have to make a claim. But be sure to read the fine print and know exactly what you are covered for and what you have to do to make a claim. It's usually necessary to report any loss to the local police, for instance, and to make the claim within a fixed time period.

There are a wide range of policies available and the cover varies greatly: as does the cost. Travel agents normally offer insurance with their holidays and may charge an extra fee — perhaps £5 — if it is not taken out. But it can still be worthwhile shopping around. It is not too difficult to save £5 on a holiday insurance premium and still get wider cover. Don't forget that you may already have insurance cover for some risks. You may

Holiday checklist

A bit of advance planning can help you avoid some unpleasant financial surprises while on holiday. The following are some pointers:

Credit cards:

- Increase your credit limit just in case you need it — unless, of course, that might prove too much of a temptation to overspend.

- Check that the magnetic strip is in good order.

- Get additional cards for your partner.

- Get the PIN number to use for withdrawing cash if you don't already have it. If you haven't lodged money to your account in advance it can be an expensive way of getting cash but useful in an emergency.

- Make a note of all your card numbers and details of where you have to ring to report their loss. Keep a couple of copies so that you can report any loss quickly.

Form E111: If you're going to a country within the European Community make sure to get a Form E111 from your local Health Board. It will ensure that you get the same sort of free medical insurance as the locals in whatever country you go to. You can pick up a blank form at your local health centre or dispensary. You need to fill it in and get it stamped. That can take a few weeks.

BUPA/VHI: If you have medical insurance check what cover it provides when abroad and make a note of any special contact telephone numbers to be used. It's not an alternative to travel insurance but it is a very useful addition.

Travel insurance: Don't forget to take out some form of travel insurance. The insurance offered by the travel agency may not be the cheapest or best. It can be worthwhile getting your insurance elsewhere even if the travel agent charges you a small fee for allowing you to do so. Read the section on page 41.

Cancel the milk and the newspaper deliveries, leave some washing on the line, turn off the water, ask a neighbour to keep an eye on the house and have a good holiday.

have items like jewellery, cameras etc. covered for "all risks" on your household policy.

People who travel a lot should consider taking out an annual policy rather than one for each trip. There's certainly a saving to be made if you make three or more trips a year.

You may want cover for the potential loss of having to cancel a holiday in the event of the death of a close relative. This cover is usually fairly restrictive. You also need cover for medical expenses. BUPA and VHI provide some cover but not enough. Most policies also provide cover for delays and the loss of baggage and personal belongings.

The Irish League of Credit Unions offer travel insurance through member credit unions. A summary of the cover it provides can be used as a guide to what's available. At a cost of £7.50 for up to 18 days holiday in Ireland, £10 for holidays in Britain; £16 elsewhere in Europe and £36 world-wide, the policy will pay out up to £2 million for medical expenses, £3,000 if you have to cancel because of the death of a spouse or close relative, jury service or the burglary of your home or business, £2 million for personal liability, up to £1,500 for loss of baggage and up to £500 for loss of cash.

There is a 10 per cent discount for people taking out holiday loans through the credit union. Holidays involving winter sports attract twice the premiums listed above. The basic rates apply up to age 75 — many insurance policies charge an extra premium for anyone over 70.

Save&Invest

Investing for the future

At its simplest saving may only involve holding onto some money to meet the occasional expense that arises less regularly than paydays — a holiday, the car or house insurance, even the ESB or gas bills. But that type of saving has more to do with managing your money — a topic dealt with in the last chapter. The sums involved are generally small and the money is only been kept for relatively short periods so the main considerations are convenience and ease of access. But when larger sums of money are being put away for longer periods different factors come into play — most importantly the rate of return and the risk involved.

In general the lower the expected rate of return the smaller the risk. The return on a bank deposit, for instance, is more secure than the likely return on an investment in shares. While the investment in shares may yield a far higher return than the money in a bank account there is always the risk that it will yield no return and that the shares may even go down in value.

With Irish interest rates now down at central European levels, investors are being encouraged to take more risks with their savings since the more secure deposit outlets offer too low a return. Certainly the return on deposits and similar safe investments such as the Post Office scheme have fallen although it is still just about possible to get a safe return that will at least maintain the purchasing power of a nest egg i.e. a rate of return above the rate of inflation.

That hasn't always been the case in Ireland. There were periods when, although interest rates were far higher than at present, the rate of inflation was even higher — above 20 per cent a year at one stage. The purchasing power of savings dropped signifi-

Getting the best from financial advisors

The old legal adage of *caveat emptor* or let the buyer beware has not been supplanted by the range of consumer protection legislation enacted in recent years. There is still little enough protection in the financial services area and wrong decisions can be very costly for consumers. Taking out the wrong insurance policy or making the wrong investment can be very expensive and it is not necessary to take out a "bad" policy or make a "bad" investment to lose out. Just as there are horses for courses, there are policies and investments which, while excellent in some circumstances, may be disastrous in others. And the salesman or advisor may err simply by not knowing enough or not having access to a wide range of products. There is no shortage of one-product salesmen in the financial area who are simply geared to sell that product irrespective of the client's needs.

The first bit of advice is to be wary of the advisor who does not ask you a lot of questions to start with. To give adequate advice, a financial advisor needs to know something of his client's circumstances: a broad idea of income and responsibilities, tax situation, attitude to risk etc. It is also up to the client to ask some questions of his own. Make sure that you understand the answers.

1. WHAT — **What do I need?**

2. HOW — **How is the product going to supply that need?**

3. WHY — **Why that product rather than something else?**

4. WHEN — **Don't be rushed?**

The "What?" question is one that you have to ask yourself. Supermarkets and shops are very much into encouraging impulse buying. That can be discouraged by making a shopping list and sticking to it. The same is true in the financial area. It's up to you to decide what **you** want. Don't let the salesman decide for you. He or she may make suggestions but make sure that you make the decisions. Before you take any advice decide what you want yourself — if only in very broad terms, such as "I need to save for the children's education" or "I need insurance cover".

Then try to go a bit further than that. If the product is insurance what cover do you need? Do you need it on yourself or your spouse or both? Try to put broad figures on your needs. For instance, if you are considering saving for the children's education how much are you likely to need? And when? Do you think you'll need it to pay for secondary school or third level. Fees may have been abolished but other costs remain. Why do you need it — will your income not be sufficient at the time to cover the expense? Are you willing to take a risk with your savings? How much can you afford to save? Jot down your answers. Use it as a check list to see if the salesman or advisor has got you to deviate from your original objectives. If so, did he give adequate reasons why you should?

The other three questions in your check list are asked of the salesman or the advisor. It is a matter of "how and why". How is that particular product going to satisfy your particular needs and most important, why that product rather than something else? And that includes the most important question of why one company's products rather than another's.

Make sure you get adequate answers. Do not be afraid to keep asking why or how and make sure you understand the answer. Ask about alternatives. You can be sure that there are alternatives even if you don't know what they are. The salesman or advisor should know what they are and be able to justify the alternative he has chosen for you.

And remember that if you don't understand it, it is not your fault. There is nothing so complicated in financial products that it can't be explained in simple, easily understood, language. If your salesman or advisor can't do that, maybe he doesn't understand it himself. If he or she is calling to your home it can do no harm taking out a tape-recorder explaining that you are a bit muddle headed and may forget what he has to say. Explain that you would like to be able to go over it after he has left. That should stop him making excessive claims.

The final question is "When?". That is really a reminder not to be rushed. In the financial area you may be making very expensive decisions. A premium of £5 a week seems small but it is £260 a year and £2,600 over ten years. Take your time. Sleep on it.

It is, of course, always better to get advice from more than one advisor if possible. It is usually free. Then you can compare one with the other. And, do not forget, that although the advisor or salesman is not charging you anything, he is getting some commission. In some cases it can be considerable. In the case of many savings-type insurance policies it can eat up more than half of the first year's premiums. It is similar with pension schemes. The point is not that you are paying too much — a good advisor is worth his commission. Just remember that you are actually paying — and paying adequately, even generously — for the adviser's time and knowledge. So there is no need to feel guilty about asking questions and getting answers before you make your final decision.

cantly. Even with interest rates at their current low levels it is still possible to guard against such a loss now although on some deposits the return is far below the rate of inflation so that the value of a nest egg is actually going down in terms of purchasing power. There may be more money at the end of the year but it will buy less.

Invest in paying off a loan

Paying off a loan can sometimes be the best use for some spare savings. It can yield a far higher return than any alternative safe investment. Let's use Post Office Savings Certificates as a benchmark investment. It's safe and tax free and yields an average of 2.74 per cent over five years six months.

Invest £1,000 in Savings Bonds and you effectively earn £27.40 a year in interest. Invest the same money in paying off a bank term loan — currently costing about 10 per cent — and your gain is £100 a year. It makes sense to pay off the loan. Paying off the loan does reduce your flexibility but loans are readily available at present and seem set to remain so for the foreseeable future. So if you do need the money later, you can always borrow again. Mortgages are the exception. The interest rate is low and the interest may be eligible for tax relief. The true cost of a mortgage at 5 per cent is only about 3 per cent after tax relief.

Taking the example above the gain from paying £1,000 off such a mortgage is £30 a year That is slightly more than the £27.40 to be gained from an investment in Savings Certificates but it still may not be worth using the money to pay off the mortgage. There are longer term considerations to take into account.

If you once pay off the mortgage, it's not so easy to borrow again at such a favourable rate. It would, of course, be possible to get a top up mortgage but it would not be eligible for tax relief. And there'll be set up costs. It would be rather foolish to pay off a loan on which the effective interest rate is only 3 per cent and then, perhaps, have to borrow in a year or two at 10 per cent to buy a car.

So as a rule of thumb it does make sense to use surplus cash to pay off most loans provided there are no early repayment penalties involved. The exception is a mortgage on which you are getting tax relief. It may not even be worthwhile paying off a mortgage on which you are not getting tax relief if you leave yourself in a position where you'll have to borrow again at a higher rate in the future. Assuming a mortgage rate of 6 per cent a married couple can get tax relief on mortgages up to about £100,000 while a single borrower gets relief on a loan up to £50,000. There is no tax relief on the portions of the loans above those levels.

Deposits are safe but the return is relatively low. Many people are, however, willing to take some risk in the hope of a better return. And there is a range of options open to them. Some products guarantee at least a return of the initial investment — so that the worst that can happen is that you'll get your money back. Others guarantee a minimum return with the chance of something better. But there are other investments that offer no guarantees. There is the hope of good returns but also the risk of losing part, or even all, of the initial investment.

There is no single option that is best for everyone. It all depends on individual circumstances and attitude to risk. But there are some general rules of thumb that one can follow in making a decision.

The following lists some of the options. They are outlined in more detail in the sections that follow:

- **Deposit accounts** with banks, building societies and credit unions — rates vary greatly depending on the institution, the amount involved and the period of notice required.

- **Post Office schemes** offer tax free returns, the actual rate of return depends on the scheme and the length of time the money is left in. It also has a scheme aimed specifically at regular savers. The rates of return offered on these schemes at the end of 1999 are relatively low but they are tax-free.

- **Investment funds** offer a wide range of options. Some guarantee a return of capital while others make no guarantees, the return depending solely on the performance of the underlying investments. The underlying investments range from very high risk to very low risk.

- **Investments under certain tax incentive schemes** such as the Business Expansion, Film Relief and certain property investments combine the chance of a good return, partly based on tax relief, with the risk of loss. It is important to understand the risk and not be mesmerised by the tax relief which can in some cases confer more benefit on the promoter or developer than on the investor.

Read the following sections for more details on these various investment options.

Those are some of the options. The choice depends very much on the individual and on his or her particular needs. As stressed above it depends on attitudes to risk and on what is required from the investment. There is no single best option. It all depends on individual circumstances and objectives. And, of course, the relative attractiveness of different options can change with time. So the following should only be taken as pointers.

Saving for the children

Even with fees abolished, putting children through third-level education can be a costly business and it makes sense to make some provision for that expense in advance. It is never too early to start saving whatever you can afford on a regular basis. There are a number of different alternatives:

Deposit Account: The easiest way of saving is in a bank, building society, post office, or credit union. You can put aside as much as you like and as you build up larger sums you can switch them into longer term accounts which pay higher rates of interest. The rate of return can be very small and is, of course, liable to DIRT tax at source. The rate often depends on the amount deposited, the notice required to withdraw money, and, of course, the institution taking the deposit. The rates can vary greatly so it pays to shop around. But the return at best is not going to do much more than ensuring that the purchasing power of the deposit keeps pace with inflation.

Post Office Instalment Saving: The idea is that you agree to save a regular amount — up to £300 a month — for a year and then leave it on deposit where it earns about 2.83% a year tax-free. At the end of the year you can start off again. It is risk free but the rate of return on the current scheme is not very attractive – it will barely keep pace with inflation. But for relatively small amounts, maybe some or all of the monthly child benefit money, Instalment Savings has some attractions. It can encourage a regular saving habit and the lump sum accumulated at the end of each five years can always be invested elsewhere at a better return. While it is obviously a longer term savings plan it is possible to get your money out at any time if you need it at seven days notice.

If you decided on a regular saving equity plan be sure that you can stick with it for at least five and ideally ten years

Investment funds: There is a wide range of investment funds that take regular investments. The choice of fund depends on the individual. Some of the factors to take into account are outlined in section 3.5 on page 73. Life assurance companies and other fund managers also offer savings plans with or without life insurance cover included. The life cover is usually very small but remember that it's not free. Part of your savings will be going to pay for it. There is a wide range of options available. Your savings go into an investment fund of some kind. In most cases the value of those investments can move down as well as up so that there is no certainty about the return you can expect. Some insurance companies offer with-profits savings plans that carry much less risk than unit-linked plans. There are set-up costs so it is important to be sure that you are going to stick with it. Older products generally front loaded the costs while newer ones spread the cost over a longer period but either way as a rough rule of thumb you are unlikely to get much, if any, return if you cash it in within the first five years.

It can be a good idea if you are taking out such a policy with a view to saving for a child's education to take it out on the life of a non-wage earning spouse — usually the mother. It is very common to find that there is ample life assurance on the life of the husband but little or none on the life of the wife. Yet her death can involve severe financial strain if the family is to be kept together. Replacing a non-wage earning wife with a housekeeper is a very costly business — a fact that is very often forgotten but be clear that you are making two decisions, one is to save for the future and the other is to take out some life insurance cover. Be sure that you know how much the life insurance cover is costing. Most of the "special" education plans offered by the insurance companies are based on such unit-linked policies. In fact, the same investment could be used equally well for saving for retirement or any other purpose.

Saving for retirement

The objective here is not dissimilar to saving for the children's education. Retirement is just a little further away. All the options mentioned are just as relevant but there is another very attractive option – a pension scheme. If you are already in a company scheme it may be possible to make extra contributions to improve your benefits. If you are self-employed, it is possible to organise your own scheme and changes in the law during 1999 made that option even more attractive. The great benefit is that up to generous limits, there is full tax relief on the contributions paid into the fund and the money grows tax-free within the fund. The limits were increased during 1999 to 30 per cent of annual income for those over 50 years of age. The drawback of saving within a pension plan is that the money cannot be accessed until retirement age but under the new laws there is a lot of flexibility with what can be done with it then. For more details on pensions see chapter ten on planning for retirement starting on page 167.

Income from a lump sum

With retirement or redundancy lump sums the usual objective is to provide the best net income with an acceptable degree of risk. In many cases no risk will be acceptable and that greatly limits the options. Some people may be willing to take a risk with at least some of their lump sum. It all depends on the individual. Tax may have to be taken into account. For instance, unless the recipient is over 65 or incapacitated, there is no way of claiming back the DIRT tax stopped on deposit interest even if the recipient is not liable for income tax.

Interest rates are at a low level so it is more important than ever to shop around for the best possible return. And that means continually shopping around, keeping an eye on what is available. That does not mean always keeping your money on short notices of withdrawal, but simply examining the options afresh each time you have the flexibility to switch. Let us have a brief look at some of the options. They are all dealt with in detail later in the chapter.

Pay off loans: It can sometimes make more sense to use part of a lump sum to pay off loans than to invest it. In general if you are paying a higher rate of interest on the loan than it is possible to get from an investment, then it makes sense to pay off the loan. Be careful, however, about penalties for early repayment on some loans and don't pay off a relatively cheap loan if that will leave you in a position where you may have to borrow later at a higher rate. For instance, don't pay off a mortgage on which you are getting, or may again get tax relief. You lose flexibility and you could be forced to borrow at much higher rates in the future — and without tax relief — if you need to replace your car, say, or need money urgently for something else.

Post Office Schemes: Saving Certificates offer tax-free returns with complete security and it is possible to get a six monthly income by cashing in some of the certificates. The returns are currently very low. It is always possible to withdraw some or all of your money on short notice but you can lose up to six months interest with Savings Certificates and up to a year's interest with Bonds. But depending on the timing of the withdrawal you may lose nothing. A bit of care is needed.

Deposit accounts: The rate of return on deposit accounts is also very low so even a large lump sum will provide a rather small income. It is important to shop around to get the best return not forgetting your local credit union.

Annuities: These are another alternative — particularly for elderly investors with limited means. On offer from insurance companies they provide a method of spreading a lump sum out over the rest of one's life. The company promises to pay an agreed income until death. The longer you live the better the overall return. But with interest rates currently low the returns are also low and you are locked into them. The advantage is that you know the income will continue until death no matter how long you live. The disadvantage is that there is nothing left of the investment when you die.

Annuities provide a secure way of spreading a lump sum out over the rest of one's life.

Investment funds: Some funds carry little risk and offer the hope of significantly better returns than can be got from a deposit account. With-profit bonds are the safest option — some provide guaranteed annual bonuses that can be taken as an income — but there are unit-linked funds investing in cash and bonds where the risk is low. These are all medium to long term investment options. Taking an income from a unit-linked fund usually involves cashing in some of the units. It is important to appreciate that if unit values are falling, or not rising fast enough, some or all of that income has to come out of capital.

Shares: Shares can provide some income in the form of dividends but a good part of the hoped-for return generally comes from increases in the share price — if you are lucky. But, of course, share prices can move down as well as up — sometimes quite dramatically as they did during the 1987 crash or most recently, although not quite as dramatically, during the summer of 1998. Over the long term share values tend to go up faster than inflation. But you do need to pick the right shares at the right time. If your income needs are limited and you can take a long term view, shares might be a consideration. You do need to know what you are doing.

Lump sum for growth

Investment funds: Again taking a long term view unit-linked and other investment funds can offer the prospect of good growth. But as mentioned above there are risks and they need to be appreciated. The amount of risk varies with the fund. Tracker bonds can offer at least a guarantee that you will get your money back after a set period — usually three or five years, with the promise of a return in line with some specified stock market index, or group of indices, if share values rise. But tracker bonds are not as attractive as they were when interest rates were higher. Because of lower rates most no longer promise to match the full increase in any stock market index or, if they do, they don't guarantee a full return of capital in the event of a downturn.

With-profit bonds offer minimum returns with the additional prospect of annual bonuses that, once declared, are not taken away. They are not entirely risk free but are very nearly so. Unit funds carry varying degrees of risk depending on the underlying investments. The choice is wide

Saving Certificates: These provide a fixed, safe, tax-free return with the flexibility that they can be cashed in at any time but you can lose up to six months interest if you withdraw your money at the wrong time.

Property: Maybe investment funds will have property in their portfolios and there are some funds that specialise entirely in property so it is possible to invest indirectly in property through a fund. The alternative is to invest directly perhaps adding to the amount you invest by borrowing. That adds more risk but it is usually easier to borrow on the security of property than on other investments. The returns can come both by way of rental income and capital gains if the property rises in value. But there are risks that the price won't go up as expected or that the rental income wouldn't live up to expectations. Property can also be hard to quickly convert back into cash.

Tax based schemes: There are tax reliefs available on some property investments and there is also significant tax relief available to people who invest in new or expanding manufacturing, tourism, or international traded service companies. and certain music ventures. There is always some risk involved – the scheme is still attractive but only really for someone with a direct interest in the project. Without that direct involvement in the venture the risks are unacceptably high. Full tax relief is available on up to £25,000 invested each year. You have to wait at least five years to get a return. There is also tax relief available on investment in certain film ventures and, of course, on certain property investments. The tax relief can make these investments seem very attractive but be wary of the investment that wouldn't make sense without the tax relief.

Details of the Business Expansion Scheme are given in Chapter 14 on page 290.

An Post investment

In addition to its normal savings bank activities An Post also offers a range of medium to long term investment outlets. These include Instalment Savings, Saving Certificates, and Savings Bonds. They are all State guaranteed so there is no worry from the security point of view. They all offer tax free returns — indeed the returns are not even considered to be income. That's the good news. The bad news is that the rates of return on the new issues of the schemes are relatively low although by and large competitive with similar secure saving outlets such as deposit accounts.

Those with savings in earlier issues are still benefitting from good returns and in some cases very attractive continuation returns are offered on maturity. Those with money in the earlier issues should think twice before cashing them in. Someone with new money to invest can consider An Post schemes as an alternative to other safe saving outlets. The rates on offer are fixed for three, five or five and a half years depending on the scheme. That certainty needs to be set against the uncertainty of most deposit rates. They may go up from current levels but then they might just as easily come down – that's particularly so of some of the higher rates on offer.

All the rates on secure investments are relatively low but it is worthwhile making some effort to get the best return. Remember the difference between 2 per cent and 3 per cent on an investment of £10,000 is £100 a year. But there is no way of knowing in advance which is going to be best in the long run. At the end of 1999, however, it was certainly possible to get higher returns on some bank deposits – not all – that was being offered by An Post. But there is no way of knowing whether that will continue for three or five years. While An Post rates are guaranteed for the term of the investment it is always possible to withdraw money having given seven working days notice.

An Post has a web site at www.postoffice.ie

These Bonds are a three year investment with guaranteed returns each year. It is possible to withdraw money at any time

Savings bonds

without penalty other than the fact that no interest is payable if the money is withdrawn during the first year.

The rates of return are as follows: money left in for one year, 2.0 per cent; two years, 4.2 per cent which is 2.2 per cent a year; three years 8 per cent equal to 2.6 per cent a year. That three year return is equivalent to a gross return, before DIRT tax, of 3.3 per cent. So that's the type of return you would want to be guaranteed on an alternative deposit account to equal the 2.6 per cent tax free offered by Post Office Bonds.

The minimum investment is £100 and seven working days notice is required for withdrawal. No interest is paid on money withdrawn during the first year. Thereafter the guaranteed annual rates apply together with the normal Post Office Savings Bank rate for each complete calendar month — with no DIRT tax or other tax stopped. No tax indeed is payable.

The money can be withdrawn at any time through any Post Office or by post from the Post Office Savings Bank, FREEPOST, Townsend Street, Dublin 2. Withdrawals are subject to seven working days notice.

The return is guaranteed for three years at the end of which you can leave your money in at rates determined from time to time by the Minister of Finance. At one time it made sense to take your money out at the end of each term even if it was only to re-invest it again. But in recent years the continuation rates have been set at a level which removes any incentive to do that. It is no harm to check, however, what rates are being offered.

The maximum investment in the current issue of Savings Bonds is £60,000 per individual. That is in addition to any investments held in earlier issues or other schemes. Up to £120,000 may be held in a joint account. Anyone over seven years of age can invest either on their own or jointly with others.

Saving certificates

An alternative to Savings Bonds are Saving Certificates. The current issue (sixteenth issue) is offering a tax free return of 2.74 per cent a year if held for five years and six months. That's equivalent to 3.6 per cent gross. An initial investment of £1,000 grows to be £1,160 over that period.

There are no regular interest payments on Saving Certificates — you get your return when you cash them in. Their value grows very slowly in the early years. After six months their value will have increased by 0.8 per cent and by 1.7 per cent after a year. It is possible to get a regular income from your saving certificates by cashing them in at regular intervals. But an investment of £10,000 will only yield a six-monthly income of about £137. The return on saving certificates is completely tax-free.

There is no provision for the actual payment of interest. The value of the certificate simply grows by a set amount at the end of each six months. It is important to understand this factor. Interest is only added in at six monthly intervals so, if you cash in a day before a six monthly period is up, you can lose almost six months interest. The minimum investment is £50 and the maximum is £60,000 (£120,000 in a joint account). That is in addition to any money in earlier issues or in other An Post schemes.

The annual rate is low in the initial years — 1.7 per cent in the first year and 2 per cent in the second. But it rises to 4.5 per cent in the final twelve months. You should be thinking of leaving your money for the full five and a half years and certainly try to avoid withdrawing money in the final couple of years when the returns are greatest. The value of each £1,000 goes up as follows:

6 months	£1,008	**One year**	£1,017
1½ years	£1,027	**Two years**	£1,038
2½ years	£1,050	**Three years**	£1,063
3½ years	£1,077	**Four years**	£1,092
4½ years	£1,110	**Five years**	£1,132
5½ years	£1,160		

Money may be left in after the initial five and a half year period at a rate usually fixed by the Department of Finance for three years at a time. It is based on the rate applicable to new certificates at that time.

With the interest only added in every six months, it is important — if you have to cash in — to do it as soon as possible after a six-monthly anniversary. That way you lose the least amount of interest. Only the registered owner of the certificates can cash them in. They can be cashed in either in whole or in part, with seven working days required. This facility for partial encashment can be used to provide the saver with a regular income. The accompanying table show how this might be achieved. The examples assume an investment of £10,000. That investment

Getting an income from saving certificates

The only way to get an income from savings certificates is to cash them in. So to get a regular income it is necessary to cash some of the initial investment in from time to time. This should be done at six-monthly intervals or at longer periods which are multiples of six months i.e. a year, eighteen months etc.

Given the low return available on the current issue of Saving Certificates the income that can be withdrawn while leaving the initial capital intact is very low. The income is ob-tained by partially encashing the Certificate.

If we assume an initial investment of £10,000 in the current 16 per cent issue a partial en-cashment of £130 of the initial value of the Certificate every six months would provide a six-monthly income raising from £131 after the first six months to £151 after five years and six months leaving £9,941 remaining at the end. The figures are shown in the table be-low.

This is, of course, only an example. There is no need to decide in advance or to take any in-come at all. Encashments should ideally be made soon after a six-monthly anniversary of the initial investment since that is when the return is effectively added in. You can lose in-terest by encashing at the wrong time.

	Initial value of Cert encashed	Value at time of encashment	Value of remaining certificate
Initially			£10,000
6 months	£130	£131	£9,949
one year	£130	£132	£9,906
18 months	£130	£134	£9,869
two years	£130	£135	£9,840
2½ years	£130	£137	£9,818
three years	£130	£138	£9,801
3½ years	£130	£140	£9,790
four years	£130	£142	£9,784
4½ years	£130	£144	£9,801
five years	£130	£147	£9,848
5½ years	£130	£151	£9,941

appears as one lump sum on the certificate but that does not prevent the saver from making partial encashments. They are simply written on the back of the certificate.

By varying the rate of encashment, the saver can get either a fairly static income every six months or alternatively a rising or even a declining one. There is, of course, no need to keep to a specified plan. Partial encashments can be made at any time. The rate on Saving Certificates is relatively attractive in the last two years so it is best to leave the money in for the full term. The return on the current issue is far from attractive but it is better than the after-tax return offered on some deposit accounts.

Seven working days notice of withdrawal is required.

Instalment savings

An Post also has an instalment savings scheme aimed at the person who can put some money away regularly with the intention of leaving it for some years. This National Instalment Saving Scheme is primarily aimed at those savers who can save a fixed amount each month for a year. As a scheme for encouraging savings it's great and the returns are not bad considering that only relatively small sums are being deposited. The saver — who must be over 7 years of age — agrees to save a stated amount each month for twelve consecutive months. The minimum monthly saving is £20 and the maximum £300.

At the end of the 12 months period, the total amount saved is left on deposit. After that interest starts to accrue at a guaranteed rate which rises over the years and averages 2.83 per cent over five years not taking the twelve month saving period into account. The annual returns after the saving year are as follows:

The Instalment Savings Scheme is an option for those wanting to save a fixed amount regularly each month.

year one	2%
year two	2%
year three	2.5%
year four	3.2%
year five	4.5%

So once started there is obviously a growing incentive not to withdraw the savings until the end of the five year period. The annual return in the final three years is far better.

The instalment saving scheme is about the most attractive of the An Post schemes for the target market of relatively small regular savers. The return is not great but it does provide an incentive to save. If the savings are left for five years after the initial year's saving period you are guaranteed your money back plus 15 per cent — that works out at only 2.83 per cent a year. But that is tax free and equivalent to 3.7 per cent before tax. So you'd have to be getting 3.7 per cent on a deposit account to be doing as well and that is not a rate readily available at the end of 1999 on small savings.

A number of points to bear in mind:-

If you fail to keep up your twelve monthly payments and withdraw your money before the end of the year, you get no interest at all. If you miss a monthly payment you can continue on with the scheme. Interest will start to accrue on the total amount saved during the twelve months from the beginning of the month following your final instalment.

If you withdraw your money after the initial twelve months you get the guaranteed bonus for each complete year together with the Post Office Savings Bank rate of interest for each additional full calendar month.

The guaranteed rates cover the first five years. Extension terms may then be offered based on market interest rates at the time. That's a good time to shop around and examine the alternatives.

Nothing is totally risk free but the nearest you can get in the form of an investment is a deposit account – after, of course, An Post schemes which must rank safest of all thanks to their Government guarantee. There are other relatively safe investments such as the guaranteed bonds issued by many insurance companies and annuities also issued by some insurance companies. With any of those options there is little chance of losing your capital. In some cases the return is variable, it may go up or down. In other cases it is fixed. But in all cases the return is relatively low. The cost of security is generally a low return.

Banks, building societies and credit unions all pay interest on deposits. The rates vary with the size of the deposit and with the length of notice required to withdraw the money. They also vary from institution to institution and, of course, over time. There are rates fixed for a set time and variable rates that can be changed from day-to-day without notice. It is important to shop around to get the best rate. The newspapers carry weekly lists of the rates available but it is as well to check by phone as well since rates can change frequently. That's also a good reason for regularly reviewing your deposits ensuring that you continue to get the best rate available.

Competition for deposits intensified towards the end of 1999 and a wide gap opened up between the lowest and the highest rates available, particularly on smaller amounts. It's important to shop around, not only when you are initially putting the money on deposit but regularly thereafter to ensure that you are still getting the best rate available.

DIRT tax is levied at the standard income tax rate — 22 per cent from April 2000 — on most deposit interest. No further tax is due on deposit interest even if the recipient is liable to a higher rate of income tax. A lower 20 per cent rate of DIRT applies to special savings accounts – more on them below. People who are not liable for income tax and who are either over 65 years of age or disabled can claim back the tax. No DIRT is currently stopped on credit union accounts although a recipient

Deposit accounts

Deposit accounts need to be constantly reviewed to ensure that you continue to get the best available return.

who is liable for tax is required to make a return of the interest and pay the tax.

Special savings accounts

Special savings accounts (SSAs) benefit from a lower rate of DIRT than normal accounts but the difference is very slight. When first introduced the DIRT on SSAs was only 10 per cent but that was raised to 20 per cent – not much below the standard rate of DIRT. But some financial institutions offer slightly higher rates on special savings accounts which gives them a small extra attraction.

That higher interest rate reflects to some extent the notice conditions on the accounts. To qualify for the lower rate of DIRT tax a savings account must meet with conditions laid down by the Revenue Commissioners. No withdrawals can be allowed within the first three months of the account being opened and at least thirty days notice is required for any withdrawal thereafter. Some accounts guarantee fixed rates for a set period but the rules stipulate that the rates cannot be fixed in advance for a period of more than two years.

In addition depositors must be over 18 years of age and can have only one special savings account at any one time. There is an upper limit of £75,000 which may be kept in the account and that includes any interest earned. For a married couple the upper limit is £150,000 which may be either in a single or joint accounts.

On opening a special savings account, the depositor is required to give a signed declaration which is kept by the financial institution for at least six years and may be inspected by the Revenue Commissioners. The declaration states that the conditions of the scheme are being met; gives the full name and address of the individual who is entitled to the interest on the account; and contains an undertaking that the individual will immediately notify the bank or other financial institution if he or she ceases to meet the requirements of the scheme.

All types of deposit accounts can, of course, meet those conditions. So a whole range of alternatives is available not only in terms of interest rates. Some financial institutions require a minimum deposit, others do not. Various income options are also available.

Credit unions

Many credit unions offer very attractive dividend rates on members' shares. They are not strictly deposit accounts and the rate is not fixed in advance. It depends on the dividend declared and agreed by members each year. That, in turn, of course, depends on the finances of the credit union. But with relatively low costs credit unions can operate on relatively tight margins between the rate they charge on borrowings and the return they provide for their saver/shareholders. While they are under pressure to reduce the interest rate they charge on borrowings from the standard 12.7 per cent it is likely that they will continue to be able to pay better rates on savings than banks or other financial institutions whose primary objective is to maximise profit. Most credit unions also offer the alternative of deposit accounts on which the return may be fixed in advance. As mentioned above credit unions are not required to stop DIRT but the returns are liable for tax.

Reclaiming DIRT tax

If you are not liable for income tax and you are either over 65 years of age or permanently incapacitated, then you are entitled to claim back any DIRT tax stopped on deposit interest you have earned. In the case of a married couple, it is sufficient for either partner to be over 65 years of age.

The claim has to be made on a simple form which you can get in any tax office, at larger post offices or from wherever you have your savings. You also need a certificate from the bank or building society giving details of the DIRT tax stopped. Fill out the form, attach the certificate of tax stopped, and send it off to the tax office — the address is on the form.

Guaranteed bonds

Guaranteed bonds issued by insurance companies are much the same as term deposits i.e. deposits for a fixed period of time. The fixed term is seldom less than a year and is more often three to five years although it can be longer. The rate of return is normally fixed at the outset and is guaranteed. Early encashment penalties can be heavy so it is essential to be reasonably sure that you won't require access to your money during the set term of the bond.

Some bonds provide a facility for taking a regular income. It may even be possible to take an income larger than the interest been accumulated. In which case, of course, you are eating into your capital.

Income from annuities

An annuity is a way of using a lump sum to provide an income for life. It was the commonest way of providing an income during retirement mainly because it was the only option open to those with personal pension money to invest. But that is no longer the case for the self-employed, directors of family firms, and those not in company pension schemes. But while people with pension funds to invest are no longer required to purchase an annuity, they are still there as an option – an option that may be attractive to some.

Annuities may have an appeal to anyone with limited capital that they want to spread out as income over the post-retirement years. The basic idea behind an annuity is that in return for a lump sum investment it provides a guaranteed income until death.

Around that central idea there are a fair number of options. In all cases the income is guaranteed for an uncertain period. The assurance companies that sell annuities do not know when the person is going to die. But they have an idea of the average life expectancy of annuity purchasers. In money terms those who live longer get a very good return while those who die younger do not. But in all cases there is the security of knowing that the income will continue until death.

Annuity rates can vary. It is worthwhile shopping around for the best rate.

When interest rates are low, annuity rates are also low and that is the situation early in 2000. A man aged 60 would require about £100,000 to buy an income of £8,000 a year for life. The initial payment would be smaller if the income is to subsequently rise with inflation. The commonest standard annuity provides for the first interest payment to be made six months after the annuity is purchased. Thereafter the payments are made at six monthly intervals. If the first interest payment is required straight away the rate of return is slightly lower. It is usual to guarantee at least five years payments whether the purchaser dies during that time or not but if you do not want the guarantee the rate is slightly higher.

There are also annuities suitable for couples. Known as **"joint survivor annuities"** they are taken out on the joint lives of the couple. On the death of one the income continues at a reduced rate until the death of the other. The rate of return on joint survivor annuities is, of course, lower than on a single life annuity — about 20 per cent less in the case of a husband aged 65 whose wife is 61 when the annuity is taken out. This 20 per cent reduction also assumes that the income is halved on the death of one partner.

People with medical conditions likely to shorten their life span can, in some cases, get higher returns than those in good health. Most companies, however, refuse to take medical history into account even thought they would make sure to do so in setting life insurance premiums. Some companies do, however, offer what as known as **"impaired life annuities"**. If appropriate it is worth searching them out. The annuity rates can be significantly higher.

But in all cases those blessed with longevity do well from annuities but then not everyone is so blessed. Many pensioners have in the past got very bad value for their money. There is always a chance in buying an annuity. And most people are willing to take the chance in the hope that they will live long and get a good return. There are other options for those who either don't expect to live long or who are willing to accept a reduced pension in order to leave something behind them for their children.

It is possible for those in bad health to get better annuity rates.

Retirement Cashback Bonds, **Capital Preserved Annuities**, and **With-profit Annuities** provide further alternatives. The Cashback Bond is a way of accepting a smaller pension in order to leave money for dependants after death. It is essentially a whole of life assurance policy that pays out on the death of the pensioner. The single premium is paid out of the pension fund at the time of retiring. Since there is less money in the fund the pension it buys is smaller.

The Revenue require that the initial life cover is no more than twice the pensioner's final remuneration and that the annuity purchased is only on a single life with no guaranteed minimum payment i.e. no minimum payment for five years.

Capital Preserved Annuities are more suited to those in ill health who are willing to take a lower pension to ensure that some of their pension fund will remain for their estate. While the benefit is similar to a life assurance there is no underwriting involved and therefore no medical is required. The pensioner can opt to have the entire retirement fund left for his or her estate or take a higher pension and have a declining lump sum remaining to the estate on death.

With-profit annuities provide an income that varies with the performance of the underlying fund. It can go down as well as up.

Within those various options the rates of return offered on annuities vary from week to week and from company to company. It is essential to shop around since once the annuity is bought the terms are fixed. The return offered does, of course, vary with the age of the person or couple involved. But the returns are better than could be obtained by simply putting the money on deposit somewhere. And there are certain tax advantages. Part of the annual income — usually about a third — is considered to be the repayment of the initial capital sum and, as such, is not liable for tax. The amount varies with the current rate of interest, and it is constantly changing. On the non-capital element of the payment — approximately the other two-thirds — the recipient is liable to pay income tax if he or she is in the tax net. If they are on a relatively low income, they may be exempt from income tax entirely — see chapter 13, page 232, or Appendix 1, page 312, for tax exemption levels.

WITH interest rates close to historical lows in Ireland there has been a growing interest in investing in shares. It has been encouraged by flotation on the Irish stock exchange of building societies, mutual insurance companies and, Eircom – the former Telecom Éireann. New investors have had mixed experiences as share prices slipped back from their highs, the Eircom shares sank below its issue price at one stage but the general expectations is for share values to tend upwards for the foreseeable future.

Taking a long term view Irish shares have performed very well in the past — outpacing most other investments. There can be sharp swings but provided you don't buy at the very top of a cycle and can take a long-term view it is possible to achieve very good returns. There can, however, be no certainty. Values on the Irish exchange have risen over three fold during the 1990s but the trend was not uniformly upwards. During 1999 for instance share values moved within a wide range – the low point was some 20 per cent down on the high for the year. So there can be a good deal of volatility and some shares will experience a greater degree of volatility than others. Even when the market is tending upwards there will always be some shares moving in the opposite direction.

Irish investors are not, of course, restricted to investing on the Irish stock exchange. But investing abroad outside the euro-zone involves an extra risk. Non-euro shares have to be bought in foreign currency and there is always the risk that the Irish pound will devalue against that currency.

Whatever the prospects, small investors must always be wary of investing in shares. They cannot spread their money over a wide range of shares in order to spread the risk and they must realise that share values can go down as well as up. But for those willing to take a gamble there is money to be made provided they realise and accept that there can be no certainty.

It can be argued that the small investor is better advised to invest indirectly in shares on the stock market through invest-

Stock market investment

The small investor may be better spreading the risk by investing in shares indirectly through a managed fund.

The stock market — understanding the jargon

Par Price: Every share has a par price fixed at the time of its issue. Thereafter it ceases to have very much meaning. The price at which a share is bought or sold is determined by what people are willing to pay, and the par price has no bearing on this.

Dividend Yield: Dividends are declared in euro cents per share now that all share prices are quoted in euros since January 1, 1999 — the amount being after a charge of income tax. However, most sources still calculate dividend yield as a before-tax figure. In effect, the dividend yield tells you the rate of return you can expect on the amount of money you have invested in the company if it continues to pay dividends at its current rate. For example, if the dividend yield of a company is 3.5 per cent at the current price of the shares, then if you laid out £100 in purchasing shares at the current price the dividends would provide you with an annual income of £3.50 per £100, 3.5p on a pound or 3.5 cents on a euro.

Earnings Per Share: The dividend is only one part of the story. Investors are hoping for some rise in share value in addition to the dividend income. And share price is as much determined by profits as by dividend pay-out. But profits can be distorted in any year by extraordinary, once-off, losses or windfall profits. These are ignored in calculating the earnings figure. It is an indication of underlying profits. Earnings are divided by the number of shares on issue to give an earnings per share figure.

Cover: This is the number of times the dividend pay-out is covered by earnings. It is a guide to the likely stability of the dividend pay-out. If earnings per share are twice the dividend — a cover of two — then the dividend could be maintained even if earnings were to halve in any one year.

P/E Ratio: This is the price earning ratio. Usually given as a net (after tax) figure, the P/E ratio is the price of the share divided by earnings per share. It is much the same as a "years purchase" figure, i.e. how many years of earnings does the current price represent. A sound secure company will normally be standing at a high P/E, while a more doubtful one will stand at a low P/E.

ments funds. These are considered in the next section. By investing in a fund rather than directly in individual shares the investor gets the benefit of skilled management and also gets to spread the risk to a far greater degree than would be feasible by investing in individual shares. A knowledgeable, or lucky, individual can always hope to do better than a fund manager, of course, and he or she might be able to do just that. But it does require time and knowledge, not only of how the stock market works – that's the easy bit – but also an insight into how economic trends are going to impact on sectors and individual companies. You'll need to be able to pick the winners and the losers or, at least, some of them.

Investing in a company on the Stock Exchange gives you a part ownership in the company concerned. The return on this part ownership depends on the performance of the company, so together with the prospect of a high return, goes the risk of no return. The degree of risk varies with the type of share and with the company.

There are debentures and preference shares which carry a fixed rate of interest and have first claim on a company's profits, and then there are ordinary shares, which are the real ownership shares, and carry with them full risks of ownership and the full prospects. If the company makes no profits, they get no dividend; if it prospers, they get all the cream.

To the outsider a certain aura of mystery surrounds the Stock Exchange, but the fact is that one can buy shares as easily — perhaps more easily — than lodging money in the bank. It is even possible to buy and sell shares directly over the phone or on the internet although Irish brokers have yet to fully develop this side of the business.

How to buy the shares

The first question which enters the heads of most potential Stock Exchange investors is: "How much do I need?" There is no hard and fast answer. Some stockbrokers would put the minimum at about £1,000: some would accept a lower figure but with a minimum commission of perhaps £40 per transaction it does not make sense to invest very small amounts.

It is better to deal directly with a stockbroker although you could use your bank manager as an intermediary. A list of stockbrokers may be obtained from The General Manager, Irish Stock Exchange, Anglesea Street, Dublin 2. In addition to buying or selling your shares for you, the stockbroker will also give advice on what and when to buy and sell. His commission is relatively small — about $1\frac{1}{2}$ per cent of the sale or purchase price subject to a minimum. Where the minimum applies, of course, the percentage is higher. There is also a Government stamp duty of 1 per cent on all purchases.

Brokers may not get over-enthusiastic about small investors, but a potential investor who can give a brief outline of what he requires will normally get a sympathetic hearing.

Government stock

Government stock, or gilts as they are sometimes called, can be an attractive investment for the ordinary investor. They are not something solely for the high flier. There is nothing mysterious about them. One of their attractions is that no DIRT tax is stopped on the interest so they can be particularly attractive to the non-taxpayer who, being under 65 years of age and not incapacitated, is unable to reclaim the DIRT tax stopped on normal deposit interest.

Although the price of Government stock can move up and down, the investor who can hold on until the redemption date of the particular stock takes no risk. So it is possible to invest on a no-risk basis. Unfortunately many people are put off by the very idea of investing on the Stock Exchange — either in shares or gilts. But there is no need to be. It is all quite simple. First an explanation of what a Government stock is. When the Government borrows from the public, the financial institutions, or the banks on a long-term basis, it does so by "selling" new Government stock. The stock can be thought of as an IOU. In return for the loan the Government gives out this IOU promising to pay the lender so much interest every six months and to repay the full amount of the loan at some time in the future. Usually the repayment date is left a little flexible. It may be set as between the year 2000 and 2005, for instance. In such a case it is usually assumed that the loan will be repaid at the later date i.e. 2005.

You can buy government stock at no risk if you are willing to hold them until they are redeemed by the government. You know exactly how much you will get and what interest you get in the meanwhile.

The person, or institution, who initially gave the loan, now owns a valuable IOU which gives the bearer the right to an interest payment every six months and a lump sum at some date in the future. It is those IOUs which are sold on the Stock Exchange. But their value can vary from day to day and from week to week. Let us see why that should be the case.

Suppose someone lent the Government £100 some years ago, say by buying a 6 per cent stock redeemable in 2005. What he got was one of the IOUs promising to pay him 8 per cent a year up until 2005 and then to give him back £100. How much is that IOU worth now? It entitles the bearer to £8 a year in interest payments but with interest rates at about 3 per cent, a would be purchaser would need to put £200 on deposit to get an annual income of £8. Of course, he also knows that he will only get £100 in 2005. But that is a long way off.

So the purchaser will not be willing to pay £100 for the IOU at this time. If he buys it for £110 he will get an interest return of 5.4 per cent on his investment (£6 interest on £110 investment) and he also has the certainty of getting £100 back in 2005. If he holds the Government stock — or the IOU as we have been calling it — until 2005, he knows for certain what his return will be and he takes no risk. If he has to sell the IOU before then, he cannot be sure what it will fetch. Its price will always be determined by the alternative investments available and that, in turn, will be determined by the general level of interest rates.

There are so many government stocks, however, that the small investor should always be able to pick one with the right number of years to go until redemption to suit his particular requirements. It's an investment option for someone with a redundancy lump sum, for instance, who knows that he is not going to be in the income tax net and wants to get a secure income on his money which is not going to be subject to DIRT tax. But the return, while secure, is low reflecting the low level of interest rates generally.

When interest rates are rising the value of government stocks goes down. But when interest rates are falling, their value rises. So they are a particularly attractive investment when interest rates are high and expected to fall. At the end of 1999 interest rates were close to a historical low and seemed set to rise. So it is unlikely that stock values will rise in the foreseeable future. But government stocks can provide a secure, tax free income to the non-taxpayer who would have to pay DIRT on deposit interest. If interest rates rise the value of the stock will fall but that is not a worry to an investor who is willing to wait until it matures and has taken that into his or her calculations.

Buying stock

Government stock can be bought through a stockbroker or, indeed, a bank manager. The cost of buying stocks is very low although there is no fixed rate of commission. Stockbrokers charge a commission of about 1 per cent on buying or selling government stocks and there is no stamp duty. But they would expect you to be investing a few thousand pounds at the very least.

Bed and breakfast

If you buy shares at one price and sell them later at a higher price you have made a capital gain and may be liable for Capital Gains Tax. That tax is completely separate from income tax and levied at a standard rate of 20p in the pound. A full account is given in Chapter 14, page 259. The tax is not quite as onerous as it seems since allowance is made for inflation and there is no tax payable on the first £1,000 of gains made by an individual in any tax year.

The inflation adjustment comes automatically but you need to take action to ensure that you make the maximum use of the annual exemption. You only benefit from the exemption when you actually make a gain so the trick is to make gains up to the exemption limit every year even if that means selling your shares and immediately buying them back again. This type of "bed and breakfast" deal, as it is sometimes called, is not as complicated as it sounds. Stockbrokers are used to looking after the mechanics.

The annual exemption only applies when gains are actually disposed of. So if you hold shares for one year, five years or ten years before selling them you only get the benefit of one annual exemption limit. Suppose you have made a gain of £1,000 on an investment and have no other capital gains it makes a lot of sense to do a 'sell and buy' deal with yourself. In effect you sell the shares to yourself. You end up with the same shares that you had but the benefit comes in raising the base value of your shareholding for tax purposes. Suppose you originally bought the shares for £3,000 a few months earlier and they are now worth £4,000. By selling and buying them you raise the base price for tax purposes from £3,000 to £4,000. The £1,000 gain you make is exempt from tax and for future tax calculations you are assumed to have acquired the shares at £4,000.

Investment funds

While the stock exchange is not for everyone more and more people are looking beyond basic deposit accounts as a home for their next eggs. One option is to invest directly in the stock market, land or property but it requires time, knowledge and skill to ensure a good return. There is no doubt that in the long run both stock market and property investments have outperformed the return on deposit accounts, But that is on average and over time. Some investments fall far short of the average and the total market in shares or property can sometimes fall significantly. Those risks of direct investment can be reduced, but not entirely eliminated by investing indirectly through an investment fund. And there are a wide range of funds to choose from. Most allow for lump sum investment and some accept regular savings.

All investment funds have one thing in common. They are pooled investments. Each individual investor's money is pooled with that of other investors and professional managers manage the whole fund on their behalf. Those managers have to be paid, of course, and the companies they work for have to make a profit, so there are charges involved. There is always an annual management charge usually imposed as a percentage of the fund. In addition there is often an initial set-up charge. Funds with high set-up charges generally have lower management charges and vice-versa.

In all cases the investor should be looking to the medium or long-term in order to achieve a sufficient return to offset the costs and ensure some levelling out of the ups and downs. Investors should be prepared to leave their lump sum investments for at least five years while regular savers should be thinking in terms of at least ten years.

The choice is wide. There are various different types of investment funds and within each type there is a very wide range of individual funds offering varying degrees of risk. So what are the basic options? Funds can be categorised within the following types:

- Unit funds including unit trusts, PEPs and PIPs,

- With profit funds,
- Tracker bonds,

Unit funds

The term unit fund covers a multitude. They are operated by banks, insurance companies, building societies, and other financial institutions. Investors' money is pooled and managed on their behalf by professional fund managers. There is every conceivable type of fund. You can choose to have your money invested in almost any category of shares in a range of markets. So you can have all your money invested on the Japanese or Australian stock exchange or you can choose a wider option. There are also funds invested solely in property and others invested solely in government funds. You take your pick and usually you can switch to a different fund operated by the same company if and when you like. There may be some cost involved but usually at least some switching is allowed without any additional charge.

Each investor is allocated so many units in the total fund. Their value changes daily or weekly as the value of the underlying investments change. With most funds the movement can be down as well as up but some funds put a floor under your potential losses by guaranteeing a minimum return. The returns are liable to income tax stopped at source similar to the way DIRT is stopped on deposit interest.

In most cases returns are taxed at the standard rate but where the fund is at least 55 per cent invested in Irish equities a special lower tax of 20 per cent applies – a relatively small concession. The various types of unit funds are called different names by different companies and the same name may, in some cases, mean different things. The following are some of the terms with a brief explanation of what they usually mean.

Unit-linked funds: These are insurance linked unit investments. The life insurance element is usually very small but it allows for the fund to be set up under life insurance legislation. Different companies call their funds by different names.

Unit trusts: These are unit funds set up under a trust deed. From the point of view of the investor there is little difference between unit trusts and unit linked funds. The differences have more to do with how they are set up and administered.

Be wary of an investment adviser who does not spend some time asking personal questions about your tax position, your financial position, your needs, pensions entitlement etc. Unless he knows your requirements he cannot weigh up all the options and be sure of giving the best advice. Always make the cheque out to the company running the fund and not to the broker.

Managed funds: These are unit funds with a mix of investments. The term is usually applied to run funds carrying a medium degree of risk because of their wide spread but there is no strict definition and the term could equally apply to a fund invested in a mix of riskier investments.

Specialised funds: While a managed fund usually offers a spread of investments over a range of sectors, the specialised fund targets a particular sector, country or investment areas. The investor is putting all of his or her eggs into the one basket. If the chosen investment area does well, then the returns will reflect that.

Personal Equity Fund (PEP): PEP can mean different things to different people. But in all cases it is a fund invested entirely in equities usually with a sufficient proportion in Irish shares to qualify for the lower rate of tax.

Personal Investment Funds (PIP): The essential difference between a PEP and a PIP is that a PIP may not be entirely invested in equities. In addition the term PIP is usually used to describe a fund open to regular savers rather than lump sum investors.

Some funds offer a discount for larger investors while others operate a smaller spread between bid and offer prices while imposing a higher annual management fee. Because of those costs it is essential to think of pooled investments as at least a medium term investment - five years at the very least and ideally ten.

Offered by mutual life assurance companies these investments are linked to the company's own internal funds and, unlike most unit linked investments, offer a minimum guaranteed return plus bonuses. The minimum return may only be your capital back at the end of a set term and the level of bonus can differ from year to year and from company to company but it is very rare for no bonus to be paid. A terminal bonus, usually bigger than the annual bonuses, is paid at the end of the term agreed when the policy is taken out. So it can be costly to cash in before the end of the agreed term which is seldom less than five years.

With-profit funds level out the return over the years. The value keeps going up or, at the very worse, stays static while the value of unit funds may be moving up and down with great volatility.

Investment funds must be viewed as medium to long-term investments.

With profit funds

Many funds allow the investor to take the annual bonus as an income. With profit funds are not entirely risk-free. Issuers generally reserve the right to apply what is known as a "market value adjustment" to encashment values should they be faced with a major drop in market values and/or a significant number of investors seeking to cash in at the one time. The risk is not high and is only likely to apply during a market slump when alternative pooled investments would be suffering major downturns.

Tracker bonds

Tracker bonds are fixed term investments generally over three or five years. There is a range of different options. Most offer a guarantee that the investor will at least get his or her money back at the end of the agreed period. Some offer a minimum return on top of that basic guarantee. The maximum return possible is usually based on the performance of some stock exchange index or mix of indices. For instance the return may be linked to the performance of the FTSE100 index of British stock market prices.

Tracker bonds are less attractive than they once were.

So for example a person making an investment of £2,000 might be guaranteed the return of that money at the end of three or five years. That's the worst outcome. There may also be a guarantee that the value of the bond will rise by half of any rise in the FTSE100 index. So if it happened to rise by 50 per cent over the period then the return would be 25 per cent of £2,000. The investor would get back £2,500 less tax at the standard rate. In most cases there is a cap on the maximum return just as there is a floor under the potential loss. Bonds are opened for investment from time to time. There is usually a range to choose from at any one time but with the guarantees reduced as a result of declining interest rates the interest in them has waned somewhat. They should be viewed as a fixed term investment. There can be heavy penalties for withdrawing money too soon.

Which is best for you?

The type of investment to choose depends very much on the person's own circumstances and attitude to risk. Specialised unit-linked investments offer the best chance of high return, but there is a risk that it will not materialise. If, for instance, the fund is invested in equities, the amount eventually paid out will depend on the state of the stock market at the time of the payment. And who is to say what market conditions will be like ten years hence.

With-profit policies offer a chance of participating in the insurance company's own profit and usually once bonuses are declared, they can't be taken back. But many of them declare their largest bonuses as 'terminal' ones i.e. at the end of the policy period. And some of those terminal bonuses have been cut back in recent times. So there is a risk of getting a lower return than expected but the risk is less than with unit-linked policies - although the chance of a really high return is also less.

With all of these investments it is important to take a medium to long term outlook. It can be costly to withdraw too early. While the set-up costs for lump sum investments is not too great, it is sufficiently high that the investor should be thinking of leaving his money for a reasonably lengthy period. With unit funds most companies allow investors to switch without cost from one fund to another within their own stable – usually at least once a year. But switching from one company's funds to another always entails a significant cost. And that is something to watch. The switching option doesn't arise with tracker bonds or with-profit funds.

Normally with the unit funds, any income earned on the fund is reinvested to the benefit of the investors – although there are provisions in some plans for the investor to get a regular income. This is arranged, however, by the sale of units and there is no guarantee that the remaining units will continue to be worth as much as the initial investment. In other words, the income could, in some cases, be paid out of capital. This could also be the case with the income from a with-profit fund if the bonuses do not come up to expectations. The performance of each fund may be subject to short-term fluctuations so it is best judged over a period of a few years. But the past performance of a fund may not be a good guide to future prospects. The sophisticated investor will also want to look at the mix of investments within each fund. This can vary greatly from one fund to another.

There is no single answer to the question "which is best?" It all depends on the individual, his or her personal circumstances and attitude to risk. Before seeking advice or making a decision ask yourself what you are investing for, how much risk are you willing to take, and what are the chances of you needing speedy access to your money. Having the answers to those questions in your head will help you to make the right decision.

Some financial advisers have been known to encourage such switching, more in the interest of maximising their commission than in the interest of the investor.

Assurance

Insurance for life and death 4.

A N essential part of any family finance plan must be the protection of one's dependants against the financial loss which inevitably results from the death of a bread winner. One thinks usually of the death of the husband in this regard, and the loss of income which will result. But the early death of a wife, even if she is not an income earner, can also impose a financial burden on a widower trying to keep a family together. Life assurance offers a way of easing these financial burdens caused by death.

The provision of protection for family and other dependants is the first and primary role of life assurance. But, as outlined in the chapter on medium and long-term saving, many life assurance policies involve more than basic life insurance. They combine cover for dependants in the event of death with a way of saving for the future — for retirement, educating the children, or even marriage. Most assurance policies satisfy both needs to some extent. Some are aimed more at protection while others are aimed more at saving. Some, of course only offer protection with no monetary return if the insured person lives beyond a certain age.

It is important for people taking out the insurance to be clear on what they need from the policy and to keep the distinction between protection and saving in mind. The insurance industry is pledged to emphasise the differences, in response to the complaints over a lack of clarity in the past. Let's first have a look at the type of policies generally available, and then examine how they can be used to satisfy the average family's needs.

There are four basic types of life assurance.

- Term or temporary insurance.

- Whole of life assurance.
- Endowment assurance.
- Disability and illness insurance.

Term insurance

Pure life assurance which pays out only if death occurs during a fixed period of years is relatively cheap.

A man aged 30 can ensure that his dependents receive £100,000 if he dies within the next ten years at a premium cost of about £11 a month. That is not bad value. Mind you if he goes to the wrong insurance company he could pay twice that for the same cover. The very big difference between the cheapest and the dearest highlights the necessity of shopping around either by getting a range of quotes yourself or by getting an independent broker to do the job for you.

This type of insurance is called term insurance and all too little of it is sold. We tend to spend a lot on life insurance compared to our counterparts in other countries but we favour savings type policies which are really geared towards saving for the future and which only pay out a relatively small amount in the event of early death.

Term insurance pays out nothing if the insured person lives for the set term of years. Suppose like our example above, you are thirty years of age and take out a ten year policy. If you live until you are forty, the policy ends and you get nothing back. But it is not a complete loss. Indeed it is no loss. What you have bought during the ten years is peace of mind: the knowledge that should you die your dependants will be provided with some financial resources. That peace of mind is worth buying.

Not everyone needs term insurance. But there are certainly a lot of people who need it and do not have it. If you are in a company pension scheme you are possibly covered fairly well for life insurance within the scheme. But it is worth checking out how high the cover is and considering whether or not you should take out a little more. Then what about insurance on the stay-at-home spouse. The financial cost of keeping a family together following the death of a wife and mother can be substantial. A lump sum would certainly make living more bearable. It has been estimated that employing someone to carry out all of the duties of a housewife would cost in the region of £350 a week. That's clearly an underestimate although it is a little less than average industrial earnings which in 1999 stood at £313 a week.

A survey conducted for Ark Life Assurance indicated that full time housewives spend an average of 86 hours a week on household tasks including childcare, preparation of meals, general cleaning duties etc. If the average industrial wage was applied the weekly cost would be £673 a week.

Term insurance may also be important for people who lose their jobs. The loss of the job may also mean the loss of the insurance cover provided within a pension scheme. In some cases employers will keep the insurance cover in place for a short time, or it may be possible for the redundant worker to keep up payments himself. There are a wide range of term insurance options to choose from. You can pick the term of years and the size of the cover. The older the person is when the policy is taken out, the higher the premiums. Term insurance is the cheapest way of providing real financial protection for dependants and it is the first type of policy a young family man on slender means should consider. Within this general category there are a number of different possibilities.

Level Term: In this case the sum insured remains fixed for the term of the policy. If the person insured survives the term no payment is made by the insurance company. If he or she dies during the term, then the sum insured is paid out. Even if there is no pay-out, and hopefully that will be the case, the policy offers value for money in the peace of mind it provides.

It could cost up to £660 a week to employ someone to carry out the duties of a housewife.

Convertible Term: This provides the same basic insurance cover as level term assurance, but there is an option to convert the policy into another type. Usually the assurance company allows conversion at any time during the life of the policy and agrees not to require any further medical test or proof of good health. The policy into which you convert will operate from the date of conversion and will be at the normal premium rates applied to such policies given the insured person's age at the time of conversion. A convertible term assurance policy need not cost much more than a level term policy — particularly if it is a relatively long term policy.

Unless your means are very slender and unlikely to improve over time, convertible term assurance makes much more sense than level term. It provides flexibility in the future when life cover may be less importance.

Mortgage protection
policies are an
example of term
insurance.

Decreasing Term: This type of policy is often referred to as a mortgage protection policy since they are often taken out for this purpose. The life cover gradually decreases over the term of the policy. For instance a policy may provide initial cover of £50,000 declining over twenty years. If the insured person dies in the first year his family would get the full £50,000, but by year ten it has reduced to £39,750 and in the last year the cover is only £6,000. This, of course, is an ideal way of providing for the repayment of a house mortgage in the event of death. The sum owing to the building society is decreasing year by year as repayments are made and the sum payable by the insurance company will more or less keep pace.

Some decreasing term policies simply guarantee to pay off the mortgage in the event of death — less any arrears — provided interest rates remain within set limits.

Banks and building societies make it a condition of granting a mortgage that the borrower takes out a mortgage protection policy. Indeed it is a legal requirement on building societies. You don't have to take out the policy with the lender's own insurance company but it is usually cheaper and easier to do so since the premium can be collected with the repayments and some lenders make it expensive to switch by imposing an additional fee on borrowers who take out the insurance elsewhere.

Family Income Benefits: This is another type of term insurance which provides, instead of a lump sum, a regular income for the family or dependants. For example, the policy on a married man might provide for the payment of £5,000 a year every year between his death and the end of a twenty year term. The payment made by the insurance company would not be liable to income tax.

Endowment assurance

With this type of policy the saving element is uppermost. Pure life insurance is kept to the minimum. The actual sum payable on death is relatively small per premium pound compared with term or whole life assurance. They are best viewed as a method of saving or investing and for this reason have been dealt with in chapter 3 on investment.

Disability insurance

Disability benefits are often included in company pension schemes. About three-quarters of all private pension schemes provide for income continuance where a member is unable to continue working due to disability or long-term illness. For those who are not covered through a company scheme there is always the option of providing the cover through what are known as Permanent Health or Income Continuance policies. Self-employed people can be particularly vulnerable to loss of income in the event of illness or disability.

As with all insurance it is well worthwhile shopping around or getting a broker to do it for you. It is important to compare not only the price but also the extent of the cover and, most importantly, what is **not** covered.

As an example of the type of cost involved one company is quoting a premium of £30 a month to insure a man aged thirty for £250 a week while he is unable, because of illness or disability, to work at his usual job. The premium goes up to £47 for a man aged forty. No benefits are paid for the first thirteen weeks of illness unless the claimant is hospitalised.

While tax relief on life assurance policies has been abolished it is still allowed in full on the premiums paid for this type of policy up to a limit of 10 per cent of income. So the true cost can be reduced by almost half for a top rate tax payer. Any benefits received, however, are taxable if the recipient is liable for tax.

Critical Illness Insurance

We usually think of disability arising as a result of an accident but, of course, it can also arise as a result of serious illness. And serious illness can put many strains on a families' finances. Over the past couple of years the insurance companies have been vying with one another in devising ever more elaborate policies providing lump sums in the event of the insured person suffering a serious or critical illness. Payment is usually only made if the person survives for fourteen days after being diagnosed as suffering from one of a stated list of illnesses. Not all illnesses are covered so it is important to read the fine print.

This type of policy should not be seen as an alternative to medical insurance such as VHI or BUPA designed to cover the cost of medical care. Neither is it an alternative to permanent health insurance designed to pay an income if you are unable to work because of an illness or disability. It is not really an alternative to basic life assurance either.

But it does pay out a lump sum which may be used for any purpose. It may help to pay medical expenses or to supplement income. But there is no need to show that the medical expenses have been incurred or that you have lost income. The claim is allowed provided you have suffered one of the designated illnesses and survived for more than fourteen days. The vast bulk of claims in Ireland are made in respect of cancer followed by heart problems and multiple sclerosis.

With some policies premium levels are fixed and guaranteed for the term of the policy. With others the premium is reviewed from time to time and you may be called upon to increase the premium or else accept a reduction in the level of cover. With this second type of policy, part of each premium is invested and the policy may build up a surrender value. The level of future premiums, after an initial fixed period, depends on the performance of the investment fund.

There is heavy competition among the companies so it is well worthwhile shopping around for the widest cover at the cheapest price if you feel that you need this cover.

Products are changing. But by way of illustration, a man of 45 should be able to get cover for £50,000 in respect of serious illness or total permanent disability for a monthly premium of about £27 but some companies quote premiums as high as £48 a month. Conditions vary from policy to policy so you can't compare on a strictly like-with-like basis. You can shop around, however, by yourself or through a broker. A good broker should be able to justify his or her recommendation. Just ask, why this product rather than another and make sure you get a credible answer.

Whole of life assurance

Term assurance is pure protection. There is no element of saving since no payments are made if the insured person survives the term. With whole of life assurance there is an element of saving, although it is saving for your dependents after your death. The insurance company undertakes to pay the agreed sum — plus bonuses if you go for a with-profits policy — whenever you die. So unlike term assurance, the payment is made at some time.

Obviously the premiums payable for a given life cover are higher in this case than a similar term assurance. You can opt to pay premiums up to death or else elect to stop paying premiums at a certain age. For most people, whose incomes fall after retirement at 65, it is a good idea to have premium payments stopping then.

No family should be without some form of life assurance. As mentioned in the introduction to this chapter the early death of husband or wife can impose severe financial burdens on the surviving spouse. And for a relatively small sum, life assurance can provide some protection and a certain amount of peace of mind. Remember, that even if you live to pay all the premiums on a term assurance, and therefore get no monetary gain, you have still got a return in the peace of mind you have enjoyed over the years knowing that your family has some protection against the financial loss they would suffer through your early death.

It is important, however, to get the right type of assurance geared to your own particular circumstances. There can be no hard and fast rules. Every family's circumstances are different, but here are some guidelines to follow. Protection is obviously the first consideration. And the newly married couple on a tight budget can get this through term assurance. Unless the budget is extremely tight, convertible term assurance offers the best bet providing the flexibility to convert into other types of assurance as the family circumstances, and possibly budget, improve.

So the first policy should be a convertible term assurance providing a lump sum on the death of either spouse but particularly on the death of the principal earner or, alternatively, guarantee of a regular income over a set number of years. This basic cover may well be provided as part of an occupational pension scheme. In that case the term insurance may not be needed.

So, first check if there is adequate cover through an occupational pension scheme. If not, then term assurance is the cheapest way to get protection. A 25 year old might take a policy over a 25 year term — by the end of which the need for cover may have declined as children mature. If money is really tight a shorter term policy can provide similar cover at a lower premium.

If a house is being purchased on a mortgage the lender will undoubtedly require a mortgage protection policy. For a very low premium this will provide enough funds to pay off the mort-

What to choose

Life assurance is primarily concerned with providing protection for your family and dependents in the event of early death.

gage should the breadwinner or, in most cases now, either spouse die within the set term. Basically it is a declining balance term assurance i.e. the amount paid out on death goes down each year in line with the reduced indebtedness to the provider of the mortgage.

It is also possible to get a term assurance to cover the full value of the house without any decline in the amount payable on death, but this is more expensive.

Even if both spouses are not earning it is important to consider having insurance on both. A mortgage protection policy will usually be on the joint lives ensuring that the mortgage is paid off in the event of either dying. But even with the mortgage paid off a surviving spouse with children can be faced with a lot of additional expense while at the same time the family may have lost the earnings of the deceased spouse. Few people think of the costs imposed on a family by the death of a parent even if he or she was not wage-earning. The surviving spouse who wishes to keep the family together might need to employ a housekeeper and will certainly be involved in some expense in looking after the children.

One approach is to combine a mortgage protection policy on the joint lives of the spouses with a term insurance on the life of the principal earner and a ten to fifteen year endowment policy on the life of the lower earning or non-earning spouse. The endowment policy provides a lump sum in the event of death but if the spouse is still alive at the end of the ten or fifteen year term, as hopefully he or she will, then the policy will pay out a useful lump sum which can be put towards the children's education.

But the main aim of life insurance must never be lost sight of. The objective must be to provide financial cover in the event of premature death. While that can be combined with saving for the future through endowment policies there are many other ways of saving. It is important to separate the twin objectives of protection for dependants and saving for the future. Be sure of what you need and what you are buying.

These are just some general guidelines for deciding what type of policy you need. So how best to go about taking them out and what about the fine print? Let us look first at the usual conditions applying to life assurance.

Commission
— the cost

It is important to shop around for the best policy. There can be a wide variation in the cover and cost. A good independent broker can help you in making the choice and can provide information on what is available and why one policy may be better suited to your needs than another. He or she can also help you to decide on the type of policy you need. The broker gets paid for those efforts by way of a commission and is worth the price if the job has been done well. Some advisers charge clients a fee and pass the commission back to the client. There may be little difference in the cost to the person taking out the insurance and it's very hard for the average buyer to do the necessary comparisons. Hopefully that is going to change during 2000.

Before 1989 life insurance companies often competed against one another on the basis of commission — not by offering lower commission but by offering higher commission. They believed — often rightly — that higher commissions would entice brokers to sell their products rather than someone else's. Many customers lost out as a result and the insurance industry itself began to lose out as the abuse was publicised.

Under a voluntary agreement maximum commission levels were agreed by the vast majority of life insurance companies and that agreement continued with some changes until it was abolished in 1998 by the Competition Authority. There is now no control, voluntary or otherwise, on the amount of commission insurance companies can pay to brokers, agents or their own salespeople. So competition by way of commission levels is once again a possibility. Indeed there are already variations in the amount of commission different companies are paying.

A ministerial order requiring insurance companies and intermediaries to disclose the full range of charges applying to life insurance policies is being drafted. The disclosure will include commission. It is expected that the order will be made during 2000.

Until the ministerial order is made the consumer is unprotected. There is no agreement on maximum commission levels and there is no right to a full disclosure of charges and commissions. But there is nothing to stop a customer asking for information on charges and commissions and a full explanation of both.

The table below outlines the maximum commission levels that applied under the now defunct commissions agreement. The initial commission on savings type policies and regular premium pension plans was capped at 50 per cent of the annual premium with an annual renewal commission of 4 per cent. The commission, of course, is the broker's pay for advice and the administration of the policy so it can be money well spent if the broker has been doing his or her job.

There is also commission, of course, on single premium products. These include both pensions and investment bonds. The commission on single premium pension plans was set at 5 per cent while the rate on other single premium investment bonds was set at 3 per cent with an extra half per cent coming out of the fund value each year.

Commission has been the traditional source of income for insurance brokers and financial advisers but there are some who operate on a fee basis and take no commission. As mentioned above the end result for the client may be much the same in either case. What's saved on commission may well go on the fee.

Commissions on life assurance policies

The maxima provided for in the now defunct commissions agreement – useful as a guide to the most you should be paying

Policy type	Commission
Savings type policies.	An initial 2½ per cent of first year's premium for each year of the policy subject to a maximum of 50 per cent, plus an annual commission of 4 per cent of each year's premium payable thereafter.
Protection policies — term, permanent health and critical illness.	An initial 10 per cent of the first year's premium for each year of the policy subject to a maximum of 90 per cent, plus an annual 3 per cent payable on each annual renewal.
Pension policies.	An initial 2½ per cent of the first year's premium for each year of the policy subject to a maximum of 50 per cent plus 4 per cent of annual premium pay on each renewal.
Single Premiums.	5 per cent of the premium paid on pension policies. 3 per cent of the initial sum on life assurance bonds plus ½ per cent of the fund value each year.

An argument in favour of fee-based charging is that the adviser cannot be influenced by commission considerations — a factor that may be more important now that the commissions agreement has ended. He gets the same fee whatever he advises so the advice wouldn't be coloured by any desire to maximise commission.

The counter-argument is that disclosure of commission, and other charges, will enable the customer to recognise that type of abuse and that transparency may force all companies to provide the same commission to the broker but, of course, commission rates can differ between products and customers may find it very hard to understand the information they get.

There is a different commission arrangement for protection type policies — the type which only pays out on death or for illness or disability. Under the terms of the old agreement the initial commission was calculated on the basis of 10 per cent multiplied by the term of the policy subject to a maximum of 90 per cent. So a five year policy paid a commission of 50 per cent with an ongoing commission each year of 3 per cent of the annual premium.

The fine print

The first point to bear in mind with all insurance policies is the condition of 'utmost good faith' implied in all contracts. This simply means that you are required to tell the assurance company all the facts relevant to its assessment of the risk it is undertaking in assuring your life. If you withhold a relevant fact then the policy can be declared null and void and no payment will be made.

Recent court judgements have made the law less certain on this matter and the insurance companies are taking more care in asking the right questions and stressing the need for full disclosure of relevant details. But it is obviously important to give full details of past illnesses etc. There is no need, however, to get unduly worried if you forget to declare some minor illness.

A further point is that you can only take out a life assurance policy on someone whose death will clearly involve you in financial loss. You must have an insurable interest in the person's life. A husband or wife is considered to have an infinite insurable interest in the life of his or her spouse and a child, of course, has an insurable interest in its parents.

But the insurable interest of parents in their children is consid-ered to be very small. This last point was written into law many years ago to prevent unscrupulous parents from taking out large assurance policies on their children and then being tempted to murder them.

With life assurance the other sections of the policy are usually straightforward enough. They contain details of who is insured; conditions on the payment of premiums; how claims are to be made and paid. A point to bear in mind is that the name on the policy should coincide with the person's name on their birth certificate. Otherwise problems can sometimes arise.

There will also be provisions on surrender values, conversion rights if applicable, and options available should you be unable to keep up your premium payments.

Let's have a look at these in more detail as they can sometimes lead to difficulties and misunderstandings.

Surrender Values: Most policies provide for an early cashing in. But it is not something to be considered except as an abso-lutely last resort. The surrender value of a policy is usually less than the amount of premiums already paid so that an early cash-ing in involves you in a definite loss. In a way this is under-standable. An assurance policy is rightly viewed as a long-term contract — a good reason for making the right decision in the first place — and the assurance company is involved in some heavy costs in preparing the initial contract.

On term assurance there is often no surrender value and cer-tainly in the early years of a whole of life or endowment policy the surrender values are very small. So if at all possible forget about surrendering your policy. There are other options if you are unable to keep up your premiums.

Paid-Up Policy: If you find that you can no longer meet the premiums it is usually possible to convert the policy into one that is 'fully-paid up'. Suppose you have a twenty-year endow-ment policy on which you have paid premiums for ten years and the life cover is £2,000. It is usually possible to stop paying premiums and continue to have a policy covering you for half (ten-twentieths) of the original sum assured.

Only surrender assurance policies as a last resort. There are various other options worth considering if you can no longer afford the premiums or need to get some money.

Conversion Rights: If you have a policy carrying conversion rights — say a convertible term assurance — bear it in mind when you come to take out fresh assurance. You may have reached the stage where you can afford higher premiums so consider first whether it is better to convert an existing policy rather than take out a new one. If your health is failing this option may be particularly valuable as you will not usually have to undergo a new medical test.

Loans: If you find yourself unable to meet the premiums on a policy or if you have a need for ready cash, it is sometimes possible to obtain a loan from the assurance company on endowment policies. Some companies give loans up to the full surrender value of the policy. Others draw the line at 90 per cent. Interest rates on these loans are normally very competitive and, very often the interest does not have to be paid as it is taken out of the benefit due at the end of the term. Loans are not given on term or unit linked policies.

A policy with a surrender value is good security for a loan. In some cases insurance companies themselves lend money on them.

Selling a policy: If you have an endowment policy which you have to surrender it may be possible to sell it to an investor for rates up to 25 per cent higher than the surrender value. It's better not to surrender a policy at all but if you have to it can be well worth while shopping around and not simply surrendering it back to the insurance company. There are companies specialising in arranging this type of sale.

How to buy assurance

Buying life assurance can be a far bigger financial decision than many people realise. It is a long-term contract which can cost a lot over the years and can involve considerable loss if cancelled too soon. So it is essential to make the right decisions at the start. Don't be afraid to shop around, ask questions, and take your time over decisions. Take advice from more than one person before committing yourself.

The earlier part of this chapter provides some guide to the type of policy you may need to suit your particular circumstances. Work out for yourself the type of policy you think you need and have the reasons clear in your mind.

Only then approach the insurance sellers. They fall into three broad categories and by law they must declare which category they fall into. There are "tied agents" who only sell the products of one assurance company; "agents" who sell the products of up to four companies; and "brokers" who should give independent advice and write policies for at least five different companies.

Let us have a look at these three in more detail.

Tied Agents: In general tied agents are trained to sell the products of their own company and may or may not know all that much about the global technicalities of assurance. They are, of course, out to sell their own company's products and they may have an incentive to sell a particular type of policy because it provides them with a higher commission or the company simply wants to sell that product. But they can only do this to a limited extent. Most companies are jealous of their good name — looking to ongoing business — and would quickly weed out any agent who was obviously misselling policies in order to boost his or her commission.

Agents: Some of these are part-timers who may be expert in their own fields of law, accounting, or what have you, but can only have a limited knowledge of assurance. But their expertise may be more than adequate and they have to be able to choose from at least two companies' products.

Brokers: By law brokers must either be members of a recognised broker organisation or else registered with the Irish Insurance Compliance Bureau — an overseeing body run by the insurance companies. If good, he is in an ideal position to advise you, given the fact that he is independent of the assurance companies and can pick from the policies offered by at least five companies. But care must be taken in picking your broker. Be particularly wary of brokers who advertise one particular policy to the exclusion of others.

Remember, the broker can only be good if he takes stock of your personal circumstances first before trying to sell you a policy. There is no easy guide to picking the right intermediary. For preference go to a reputable firm which can obviously provide sound back-up service.

Ask around for advice about who other people have found reputable. If in doubt, seek the advice of more than one broker or agent. Get details of policies direct from the companies concerned. Write to other companies asking for details of their similar type policies. In all cases, take your time.

With life assurance, a good broker or agent will want to know details of your financial position; any other assurance cover you have; your prospects for the future; the size of your family; and your plans for them. If he does not ask for such details, be wary, since he cannot possibly give sound advice without knowing details of your personal circumstances.

There are systems for dealing with complaints —see chapter 11.

Medical Insurance

While every Irish citizen is entitled to basic health care free of charge it may be possible to get speedier treatment if you are able to pay your own way. You also have a wider choice of consultant and of hospital accommodation. Private medical care can, however, be very expensive and would be beyond the reach of most people in the absence of an insurance scheme.

The VHI (Voluntary Health Insurance) had a near monopoly of the provision of medical insurance up until January 1997 when the law was changed allowing for competition. At the time a restriction of 'community rating' was imposed on all new entrants. This requires that insurers in this category provide cover at the same premium rates to all adults seeking it.

The British based BUPA set up an Irish subsidiary during 1997 and has since developed a range of products similar, but not directly comparable, with those offered by the VHI. VHI responded by extending its range with the introduction of optional enhancements to its existing plans. Both companies have added refinements to their products since then. As a result the consumer is left with a confusing range of options.

VHI has five basic plans, each of which can be extended with what are known as "options". So there are in effect two different products. BUPA Ireland offers three basic plans.

The VHI's basic plans provide different levels of cover related to the type of hospital accommodation required. Plan A covers semi-private accommodation in public hospitals while at the other end of the scale Plan E covers accommodation in the Blackrock Clinic and Mater Private Hospital. VHI does not guarantee to cover all the medical costs involved in all procedures but it does supply a list of medical consultants — about 97 per cent of the total number — who do accept VHI rates as full settlement of their fees. Other consultants may charge more than the VHI payment rates. Your doctor will be able to tell you whether a consultant is in the VHI scheme. Don't be afraid to ask.

There are limits to the amount of cover. Those limits can be eased and extra cover obtained by an additional *option* premium. There are also time limits on pre-existing ailments which apply both to new members and those rejoining after a lapse of membership. If you do not pay your subscription within fifteen days of the due date your policy can be lapsed — so be careful.

Those joining VHI under 55 are not covered for pre-existing ailments for the first five years after joining and get no benefits for ailments arising in the first 26 weeks. Those aged between 55 and 59 on joining are not covered for existing ailments for seven years and get no benefits for ailments arising in the first 18 weeks. For those joining over the age of 60, there is no cover for pre-existing ailments for ten years and no benefits for ailments arising in the first 52 weeks.

BUPA Ireland offers three alternatives, Essential, Essential Plus, and BUPA Gold. The Essential Plan covers semi-private accommodation in participating public hospitals. Essential Plus private accommodation in those public hospitals and semi-private in other participating hospitals while Essential Gold covers private accommodation in all participating hospitals including the Mater Private, St Vincent's Private Hospital and the Blackrock Clinic.

Cover for certain heart surgery procedures in the Mater Private and Blackrock Clinic is provided in all the plans. But they all differ in the amount of out-patient cover provided.

The Essential Plus plan is the most popular and is often compared with VHI's most popular plan – Plan B with options.

But the two are not directly comparable. There is no easy way of deciding which is best. It very must depends on individual preferences. There is not a great deal of difference in terms of cost except where there are full-time students over eighteen years of age in a family. BUPA charges for such students at the child rate while VHI charge a premium rate somewhere between the child and full adult rate.

Both VHI and BUPA give a 10 per cent reduction in premiums for those in group schemes. Many credit unions operate group schemes which are open to self-employed people provided they join the credit union. Not only do they get a 10 per cent saving on the premium but the credit union may also provide them with a cost-free facility for paying the premium in monthly instalments.

Borrowing

Borrowing — the best deals 5.1

Sensible borrowing has always had an important and beneficial role to play in family finance. But there is a cost involved. Interest rates rose slightly again towards the end of 1999 but they are still close to their lowest levels for decades having converged with central European rates following the creation of the pan-European currency, the euro. They seem set to remain low — at least by historical Irish standards — for the foreseeable future. But when considering the level of interest rates it is important to take inflation into account. Consumer prices are currently rising at a slow pace so that many personal borrowers are paying real interest rates as high as they ever were.

But borrowing can often make sense even after taking account of the low level of inflation. Against the cost there can be offsetting benefits i.e. the benefit of buying something now rather than having to wait until you have saved up the money. Tax relief can reduce the cost of loans used to buy, maintain or improve your principal residence or to buy shares in your own company. Mortgage tax relief is detailed in Chapter 6.3 on page 131.

But in all cases you should be aware of the cost. Make up your own mind whether the benefits outweigh it. Be clear that you can afford the repayments. Know what the repayments are and when they are payable. Are you sure you will be able to meet them as they fall due? What is the likelihood of you hitting a bad patch — an unforeseen expense or drop in income — which might make repayment of the loan difficult or impossible?

Having assured yourself of all that the final step is to shop around for the cheapest possible loan.

Each individual will exercise a different degree of caution, but there is no need to be cautious to the point of not borrowing at all. Most reputable lenders will allow a degree of flexibility to help a borrower over an unexpected bad patch.

There is a wide range of options open to the would-be borrower: bank loans, finance houses, credit sales, budget accounts, H.P., etc.. And the cost can vary greatly. All those providing credit, either by way of loans or by way of credit sales, are required to show the true rate of interest being charged on their loans. All but the most general advertisements for loans are required to show interest rates. So it is possible to shop around by just keeping your eyes open and comparing rates. The difference between the dearest and cheapest loan can be significant. Getting the cheapest available can save you a lot of money and remember that the lender really wants to lend money. That is how they make a profit. If nobody borrowed they would go out of business.

Where the loan is arranged by the provider of a product or service that you are buying don't forget to check carefully the price you are being charged for the goods or services. It's no good saving on the loan and ending up paying over the odds for whatever you are buying. Similar caution is necessary when buying goods or services on credit, perhaps paying by instalments. Even if the credit is claimed to be free there's very likely a hidden cost in the price of the goods or service being bought. So shop around not only for the cheapest loan but also for the cheapest goods and service.

Shopping around

Borrowing is a normal business transaction, in which the buyer is buying a commodity from the seller. The commodity in this case is money. It might be more correct to say that the borrower is hiring the use of the money for a period and will be paying a rental — the interest — for the use of it. The lender has one thought in mind — will he get the money back? This is the risk factor, and the higher the risk he considers he is taking the higher the interest he will charge. The longer the period of the loan, the greater is the risk he foresees: so normally the longer the term of the loan, the higher the interest rate. The major exception to this rule are mortgage loans on which rates are relatively low because of the security provided.

Most lenders, of course, have their interest rates fixed at any particular time and, as a result, have a set idea about the risk they are willing to take, or, in other words, the type of person they will lend to. So the would-be borrower should be ready to fortify the lender's faith in his ability to repay. As we said, the lender wants to lend the money — he just needs convincing that you are a good risk.

Obviously, you want to pay the lowest interest rate possible, and as a rough guide the rates will go up as you move along the following list: building societies (for mortgages), the major banks, credit unions, finance houses, credit accounts, hire purchase, money lenders. It used to be very difficult for the uninitiated to compare the interest rates being charged on alternative loans but this difficulty has been overcome with the requirement that all lenders show the annual percentage rate (APR) charged on their loans. This can be defined as the true rate of interest and can be used to compare alternatives. The APR shown on loan advertisements, shop notices and loan agreements has to be based on the global cost of the loan — interest and other charges. So it is ideal for comparing one source of finance with another — the lower the APR, the cheaper the loan.

In the past lenders declared their interest rates in all sorts of different ways which were not comparable. Some quoted rates close to the true annual rate of interest; others quoted monthly rates; others a rate on the initial sum borrowed; or some other such device aimed at making comparison almost impossible.

It is no harm having some understanding of what a true rate of interest is. Suppose you get £100 now and repay £110 this day next year — i.e., the initial £100 plus £10 interest — that is a true rate of interest of 10 per cent — £10 on £100. But suppose that instead of repaying in a lump sum, the repayments are spread over the full year and you still repay a total of £110, that is nearer a 20 per cent rate of interest, since you did not have the use of the £100 for the full year. Indeed, you only had, on average, the use of £50 for the full year, since you had more than £50 for the first six months, but progressively less than £50 for the second six months.

It does not matter a lot how the rate of interest is actually calculated as long as they are all calculated in the same way so that the borrower is comparing like with like. The APR allows you to do this since it has to be calculated in the same way by all

Lenders, be they banks, finance companies or pawnbrokers, want to lend money. That is their business and that is how they make their profit. There is no need to go out with the begging bowl.

lenders. Some of them may still be quoting rates calculated in different ways but they have to quote the APR as well. The best advice is to ignore any other rate except the APR.

As mentioned above the borrower has a wide number of options open to him and the cost difference between the cheapest and dearest loans can be considerable. So it pays to consider carefully the various options and to try the cheapest first.

Overdrafts

Overdrafts used to be the preserve of the Associated Banks i.e. the four largest banks — Allied Irish Banks, Bank of Ireland, National Irish, and Ulster Bank, but they are now available from range of other banks such as the ACCBank, TSB, Irish Permanent, and Tusa, the new banking operation linked with Superquinn. An overdraft is usually the cheapest type of bank loan because of its flexibility. But it can prove expensive in some circumstances. Running up an overdraft will usually lose the customer the benefit of free banking. Someone who keeps his current account in credit may be exempt from bank charges on his transactions but once the account runs into overdraft — even for a short period — it can mean having to pay bank charges for a full three months. Those charges must be considered as additional to the interest in working out the true cost of an overdraft. Some lenders also impose an arrangement fee. Allied Irish Bank and Ulster Bank charge £20 for arranging an overdraft permission. Bank of Ireland charges £12. So the costs can be significant but that can be offset by the greater flexibility.

Overdrafts are the most flexible way of borrowing and they can be one of the cheapest.

Once an overdraft permission has been granted, it can be drawn on at any time without fresh recourse to the bank. That convenience has some value and there is a very tangible gain as well. Every penny put into the account immediately reduces the amount of the loan and since interest is charged on the amount outstanding each day there can be a significant saving.

Suppose, for instance, the borrower has his or her wages paid into the bank each month. Let's suppose that a net £1,000 is lodged. If that money is spent evenly over the month the customer has a net £500 on average in the account over the year — more than £500 early in the month and less than £500 later in the month but an average of £500. That's automatically reducing the size of the overdraft. At 10 per cent a year the interest saving would be £50 to help offset the extra charges which might be incurred.

To avail of an overdraft you need to have a current i.e. cheque book account. In effect you ask your bank manager if you can overdraw your account to a specified sum. If he agrees you can then write cheques for that amount over and above the funds you have in your account. You only pay interest on the actual amount you have drawn and, as mentioned above, interest is calculated on a day-to-day basis. If you don't make use of the overdraft permission you pay no interest.

Overdraft permissions, however, are only given to cover short-term borrowing requirements. There are no set repayments, but the account has to be back in credit at least within a year and the bank manager will want some assurance that you will be able to clear off the debt within that period. So overdrafts generally have a limited use. They are particularly useful to cover the odd bad month when a number of large payments fall due. In other words it should be viewed like an advance, or a "sub" on your salary or wages which will have to be paid off on the next pay day or at least over a few pay periods.

- **Budget Accounts:** Some banks and credit unions run budget type accounts where the customer sets out his spending requirements in advance. They are not unlike formalised overdrafts. The spending needs will not, of course, be spread evenly over the year but the bank allows for overdraft type loans to cover the lean periods while requiring fixed regular payments. It is simply a way of balancing out one's cash flow. But it is fixed and formalised — unlike the normal overdraft.

Three of the big four banks offer budget accounts which are a sort of formalised overdraft. Allied Irish Banks has "Masterplan"; Bank of Ireland has "Budget Saver" and National Irish has "Home Management". In all three the borrower makes out a budget for the year ahead listing the bills which he wants covered. Those are then totalled up, divided by twelve, and he pays that much into the account each month. As bills fall due, he can draw out sufficient money to pay them, borrowing automatically any excess needed when his savings fall short of what has to be paid. There are charges to pay in addition to the interest on the amounts needed to be borrowed but they are relatively small.

Term loans

Unlike overdrafts, term loans have fixed repayment commitments. Also, unlike an overdraft, the full amount of the loan is handed out to you or transferred into your current account and interest liability begins to accrue immediately. Interest rates can vary greatly depending on the lender, the borrower, the term of the loan, and even, in some cases, what the loan is for. It is up to the borrower to shop around and take care. The Central Bank used to set an upper limit to the amount a lender could charge but that control was abolished during 1999. It worked by linking the top rate a bank could charge for loans to the lowest rate charged to business customers. The idea was that competitive pressures exercised by large business borrowers would keep the lowest rates low and that personal borrowers with less clout in the market place would share in the benefits.

With that control gone personal borrowers need to take extra care.

While lenders do have schedules of interest rates that apply in most cases, they can and do charge higher rates to some customers and for some purposes. So it is important to check around. In general the larger banks charge the same rate for normal term loans as they do for overdrafts but ignoring the impact of bank charges — as mentioned above — a term loan may prove more expensive for short term borrowing since you do not have the flexibility of drawing down only what you need. But overdrafts normally have to be cleared off at least once a year so they are not suitable for those keeping funds over a longer period.

Repayments are normally set in monthly amounts extending over a fixed period.

Most term loans are given at variable rates of interest. The rate charged may change during the term of the loan in line with changes in wholesale interest rates. The rate may go up or down. If rates go up some lenders will leave repayment levels unchanged and add some extra repayments at the end to cover the higher interest rate. Others may require an immediate increase in the repayments.

Fixed rate loans are also available but there are drawbacks. If variable rates are expected to rise the fixed rate will be set higher than the initial variable rate. On average fixed rate loans will be more expensive than variable rate ones. The borrower pays a premium for the security of knowing that the interest rate will not be increased during the term of the loan. If rates do go up it will have been worthwhile but if rates decline a variable rate loan would have worked out cheaper.

The major drawback with fixed rate loans is a lack of flexibility. There are usually penalties, sometimes quite heavy, for early repayment.

Repayments (monthly) per £1,000 borrowed

Interest rate	3 years	5 years	7 years	10 years
8 per cent	£31.27	£20.21	£15.52	£12.06
8.5 per cent	£31.50	£20.44	£15.76	£12.32
9 per cent	£31.72	£20.68	£16.00	£12.58
9.5 per cent	£31.94	£20.91	£16.25	£12.84
10 per cent	£32.17	£21.14	£16.49	£13.10
10.5 per cent	£32.39	£21.38	£16.74	£13.37
11 per cent	£32.62	£21.62	£16.99	£13.63
11.5 per cent	£32.84	£21.85	£17.24	£13.90
12 per cent	£33.07	£22.09	£17.49	£14.18
12.5 per cent	£33.29	£22.33	£17.75	£14.45
13 per cent	£33.52	£22.57	£18.00	£14.73

Opting for a fixed rate loan can make sense where the borrower needs assurance the repayments levels won't increase during the term of the loan. That can often be the case with a mortgage loan where the repayments represents a large proportion of the borrowers income. But it's less likely to apply in the case of a smaller term loan. The extra flexibility and potential lower cost of a variable rate loan usually makes it the best option.

Term loans are available from a wide range of lenders, banks, building societies, credit unions and finance houses. Building societies better known for their mortgage finance can and do provide unsecured personal loans. Credit Unions are ever increasing their range of services. They are treated in more detail below.

Do a wealth check on your borrowings — it

Financial decisions, once made, are all too seldom reviewed. This is particularly the case with personal borrowings. Built up over time for various different reasons, it is very easy to let each loan run its course. Yet personal circumstances change, interest rates vary, and the need for the debt may diminish as other assets become available.

So it's worth doing an occasional wealth check on your borrowings. It is possible to re-finance debt in order to alter repayment schedules or avail of lower interest rates. It may be worthwhile using savings to reduce or pay off a loan. The biggest interest savings can be made by rolling up a number of loans into a mortgage top-up. The interest rates are the lowest available and the repayments can be spread over as long as twenty years. It's an option which needs very careful consideration and it's not the only change which can produce savings. Before you can make any decisions, of course, you need to take a little time to itemise your current loans and work out what they are costing you. Then you can start looking at the alternatives.

But first list your loans. They are likely to fall into three main categories.

Mortgage: You know how much you initially borrowed but how much do you owe now. If it was an endowment mortgage you still owe as much as you did on the day you took out the loan but your endowment policy should be worth something. Find out how much it is worth. It's seldom worth cashing in a policy on which you have already incurred heavy set-up charges but it's nice to know where you stand.

How much equity do you have in your house? If it is worth at least 10 per cent more than the outstanding loan you should be able to get a top up mortgage. What rate of interest

Finance houses sometimes provide loans through car dealers or shops. Sometimes they are at special low rates subsidised by the retail outlet. It is important to be sure, however, that you are not paying for the cheaper loan by paying over the odds for the goods or services being bought.

In other cases it is cheaper to go direct to the finance house itself rather than take out the loan through the retailer, service provider or agent. The intermediary often takes a commission — which you pay — and in any case you are in a stronger bargaining position when buying the goods if you arrange the loan yourself. As far as the seller is concerned, you are then a cash buyer.

are you paying? Is it fixed or variable? How does it compare with the competition. It can be worth switching mortgages although it is a big step and likely to require a heavy up-front cost. See page 130.

Bank Loans: We can include credit union and finance company loans in this category. You should check what rate of interest you are paying. There isn't a lot of variation at this time between one institution and the other but if you have a loan that's a few years old you may discover that you are still paying a fixed rate that's a little over the odds. If so you need to find out if you can pay it off without penalty.

Also check your overdraft. An overdraft can be the cheapest form of bank borrowing since you only pay interest on the amount outstanding each day. So when your pay cheque is lodged to your account, your interest liability immediately goes down. A well used overdraft can be cheaper than a term loan even though the interest rates are the same on both.

But running up an occasional overdraft can be very expensive since it usually makes you immediately liable for bank charges during the relevant quarter. Running up an overdraft for just one day can prove very costly.

Credit Cards: Credit cards should ideally only be used to secure free credit by paying the bill in full each month. Occasionally letting some of the bill run on for a month or two is not too costly but on-going debt should definitely be avoided. The interest rates can be penal — over 20 per cent. It's easy to get into the habit of letting the credit card debt run on and on paying only the minimum requirement each month. The answer is to get a term loan to pay off the debt. If you then let the credit card debt run up again it may be time to bring out the scissors and cut the card in two.

Finance houses are the most likely to apply a sliding scale of interest rates on personal loans, depending on what the loan is for. Cheapest rates are usually for things like house extensions — dearest, perhaps, for second-hand cars. They are seldom in a position to check — they just ask you.

Some lenders offer a variant of the term loan known as an endowment loan. They are not very popular and are seldom actively marketed. The loans are usually for longer periods — say ten years — to be used for home improvements or education. Basically the idea is that the borrower only pays the interest on the loan during its term — say ten years. He also takes out an insurance policy which matures at the end of the ten years hopefully providing enough funds to pay off the loan and maybe even leave something over. There is a risk, of course, that the investment fund will not yield enough to pay off the loan and there are set-up costs to be borne on the insurance policy.

Endowment loans can work but the borrower needs to appreciate the risks and be willing and able to accept them.

Most banks also provide more flexible loans to suit special circumstances. There are also "loan accounts" on which there are no fixed repayments. Such loans are negotiated on a personal basis with the repayments geared to suit the circumstances. The interest rate is often no higher than that on an overdraft or term-loan but it sometimes is to reflect the higher risk.

Mortgages

Loans for house purchase are dealt with in Chapter 6, page 115 but there are other uses for loans secured with mortgages on the borrower's house or other property. Such loans are, of course, mainly used for house purchase but need not be. The interest rate is lower than on other loans but there are usually setup costs involved in taking out the mortgage — they are detailed in Chapter 6. Those costs are lower, of course, in the case of a top-up mortgage.

Topping up a mortgage sometimes involves taking out a new increased mortgage and paying off the existing one. But it is possible to take out a second mortgage while leaving the existing one. A bank or building society with an existing mortgage on the property should be able to set up a new mortgage at a lower cost. But it is important to check interest rates as well.

Because of the cost of setting up the mortgage this type of loan does not make much sense unless a fairly sizeable amount is being borrowed — say upwards of £3,000. And it is important to appreciate that the loan is secured on the property. The bank or society has the right to sell the property to get its money back if the borrower defaults on payments. It is that security which allows them to charge a lower interest rate. So in return for a cheaper loan the borrower is putting his home or other property on the line.

Borrowing by way of a mortgage can make sense where the money is being spent on a house extension or other long term investment in real assets — that can include education. But despite the lower interest rate it may not be a good idea to borrow on mortgage simply to pay off short-term debts or finance short-term purchases such as a car or a holiday.

People have been encouraged to extend their mortgages to pay off their bank and credit card debts. Their monthly repayments can go down as a result but that is partly because the debt is being spread over a longer period. In two or three years time they will still be facing many years of higher mortgage repayments while the bank and credit card debts may have again emerged. And they have put their homes up as security.

So care needs to be taken. It is usual for mortgage finance providers to charge the normal house purchase rate for personal loans related to the house. Up to an extra two percentage points may be charged on other personal loans with business loans rating three percentage points above the basic mortgage rate.

Store budget accounts

Most of the larger stores have their own budget account facilities and a growing number of smaller stores have budget accounts run for them by finance houses. The interest rate is much the same as charged by the finance houses. The best advice is to avoid them.

While a budget account is handy, it can be relatively dear to run — it is cheaper to try to get a term loan from your bank or, cheaper still, your credit union. Budget accounts are flexible, however, allowing you to spend up to the applied maximum credit level at any time.

The worst part, however, is that you have to use it in the one store, or group of stores, so there is a disincentive to shopping around. Indeed, borrowing on your credit card is likely to be as cheap while still leaving you the freedom to shop around. But in either case, of course, you may be tempted to spend more than you should, or really want to.

The advice is to try to get a bank or credit union loan for major shopping sprees. If you want to have a store card to avail of special offers or promotions try to keep it on the basis of a monthly card. That should cost you nothing.

If you actually do a lot of shopping in the one store there can be some advantage in having a card, even for credit purposes, since the card is generally free and the interest rate can be lower than that charged on a bank or building society card.

Credit unions

Credit unions are among the cheapest providers of loans but they are, of course, only available to members. Membership is open to those who are part of a "common bond" i.e. live in the locality or work in the particular firm covered by the union. To qualify for a loan it is usually necessary to be a member of some standing having shown an ability to save. But that can be well worth the effort. There are credit unions now based in most localities and in many organisations and big firms.

With the enactment of legislation in 1997 credit unions have been empowered to provide larger loans over longer periods. The standard interest rate is 1 per cent a month — an annual percentage rate of 12.6 per cent. But many credit unions now charge less than that.

Credit unions are non-profitmaking organisations. Any surplus made belongs to the members. Some credit unions use some of the surplus to give interest rate rebates to their borrowing members. Another advantage is that loan protection insurance is built-in. It provides for the repayment of the loan in the event of death or permanent disablement. Limits may apply to the size of the loan and the cover is curtailed for the over 60s and not available for the over 70s.

Another built-in insurance provides for the payment of a benefit to a member's estate in the event of death. In the case of a member aged under 55 the benefit is equal to the amount on deposit or in shares at the time of death. The benefit is lower for those over 55 and not applicable in the case of the over 70s.

Hire purchase

Hire purchase is generally an expensive way of buying on credit. Not only is the interest rate high, but there are also high administrative charges, all built into the hire purchase price. Most people who can buy goods on HP would be acceptable for at least a finance house loan — assuming they do not have a normal bank account. Either finance houses or banks would be far cheaper. The best alternative for most people tempted to borrow on hire purchase is the local credit union.

Insurance

It is sometimes possible to borrow against the surrender value of with-profits endowment life assurance policies. Most insurance companies will provide such loans and the interest rates are usually relatively low. In some cases there is no need to repay the loan, since the sum involved will be taken out of the final sum due on maturity of the policy. Indeed, the interest payments can also be rolled forward in this manner. But the policy does need to have a cash-in value higher than the size of the loan.

Credit cards

Credit cards are best seen as a means of getting short-term credit — they are a boon if used wisely in this way. They save you carrying cash; enable you to keep a record of your spending; and can provide you with a handy period of free credit. But used unwisely, they can be very expensive. If you exceed your permitted period of free credit you end up paying a fairly high rate of interest on the outstanding amount — up to twice the rate you would pay on an overdraft or term loan from one of the big-four banks. See the section on credit cards in chapter 2 on page 26.

Moneylenders

The best advice is not to borrow from moneylenders at all, whether legal or illegal. If there is no other alternative pawnbrokers are not all that expensive provided you do not make a habit of using them.

Tackling debt problems

IT is all too easy for debts to become a problem and when they do there is a strong temptation to bury your head in the sand and hope that the problem will go away. Of course, that just makes it worse. The only solution for those with debt problems — or heading that way — is to confront the difficulty head on. The quicker that is done the quicker the problems can be solved.

Mr. Micawber in Charles Dicken's novel "David Copperfield" well understood the problem of debt. His comment is often quoted. It goes like this: "Annual income twenty pounds, annual expenditure nineteen nineteen six, result happiness. Annual income twenty pounds, annual expenditure twenty pounds nought and six, result misery". It has been suggested that Charles Dickens arrived at this view himself as a result of his father's experiences. Mr. Dickens Senior spent some time in a debtors prison.

There is no debtors prison today and contrary to some popular notions it is not possible to end up in prison simply for being in debt. But you can get locked up for failing to meet debt repayments decided on by a court. Initially when a person is brought before a court for debt it will do no more than decide on equitable repayments in the context of the person's ability to pay. It is only if those repayments are not met, that a person may face jail and then only for blatantly failing to pay. A court can always be asked to adjust a repayment order if circumstances change.

But there should be no need for anyone to appear in court for debt. If action is taken soon enough and creditors kept informed of any financial difficulty then it is usually possible to reschedule repayments and sometimes even have interest charges reduced. It is important to take action as early as possible.

Debt is not a bad thing, in itself. Borrowing, indeed, has an important role to play in most families' finances. But borrowing can get out of hand. Problems start to arise when a person's — or a family's — spending needs start to outstrip their income. Initially it may seem possible to handle the problem. But it is usually only being compounded. The balance on the credit card runs up. The ESB bill is missed so that something else can be paid. There is a hope that something will turn up. But it doesn't. Postponed debts do not go away. Indeed if interest is being added on, they only get worse.

Swopping a number of small loans for one big one can be a big mistake too. You can, of course, reduce your monthly repayments by replacing some short-term expensive loans with a cheaper building society or bank mortgage spread over a longer period. But you may be only storing up problems for the future. If you do not meet the repayments on the mortgage you will be putting your home in jeopardy.

This is not the answer if you have major debt problems. If you see it as part of a solution you need to be absolutely sure that you will be able to meet the mortgage repayments and you also need to check that there are no heavy penalties involved in paying off your existing loans early. With many finance house loans there are such penalties. And there is no sense in replacing your loans with even more expensive ones. Overall there is no easy solution down this road.

Remember that you have to deal with the priority debts first. A building society will normally agree to reduce repayments so long as you are at least meeting the interest portion. In the early years this may, unfortunately, represent more than 90% of each repayment so that the possible reduction is not great. But if you are not meeting the interest, then the amount outstanding keeps going up. Banks, credit card companies, and finance houses will sometimes agree to reduce interest charges. Some of their rates are so high they can well afford to. If you feel unable to do the negotiating your local St. Vincent de Paul Society or credit union is likely to know of someone who may be able to help.

The Department of Social Welfare supports a money advice and budgeting advice service (MABS) throughout most of the country. It's a free service of course. Ask about it at your local Social Welfare Office or public library.

Another scheme administered with help from the St. Vincent de Paul Society and credit unions, provides advice on budgeting and will negotiate with creditors on behalf of borrowers. It is not there to pay off loans but rather to help people budget their way out of difficulties. In some cases arrangements may be made to pay off expensive loans and replace them with cheaper credit union loans.

The quicker you face up to debt problems the quicker they can be solved.

SIX POINT PLAN TO TACKLE DEBT

The following six step action plan boils down to facing your problem, coming clean with your creditors and making them an offer based on a full disclosure of what you can afford.

ONE: The first step is to work out exactly what your income is. Get out a copy book or a few sheets of paper and detail your income — what actually comes into the house from all sources each week or month.

TWO: Next list your total spending needs. Do not leave anything out. There are the obvious things like rent/mortgage repayments, food, fuel etc. But do not forget to include the irregular spending items — clothes, the ESB bill which only comes in every two months, insurance bills which may only come once a year etc. Bring it all down to a monthly or weekly figure.

THREE: Then compare your first list with your second. If your income exceeds your spending needs then you do not have a problem in meeting your ongoing commitments. Check your figures again. If your outgoings do exceed your income an obvious approach is to cut your spending. Divide your spending into essentials and nonessentials. Can you cut back? Is there anything you can sell to bring in money to reduce some debt — not goods that you have on HP, although if you do have goods on hire purchase and you have not paid a third of the price, the HP company may take them back.

FOUR: Examine possible ways of increasing your income. Are there any social welfare benefits you are entitled to — supplementary benefit or the family income supplement (see chapter 12). If you are on social welfare and have difficulty meeting your rent, you may be entitled to rent allowance under the supplementary benefit scheme administered by your local health board.

FIVE: List exactly how much you owe. Divide the loans into priority ones and others. The priorities would be rent/mortgage, ESB, other fuel bills. If you fall too far behind with these you could lose your house or have the electricity or gas turned off.

SIX: Lastly having gathered all that information the final step is to talk with your creditors. Summarise the figures you have listed and let them see the details of your income and spending. That way they will realise how much or how little you can afford to pay. Make an offer.

The European Consumer Centre, 13A Upper O'Connell Street, Dublin, phone (01) 809 0600 can help you prepare for a district court appearance over debts of up to £5,000. The legal adviser at the centre can help you prepare for the court appearance but will not actually represent you in court.

Home buying

Home buying
an easy guide
6.1

FOR most families the purchase of a house represents the single largest financial commitment of their lives. The purchase of the house is likely to require three or more times the average person's annual salary. And if the money to make the purchase is borrowed, the repayments will take a considerable part of the family budget. But buying a house does not simply add to household expenses. It is a major investment decision as well, and the return on the investment can be sizable. Borrowing to buy a house usually makes good financial sense even when interest rates are relatively high. Assuming that you do not pay an inflated price for the house, there is little doubt that it makes more sense to borrow and buy, rather than to rent — unless, of course, the rent is particularly low as it might be on a local authority house.

Over the longer term the value of house property can be expected to rise faster than the rate of inflation unless the economy collapses completely. Interest rates will hopefully remain low and even if they do rise from the current levels they may average out at a reasonable level over the twenty years or so during which the loan is being repaid.

So it usually makes sense to buy a house. Even the fairly heavy costs involved in making the purchase can be more than offset for first time buyers of new houses by the State grants available. You need some money for the deposit and expenses and you need to convince a lender that you will be able to meet the repayment on a loan. There are plenty of willing lenders in the market. But there are traps along the way and a lot of critical decisions to make. Unfortunately many of those decisions have to be taken on the basis of assumptions about the future rather than hard facts. So what are the options?

What are the options?

In almost all cases, it makes good financial sense to buy a house on mortgage, provided you are eligible for income tax relief on the interest paid.

The main constraint on what you can buy is the availability of finance. For most people this means simply the amount they are able to borrow. The range of borrowing options open to the house buyer has widened significantly in recent years with most lenders actively seeking mortgage business. The competition has intensified since the Bank of Scotland entered the Irish mortgage market in 1999. It is possible that other lenders will enter the market in the future.

The banks and building societies are looking for would-be borrowers. There is plenty of scope for the borrower to shop around. The choice is wide and you can never be sure of making the right decision. Borrowing by way of a mortgage is a long term decision and who can tell what is going to happen over the space of maybe twenty years. What appears to be the cheapest and best option now may prove to be otherwise over the course of time. There are a number of factors to consider:

Interest rate: It is easy enough to compare interest rates so it is not too difficult to pick the cheapest loan. Have a look at the stated interest rate first and then at the monthly repayments. The repayments are possibly the best guide since while all lenders have to show annual percentage rates of interest that take into account all the factors involved they may not be strictly comparable.

Remember that it is the interest rate over the full term of the loan that matters so do not be taken in for short-term catch all promotions. If the rate is variable it may change within months and what was cheapest when you borrowed may prove dearest in the long run. Some lenders offer a special low rate for the first year or so and that may look attractive. But the gains in the first year can very quickly be offset if the interest rate in subsequent years is higher than the competition.

It is, of course, always possible to switch lenders later but that can be costly enough – perhaps £500 to £1,000. However, switching shouldn't be ruled out because of that. Remember if you can save half a percentage point on a £100,000 mortgage the annual saving is £500 gross or £370 after allowing for tax relief. So the cost of switching can be recouped over a few years. And most mortgages run for twenty years.

Rent or Buy?

Successive governments in Ireland have sought to encourage home ownership through a combination of incentives including grants and tax reliefs. The result is that it is almost always better to buy than to rent. And this has not been changed by the tax relief of up to £500 (single), £1,000 (married) on rent paid for private accommodation. The main exception is someone who is not going to stay in the one place for too long. There are once-off costs incurred in buying which are obviously best spread over a number of years and not repeated too often.

Buying can be far cheaper than renting. A two-bedroomed house in Dublin can cost upwards of £700 a month to rent. The net monthly repayments on a £90,000 mortgage can be as low as £500 after tax.

Taking the example of a married couple buying their first house for £110,000 with a £90,000 mortgage. For the sake of simplicity we can ignore the costs of purchase, legal costs, surveys etc. At an interest rate of 4.5 per cent the gross monthly repayments on £90,000 would be £574 which after tax relief would come down to £493 for a married couple or £524 for a single buyer.

There are other factors to take into account. Someone renting a house would not need the £20,000 deposit. If they have £20,000 they can earn interest on it. That could be worth £33 a month at an interest rate of 2 per cent. That's another cost of buying. It puts the cost up to about £520 for a married buyer — still well below the cost of renting. And there's another advantage in buying. The value of the house should go up. Just going up in line with a 3 per cent inflation puts £275 a month on to the value of a £110,000 house and house values have been rising far faster than that.

Fixed or Variable: It is impossible to know which is best in advance. As a rule of thumb a fixed rate mortgage will tend to be more expensive in the long run. The lender will fix a rate on the basis of how interest rates are expected to move and then add a margin on to cover his risk. The borrower pays a little extra for the assurance that whatever happens to rates his interest rate remains unchanged.

But then it is impossible to accurately foretell the future. It may well be that the fixed rate mortgage will prove to be the cheapest.

In general those on a tight budget who would face severe difficulties if faced with rising interest rates, should consider a fixed rate mortgage. Even if it doesn't prove cheapest they will have benefited from fewer sleepless nights. Borrowers who can well handle a rise in interest rates and are not of a worrying nature should consider a variable rate.

Lender: Different lenders may be prepared to lend different amounts. The norm favoured by the Central Bank is to limit mortgage loans to $2^1/_2$ times the sum of a principal income and half of a secondary income. But some lenders will lend more than that and take a more liberal view of what constitutes "income". Lenders may also have a different propensity to raise interest rates in the future. In Britain mutual building societies have tended to have lower mortgage rates over time than more profit orientated lenders. But there can be no guarantees in this regard.

Endowment versus annuity: An annuity mortgage operates in the same as most loans. The borrower makes a monthly repayment which includes both interest and something off the loan itself. Initially most of the repayment is interest with very little going to reduce the amount owing. But as the years pass the loan goes down faster and in the later years the interest part of each repayment gets smaller. That is the way most people expect to pay off loans and it is easily understood. But it has some implications for tax relief. Tax relief is allowed on the interest paid on loans used to buy, extend or improve the borrower's own residence. The full repayment does not qualify for relief — only the interest portion. And with the annuity type mortgage the interest portion is declining over the years. So the tax relief is going down.

The decline is relatively small in the early years and even ten years into a twenty year loan three-quarters of each monthly repayment is still interest. After that it goes down at a relatively faster pace so that by year fifteen only a little more than half the repayment is interest.

With an endowment mortgage the tax relief should remain constant for the life of the loan. It should only change if the Government changes the rules or if the borrower moves into a different tax bracket. If he loses his job and ceases to be liable for tax, then there is no tax relief. But that applies, of course to both types of loan.

Endowment mortgages combine a loan with a savings-type life assurance policy. Only the interest on the loan is paid during its

The options — building societies and banks

The range of mortgage options now available is very wide. The following is an outline of the various mortgage types.

Annuity: This is the old traditional mortgage where each repayment covers the interest and also pays something off the loan. The amount owing goes down each year, slowly at first and then progressively quicker. But you are fifteen years into a twenty year mortgage before you have paid off half the loan.

Endowment: With the basic endowment mortgage the loan is not repaid until the end of the term. The borrower pays interest each year on the full amount and also pays premiums on a life insurance policy which should, at the end of the term, mature yielding at least enough to pay off the loan. Their attractiveness depends on how the insurance policy actually performs and, to a large extent, on the continuation of mortgage interest relief.

Low start: The repayments are kept at a fixed level for the first number of years — usually three or five — even though they may not be enough to even meet the interest payments on the loan. As a result, the amount borrowed may go up during that initial period. The borrower then starts paying off the higher loans in the normal way. Such loans can be useful for borrowers buying a house which is a bit beyond them now but who hope to be better off in a few years time.

Fixed Interest: The interest rate is fixed for a set number of years irrespective of movements in the market so that the borrower knows exactly what the repayments will be during those years. At the end of the set period, interest rates may be fixed for another period or the borrower may switch to normal variable rates. The borrower gambles that the fixed rate will prove lower than the market rate. Even if it doesn't there has been the security of knowing that whatever happens the repayments were not going to rise.

Pension linked: This is an endowment type mortgage linked to a pension scheme rather than an insurance policy. For a self-employed person it provides better tax relief since all of the premiums to a pension fund can be allowable for tax relief. But the contributions to the pension scheme need to be quite large since the mortgage has to be paid off from the lump-sum option on retirement leaving the bulk of the savings to buy a pension.

Foreign currency: It is possible to borrow in a foreign currency at the interest rates being charged in the country concerned but the borrower takes on the additional exchange rate risk if it's a non-eurozone currency. The loan is taken out and has to be repaid in the foreign currency.

life. But the borrower also pays premiums on a savings type life assurance policy. That policy is designed to mature at the end of the loan — say twenty years hence — and yield enough to pay off the loan. There may even be something left over.

So there are two possible advantages to endowment mortgages. Firstly, the money being saved up to pay off the loan may yield a better return as savings over the years than the interest it would save if it were used to gradually pay off the loan. Secondly, and contributing to that hope, is the possibility of getting better tax relief over the term of the loan.

Endowment mortgages involve taking some risks. They may be worth taking but you should realise what they are.

But there can be no certainty. There is always the possibility that tax relief on mortgage interest will be abolished. If it is, the hoped for extra tax saving will not emerge. And, in addition, the hoped for return on the insurance policy may not emerge. The borrower must weigh up the possible benefits and the risks. There can be no single right answer. Much depends on what view one takes of likely future developments with regard to the rate of return on insurance policies and the continuation of mortgage tax relief.

The choice of investment fund is obviously of prime importance. Some are more risky than others. Unit linked policies have, in general, performed reasonably well over the longer term although they can move sharply down at times. And the variation between best and worst is great.

There is no sure way of picking the winners although you can reduce the risk by picking a with-profits policy from one of the mutual societies mentioned above or a unit linked policy with a good long-term track record. There are, no doubt, other policies which have performed well in the past and which may perform even better in the future. If one is being recommended to you simply ask the seller, be he an insurance broker or a lender, to justify the choice. Why is he recommending that policy rather than another? That is a very simple question which is relevant to a lot more than buying an insurance policy.

In all of the financial services area the buyer should ask the seller "why this and not another". You do not have to know what the others are. Be assured that there are alternatives so why is the adviser recommending this one. And be sure that you understand the answer. Do not be put off by jargon. Do not be afraid of appearing ignorant. If the adviser cannot explain adequately it is his ignorance and not yours. The good adviser

Switching lenders could cut your costs

Most loans can be repaid at any time without penalty. So there is scope for switching lenders. Borrowing from one to repay another. Unfortunately the more expensive loans, sometimes at fixed rates, include penalty clauses. The penalty for early repayment can more than offset any potential savings on interest payments. But there should be no penalty clauses on variable rate mortgages.

So is it worthwhile switching?

Setting up a new mortgage can cost up to £1,000. It depends, of course, on the size of the mortgage, the legal costs the lender may impose, and the way it is registered. However given the current competition in the market many lenders are willing to absorb some of the costs bringing it down to perhaps below £500. So the up-front cost can be heavy. What are the potential savings?

Let's take the case of Tom and Mary who borrowed £70,000 two years ago with an annuity mortgage at a variable rate. They are currently paying 5.25 per cent — far higher than the 4.4 per cent they see one building society advertising. They are thinking of switching. Is it worthwhile?

The annual saving is simple enough to work out. It amounts to 0.85 per cent. Tom and Mary still owe almost the full £70,000 so the saving works out at about £590 a year. The real saving after tax relief would be about £440. If it costs £500 to set up the new mortgage Tom and Mary will be net winners in little more than a year.

While there is no certainty, if the current differentials remain for a little over a year they can't lose. Of course, it may be sufficient just to warn your existing lender that you intend switching unless they lower their rate. That might produce the desired result without the need to switch. That, after all, is what competition is all about.

will have looked at the alternatives and have picked the right product for you. He'll know why and be able to explain why.

Local authorities — county councils and corporations — provide house purchase loans for those on relatively low incomes and can also pay mortgage subsidies to tenants and tenant-purchasers of local authority houses who give up their houses to buy a private home. There is also a scheme whereby people on a local authority housing list can jointly buy a house

Local authority loans

with the local authority. Let us have a look at each of those schemes.

The straightforward local authority loan is only available to those who have been turned down by both a bank and a building society. Would-be borrowers have to get those refusals in writing before the local authority can consider them for loans. Just being turned down by these private institutions is not enough, however. There are other conditions to be met.

Where there is only one earner his or her gross income must have been no more than £20,000 in the last full income tax year if the applicant is the only earner in the household. A second income is also taken into account according to a set formula. The principal income is multiplied by two and a half and to the product is added the subsidiary income. The final figures must be no more than £50,000.

If we take the example of a couple, one earning £15,000 a year and the other £12,500, the sums work out like this. Two and a half times £15,000 is £37,500. Adding the £12,500 brings that up to £50,000. That's just at the £50,000 limit so the couple are eligible for a local authority loan provided, of course, they can't get a loan elsewhere.

That maximum income limit does not apply to approved applicants for, or tenants of, local authority dwellings. Neither does it apply to tenants of rental subsidiary scheme housing owned by a voluntary housing group provided the accommodation is being returned to the group.

Standard Loan: There is no minimum income requirement but the local authority must be satisfied that it is sufficient to meet the repayments. The maximum loan is normally £50,000 but loans up to £55,000 are given for houses on certain offshore islands. Within those upper limits, loans may be up to 95 per cent of the purchase price or the market value of the house (whichever is less).

The interest rate is variable and will not exceed the standard building society rate. Loans for new houses can be repaid over 30 years while the upper limit for second-hand houses is 25 years. Normally neither the borrower, nor his or her spouse, should ever have bought or built a house before. An exception is made for people living in substandard conditions.

Shared Ownership: Tenants or tenant purchasers of local authority houses wishing to give them up to buy a private house, or people on a housing list, or those who meet the income criteria mentioned above may qualify for a local authority loan to buy at least a 40 per cent share in a private house of their own choosing. The local authority buys the other share and charges an annual rent calculated at 4.5 per cent of its value, adjusted for inflation each year. Those with incomes below £12,000 enjoy a reduced rental. The maximum reduction is £1,200 a year for those with incomes below £8,500 while the minimum is £250 for those earning between £11,001 and £12,000.

Costs of getting a mortgage

Obviously, first of all, you need the cash for the deposit. As outlined above, although 90 per cent loans are available you may find it hard to get more than 80 per cent on an old house. If it is an old house which you are going to renovate, it may be possible to increase the mortgage later as alterations and additions are made. Check this with your lender.

But there are also other costs. Auctioneers fees are paid by the seller, so there is no need to worry about those, but there will be fees to the building society or other lender, legal fees and maybe stamp duty. There will also be costs involved in satisfying yourself that the house has no structural flaws.

Let us look at these in turn.

- **Fees to the lending agency:** These are not likely to break you, but it is as well to bear them in mind since they can stretch a slim budget. They include mortgage fees, survey fees, and search fees. The rates vary from lender to lender but the following provides a rough guide:

Mortgage Law Costs: 0.5 to 0.65 per cent of loan – some lenders charge a fixed fee of up to £240, others allow you to use your own solicitor.

Application Fee: From nothing to 0.2 per cent per £1,000 to a fixed £50 fee depending on the lender.

Survey Fees: About £1.50 per £1,000 although some times a fixed fee is charged. There may also be travelling expenses for the surveyor.

Search Fees: These should not amount to much more than £50 or £60.

The costs — an example

The following example assumes the purchase of a £90,000 second hand house with a mortgage of £70,000. On a new house there would be no stamp duties on the house although there would be on the mortgage. This is only an illustration of the possible costs.

Legal fees *	£1,000
Survey fees	£150
Land registry fees etc.	£250
Search fees	£60
Stamp duties on house	£2,700
Stamp duties on mortgage	£70
Total	£4,230

* There is no set scale of fees. They are negotiable. Check in advance and don't be afraid to shop around or at least haggle.

Stamp duties: Stamp duty rates on residential property were reduced from April 23, 1998. The rates are shown in the table opposite.

There is no stamp duty payable by the first purchaser of most new dwellings provided the purchaser intends to reside in the dwelling and undertakes in writing to inform the Revenue Commissioners if within the first five years of ownership the property is let. If the dwelling is let within the five years the stamp duty becomes payable.

The stamp duty exemption on new houses does not apply if the dwelling is ineligible for a State grant. If for example, its floor area is greater than 1,346 square feet (125 square metres) — then stamp duty is payable but only on the site value which is assumed to be 25 per cent of the total amount paid. The rates are given above. Stamp duty is payable on the full value of most second-hand houses and dwellings bought by non-owner occupiers. There are exemptions for certain tenants of local authority houses who buy their houses from the Authority. Your solicitor will normally arrange for the payment of it and bill you. These stamp duty rates are not charged on slices of the price. On a £100,001 house, for instance, the rate is 4 per cent

Stamp duty on house purchases

Less than £60,000	Nil
Between £60,001 and £100,000	3 per cent
Between £100,001 and £170,000	4 per cent
Between £170,001 and £250,000	5 per cent
Between £250,001 and £500,000	7 per cent
Above £500,001	9 per cent

on the full £100,001. There is also a stamp duty of 25p per £200 on mortgages over £10,000

- **Legal Fees:** There are too many possible pitfalls in buying a house for you to dispense with the services of a solicitor. Ask him in advance what his fees will be – most solicitors will tell you as a matter of course. There is no fixed rate of charges, but the Incorporated Law Society used to recommend a rate of 2 per cent of the purchase price including VAT. That recommendation was made when houses were considerably cheaper than they are now and the legal work is much the same no matter what the price of the house is. Legal fees are subject to VAT at 21 per cent. The VAT only applies to the fees — not to the stamp duty which the solicitor may also collect.

There are, of course, other — mainly non-financial — matters to be borne in mind. These are the fairly obvious considerations of location, house size, age, etc. In other words, is the house good value for money? Is it suitable for your particular requirements and are there any flaws which might make it bad value for money? Your solicitor is only concerned that the contract of sale does not put you at a disadvantage. Make sure that a check is also made for planning applications or approvals which might effect the value of the house.

The importance of location and size are matters for your own judgement, but you should never buy a house without having someone give it a professional once-over, unless it is a new house and the purchase contract provides for the making good of any structural defect appearing in the first two years. How do you go about that?

Checking the house

Monthly repayments per £1,000 borrowed

The following are the monthly repayments per £1,000 borrowed on an annuity mortgage. They include no provision for mortgage protection insurance or other extras.

Interest rate	Term of loan in years			
	10	**15**	**20**	**25**
4%	£10.28	£7.50	£6.14	£5.34
4½%	**£10.51**	**£7.74**	**£6.38**	**£5.60**
5%	£10.80	£8.03	£6.69	£5.92
5½%	**£11.06**	**£8.31**	**£6.98**	**£6.22**
6%	£11.33	£8.59	£7.27	£6.52
6½%	**£11.60**	**£8.87**	**£7.57**	**£6.84**
7%	£11.87	£9.15	£7.87	£7.16
7½%	**£12.15**	**£9.45**	**£8.18**	**£7.48**
8%	£12.42	£9.74	£8.49	£7.81
8½%	**£12.71**	**£10.04**	**£8.81**	**£8.15**
9%	£12.99	£10.34	£9.13	£8.49

The lending agency will always send out its own surveyor to examine a house before agreeing to grant a mortgage. This provides some protection, since a mortgage will not be forthcoming unless the house is reasonably sound. But remember the lending agency is only concerned that the value of the house covers 80 per cent of the price which it is lending to you. So with a second-hand house it is a good idea to engage your own surveyor to carry out a more detailed examination.

With a new house, ask your solicitor to ensure that the purchase contract contains a guarantee that any structural defects becoming evident in the first two years will be put right at the builder's expense. For preference deal with a builder who is in the National House Building Guarantee Scheme. If not, have a survey done yourself. Having satisfied yourself that the house is sound — or at least that you know of any major defects — the next thing to check is the possibility of any new building which might affect its value in the future. It could be that the person selling knows that a large block of flats is planned on a site overlooking the, seemingly private, back garden; or that a new motorway is to be built along your side wall.

So you need to check the planning applications and approvals for the area. This can be done at the offices of your local planning authority. There you can examine maps of your area showing the zonings — whether agricultural, commercial or residential — and see details of any planning approvals granted or applications pending. Such a visit is well worth making. The planning offices are usually located in the local urban or county council premises.

State housing grants

GRANTS for house purchase and improvement have been dramatically curtailed in recent years but there are some still available and a number of new schemes have been introduced. These include mortgage subsidies for tenants and tenant purchasers of local authority houses who wish to purchase private houses, and grants for improving or extending the houses of people on local authority housing lists. Local authorities can also provide subsidised sites to eligible applicants and also provide assistance to promote voluntary housing. There are grants to help the first time purchaser and grants to assist in financing some very basic home improvements — but the house needs to be in urgent need of essential repairs.

Full details can be obtained from the Department of the Environment, Housing Grants Section, Ballina, Co Mayo. The following is an outline of what is available:

House purchase grants

First time purchasers of new houses are entitled to a grant of £3,000 provided the house is built by a registered builder. 'House' in this context can mean either a house or apartment. To qualify the buyer must never have owned a house in Ireland or abroad before, and the house must not have been occupied before. An exception is made in the case of local authority tenants who buy their existing houses and also, in certain circumstances, where an earlier house was destroyed by fire, flood or such like. Where a spouse has got a recognised divorce, a civil annulment or a legal separation, the grants may also be payable if the applicant can show that he or she needs housing.

In all cases the purchaser must occupy the dwelling on completion as his or her normal place of residence on a year round basis. This excludes holiday homes, etc. Apart from the exception mentioned above, the condition of not having purchased a dwelling before applies to both the purchaser and spouse. Neither must have owned a house either individually or jointly. In addition, the dwelling must be built to a standard not inferior to that laid down by the Department.

There are also limits to the size of the house or apartment on which a grant is payable. For a house, the total floor area must be more than 38 square metres (409 square feet) and less than 125 square metres (1,346 square feet). The measurements are taken inside the external walls and exclude undeveloped attics and basements, garages and out-offices. In multi-dwelling buildings, common spaces are also excluded. The minimum floor area is the same for apartments as for houses.

The 38 square metre minimum size for apartments is laid down in guidelines issued by the Department of the Environment to local authorities for use in considering planning applications. They specify that no more than half the apartments in any development should have only one bedroom and that a proportion of larger apartments of over 70 square metres should be included in larger developments. Two bedroomed apartments should have a minimum floor area of 55 square metres while those with three or more bedrooms should have a minimum floor area of 70 square metres.

If applicable, it is advisable to make the application for a grant before the house is commenced or when a deposit is paid. A provisional approval can then be given. When the house is finished and occupied, the grant is then claimed by signing the declaration on the back of the certificate of approval and forwarding it to the Department. The payment is made directly to the purchaser.

Mortgage subsidy

A tenant or tenant purchaser of a local authority house who gives up the house and buys or builds a private house with the help of a mortgage loan of at least £10,000 can qualify for a mortgage subsidy of up to £4,500 spread over five years. It is known as a mortgage allowance and at its maximum is paid as follows. The subsidy is paid directly to the lending agency and the maximum is paid provided it doesn't exceed the actual amount of interest incurred in the year.

Year 1	£1,400	Year 4	£700
Year 2	£1,100	Year 5	£500
Year 3	£800		

The subsidy is not paid to those who buy under the local authority shared ownership scheme.

Improvement grants

Grants can be given by local authorities towards the cost of improving or extending privately owned houses occupied or intended to be occupied by an approved applicant for housing as an alternative to the provision of a local authority dwelling. The local authority pays the full cost of the works and then charges a "reasonable weekly or monthly" amount for a maximum of fifteen years. The charge is calculated in much the same way as differential rents taking into account income and the cost of the work carried out.

Local authorities can also make loans of up to £15,000 (£20,000 on offshore islands) towards upgrading the accommodation of people eligible for local authority home purchase loans. The interest rate is the same as on home purchase loans. Loans of up to £6,000 can be given without the security of a mortgage on the home.

Thatching grant

A grant of up to £2,000 is available for renewing or repairing thatched roofs on houses. The work must cost a total of at least £750 with the grant covering two-thirds of the approved cost up to that maximum of £2,000. The house must be more than ten years old; it must be structurally sound; and it must be occupied as a normal place of residence.

Mortgage tax relief

Mortgage interest relief still costs the Exchequer some £150 million a year. So it's a valuable tax relief. There have been significant changes in the relief over recent years — changes which made the calculations increasingly complicated. However they are being simplified from April 2000 with changes in the way the ceilings are calculated. No-one loses as a result of the change in the ceilings and widowed borrowers stand to gain significantly. But the relief will be worth less to some people because of the reduction in the standard rate of tax from 24p to 22p. Instead of saving 24p in tax for every pound of eligible mortgage interest, the saving will only be 22p.

First-time home buyers get extra mortgage tax relief during the first five years of the mortgage. From April 2000 a married or widowed borrower can claim tax relief at the standard rate on a maximum of £5,000 of interest. For a single person the maximum is £2,500. Those ceilings are unchanged from the 1999/2000 tax year except that the special widowed person's ceiling of £3,600 has been abolished and the widowed person can claim the full £5,000 allowed to married couples.

Other borrowers i.e. non-first time buyers, could claim relief on only 80 per cent of the interest paid during 1999/2000 subject to those interest ceilings of £5,000, £3,600 and £2,500 depending on whether they were married, widowed or single. And in addition the first £100 (single or widowed) or £200 (married) was disallowed. So a married couple whose interest payments totalled £6,000 first reduced the eligible interest to the ceiling of £5,000, then further reduced it by 20 per cent or down to £4,000.

Finally they knocked off the first £200 to bring the allowance down to £3,800. That £3,800 was the maximum relief available in 1999/2000 to a married couple who were not first-time buyers. From April, 2000 the ceilings on non-first time buyers will be £4,000 for married and widowed borrowers and £2,000 for single borrowers. They are allowed claim relief on all the interest paid up to those limits. The 80 percent rule and the disallowance of the first £100 or £200 has been abolished.

Will you get maximum tax relief?

If you're a first time buyer you're very likely to be borrowing enough to qualify for the maximum tax relief. The size of loan to bring you up to that threshold depends on the current rate of interest. The following are approximate levels for various rates based on the post-April 2000 situation. If your loan exceeds the relevant figure then you can safely assume that you are eligible for the maximum tax relief.

Interest	4%	4.5%	5%	5.5%	6%
Single	£62,500	£55,500	£50,000	£45,400	£41,600
Married	£125,000	£111,100	£100,000	£90,900	£83,300
Widowed	£125,000	£111,100	£100,000	£90,900	£83,300

How much is the maximum relief worth?

The maximum tax relief you can claim depends on your marital status and whether you're a first time buyer or not. The table shows the value of the maximum tax relief. It's the same whether you pay tax at the top or standard rate since the relief is only given at the standard rate. The reduction in the value of the relief between the two years is due to the cut in the standard rate of tax from 24p to 22p. In the case of widowed borrowers this is more than offset by an increase in the maximum interest that can be claimed.

	First time buyers		Other buyers	
	1999/2000	**2000/01**	**1999/2000**	**2000/01**
Married	£1,200	£1,100	£912	£880
Widowed	£864	£1,100	£667	£880
Single	£600	£550	£456	£440

Up to 1994 tax relief was allowed at whatever your maximum tax rate was. Since then it has only been allowed at the standard rate – 24p in 1999/2000 and 22p for the tax year 2000/2001.

The special treatment for first-time buyers was introduced in 1996 and the benefits only applied from April 1996 although the five year limit is taken to have started whenever you first claimed mortgage interest relief. For example if you first claimed interest relief in 1995/96 tax year you are entitled to the relief for the 1999/2000 tax year but not thereafter since your loan will be more than five years old. There is no provision to allow a rebate for years prior to April 1996.

- **Designated Areas:** There is additional tax relief available to the owner occupiers of homes in designated areas which meet certain conditions. The property must be the sole or main residence of the individual claiming the relief. If it is a converted premises there must be a certificate of reasonable cost. The total floor area must be between 30 and 90 square metres in the case of an apartment (up to 125 square metres in the case of a refurbished apartment). A house must be between 35 and 125 square metres.

The expenditure must have been incurred after October 1985 and before July 31, 1997.

Tax relief is allowed each year for ten years on 5 per cent of the construction cost in the case of a new premises and 10 per cent in the case of a refurbished premises. For example the construction costs of a new apartment selling for £90,000 might be about £60,000. The buyer is entitled to claim tax relief on 5 per cent of that for ten years. So relief is allowed on £3,000 a year. At 22p in the pound the actual tax saving is £660. That relief is in addition to any mortgage tax relief calculated on the basis outlined above.

Rent Relief

Since April 1995 it has been possible to claim tax relief on the rent paid for private sector accommodation. It is not available for rent paid on local authority houses or flats. In 2000/2001 the maximum amount that can be claimed by someone over 55 is £2,000 single, £3,000 widowed and £4,000 married. The relief is restricted to the standard rate. The maximum relief had stood at half of those figures since 1995 and it could be claimed at the taxpayers marginal rate of tax.

Rent relief was extended to under 55s from the 1995/96 tax year subject to the following maximum figures: £1,000 (married); £500 (single); or £750 (widowed). That relief was always restricted to the standard rate of tax. From April 2000 the limits are being increased to £750 single, £1,125 widowed and £1,500 married. It's a tax relief that is often missed because it has to be claimed. It is, of course, possible to backdate a claim for at least six years — see chapter 14.

Wills

Wills, probate and inheritance

7.

MOST people experience an understandable reluctance about drawing up a will. It brings thoughts of death and few people like to think about dying. But the failure to make a will can cause many problems for dependents. It has also resulted in many bitter family feuds. Unless there is a properly drawn up will in existence, your property will be divided up, after your death, in accordance with the dictates of the 1965 Succession Act. Such a division may not be in keeping with your wishes and could cause major problems for your spouse. A little early planning can also reduce the amount your dependents may have to pay in inheritance tax. That is particularly so if some of the beneficiaries are distant relatives or friends.

The first concern is to ensure that your wishes are known. If there is no will, the law lays down how the estate is divided up. By making a will you ensure that your property passes to the people you choose — not to the people dictated in court according to the strict rule of law. There is the added advantage that you can appoint your own executor and the administration of the estate will be much easier.

A valid will can be made by anyone over eighteen years of age — or younger if he or she is married. It must be in writing. While a simple will can be drawn up at home, it is worthwhile getting a solicitor to oversee the task. The few pounds it costs can save a lot of trouble in the long run.

If you do decide to draw up your own will, remember to word it simply and clearly. Date it, sign it, and get your signature witnessed by two people. This means that you should sign it in their presence. They do not have to read the will. Neither of the witnesses should be a beneficiary under the will. It is normal to appoint an executor or executors to carry out your wishes under the will although it is not essential. The executor can be a beneficiary under the will although he, or she, need not be. For a simple will, where the main beneficiaries are members of the immediate family, it is common to name the principal beneficiary as executor. In most cases this is the husband or wife. If either are reaching old age and might find the task difficult, it is useful to name a co-executor — perhaps an elder child or the family solicitor.

The larger banks have special departments to deal with estate matters and will normally accept being named executor for wills. Solicitors and banks, of course, make charges for this service. It can be expensive and it is usual to provide for the charges in the will. For the person leaving his estate to fairly distant relatives, it may be as well to have an outside executor who can be above any family friction which might arise. But usually a member of the family — or a friend whom you trust — is the best choice. There is nothing to stop an executor hiring a solicitor to help in administering the will if he or she thinks it necessary.

The will should, of course, be lodged in a safe place, and be sure that the executor, and some other people know where it is lodged. This is particularly important for people whose families are widely spread. There are many wills lying in solicitors' offices throughout the country forgotten and, to all intents and purposes, lost. If you are a regular user of a bank, that is possibly the best place to have the will kept.

Once made, the will remains in force until a new will is made or the person who made it gets married. On marriage an existing will becomes void and a new one should be drawn up. Remember also to review your will from time to time. Even if you do not want to change the provisions you may want to change the executor and it can be useful to reconsider the inheritance tax implications.

All married people should have a will drawn up. It costs little to have the job done correctly by a solicitor. Once made, the will should be reviewed from time to time.

Both spouses should make wills

It is now common for both spouses to share ownership in the family home. But there are still many families where the bulk of the assets — perhaps home and/or farm — are held in the husband's name. It may be thought unnecessary in such cases for the wife to make a will but nothing is further from the truth. In not making a will the assumption is that she will always have time to do so, if necessary, after her husband's death. Yet this

Where there is no will

Surviving Relatives	Distribution of estate where there is no will.
Spouse and children	Two-thirds to spouse, one third to children in equal shares with children of a deceased child getting their parent's share
Spouse, no children	Whole estate to spouse.
Children, no spouse	Whole estate to children in equal shares with children of a deceased child getting their parent's share.
Father, mother, brothers and/or sisters	One-half to each parent.
Parent, brothers and/or sisters	Whole estate to parent
Brothers and sisters	All get equal shares with children of deceased brothers and sisters getting their parent's share.
Nephews and nieces	All get equal shares.

can lead to problems in an unfortunate situation where both die together — in a car accident, for instance. It could happen in such a case that the husband dies first leaving his entire estate to his wife but that she then dies without having time to make a will. The estate would then be equally divided among the children — if there are any. That may be in accordance with their parent's wishes. But it might not, if one child, for instance, was still living at home and hoped to be left the house.

There is only one important restriction on the maker of a will. A spouse cannot be cut out of the estate unless he or she agrees to be, for instance as part of a separation agreement. Irrespective of what the will says, the spouse is legally entitled to one-third of the estate where there are surviving children, and one-half of the estate where there are no children. Apart from that restriction, however, a person may dispose of his or her property as he or she thinks fit, although the courts can overturn the provisions of a will if, for instance, a child claims that he or she has not been adequately provided for.

Rights to the family home

Both spouses have
important rights to
the family home even
if they are not
formally joint owners.

In many cases family homes are jointly owned by both spouses but even where one spouse has formal ownership the other spouse, very often a non-wage earning wife, has certain rights in the family home under existing legislation. They are not rights of ownership although in the case of a judicial separation or divorce, a court may order a transfer of property from one spouse to another. Rights in this area are provided under the Family Home Protection Act; the Married Women's Status Act; and judicial separation and divorce legislation.

The Family Home Protection Act provides that both spouses must agree to the sale or mortgaging of the family home. But where the house is in just one name, the other spouse has no right to any proceeds from a sale unless he or she has made some financial contribution to the purchase of the house or the mortgage repayments.

There are also provisions protecting the rights of a spouse against whom a barring order is being sought. The first step in getting a barring order is to get a protection order. Where that has been obtained neither spouse can remove or dispose of any household contents until a decision has been made on the barring order. A spouse must also be given the opportunity to take over the mortgage repayments on the family home where his or her partner has defaulted on the payments. And the courts can make orders for the protection of a home where it can be shown that a spouse is indulging in some actions which could lead to the loss of the home.

Under the Married Women's Status Act the Courts can be asked to rule on the ownership of property, including a family home. But the Courts will only grant ownership rights to a spouse who can show that he or she made financial contributions to the purchase of the house or to other household costs. Work done in the home or in rearing children is not taken into account.

The courts have much wider powers of discretion under the judicial separation and divorce legislation. Where a couple have been granted either a judicial separation or a divorce the court can make orders requiring the transfer of property from one spouse to another. In this case it does not matter whether or not a spouse has made a financial contribution. The courts may also make maintenance orders. Such orders can be reviewed from time to time, but orders made with regard to property are permanent and a court will only review them if it can be shown that it was deliberately misled when the original order was made.

Tax is another thing to consider when making a will. Inheritance taxes have been hitting a growing number of people. A wide range of concessions have been introduced in recent years to lessen the impact on business assets including farms. That has greatly reduced the potential liability of those with their own businesses. Traditionally this was the section of the community who worried most about the impact of the tax. But people who wouldn't necessarily perceive themselves as wealthy are now being caught by the tax. It is still not a major worry for people inheriting from parents or spouses but the tax can be onerous for the growing number of people inheriting from more distant relatives.

Details of Capital Acquisitions Tax (CAT) and Probate Tax are given in chapter 13 but broadly speaking a person can receive any amount from a spouse without tax liability while a child can receive up to £300,000 from a parent or grandparent before coming into the tax net. But the tax thresholds for gifts or inheritances from more distant relatives are much lower and because of low marriage rates in the past, particularly in some rural areas, it is not uncommon for people to receive inheritances from sisters, brothers, uncles, aunts or cousins. The tax on such inheritances can be quite steep. But it can be reduced, or eliminated, with a little advance planning.

There is a section on tax planning for inheritances in chapter 14 on page 276.

The person making a will — the testator — should always seek the consent of a person named in the will to act as executor. It is, of course, quite in order to name more than one person, but there is no obligation on the persons so named to act. A person who does not wish to accept an executorship may renounce it by signing a form of renunciation before a witness. It is usual to get a solicitor to oversee this operation. When this happens it can obviously create problems so it is essential to ensure that the executor named will act, and to review the will from time to time to ensure that this is still the case. As mentioned above, it is usual to name the principal beneficiary under the will as executor so a husband will name his wife and vice versa. If there are children over 18 years of age it can be a good

Wills and tax planning

Inheritance taxes can be avoided or reduced. It is worthwhile considering the options and getting advice.

The duties of executors

idea to name one of these as a co-executor as a way of reducing the burden on the spouse. It is not necessary to name a solicitor, accountant, or bank as a further co-executor. Professional advice can be obtained after the death, if required.

An executor may benefit under a will but he is not entitled to any payment for his services unless it is specifically stated in the will that such a payment should be made. The executor can, however, claim for expenses actually incurred in administering the will. If the person is not a beneficiary under the will provision for the payment of a fee should be made.

You don't need to hire a solicitor to take out probate on a will. You can do it yourself.

If it is decided to accept the executorship, the first move is normally to obtain a Grant of Probate from the courts. This will formally authorise the executor to collect the deceased's assets and carry out the provisions of the will. But the will itself is sufficient authorisation and even without a grant of probate the executor can immediately take charge of the deceased's assets and start to carry out the provisions of the will.

A listing of all the deceased's assets should be made and valuations obtained where necessary. It is also necessary to obtain details of any outstanding debts. Usually these are easily ascertained but, if they are not, the executor can protect himself against further claims by putting a notice in the daily newspaper asking all creditors to supply details of their claims by a certain date.

If a creditor has not made a claim by that date, he loses the right to pursue his claim against the executor although he can still proceed against the beneficiaries under the will. If the executor does not put the statutory notice in the newspaper, he may protect himself by getting the beneficiaries to give an agreement in writing to indemnify him against any claims which emerge after the distribution has taken place.

The Probate Office in the Four Courts, Dublin 7 (phone 01 8725555 ex 179) has a special application section for those who wish to take out probate themselves. Application for probate can be made there or to one of fourteen District Probate Registries. There is, in fact, no need to get a solicitor to do the job, particularly if it is a simple will. On request the probate office will send out an application form which should be completed as fully as possible and returned. The probate office will immediately acknowledge receipt of the form and will ask the applicant to call in for a preliminary meeting. At that stage the applicant should present full details of the estate, a death certificate and the original will, if there is a will. Statements of deposit accounts held by the deceased should be produced as well as details of assurance policies and all assets owned by the deceased. A second meeting will be arranged to finalise any outstanding matters and the applicant will then be required to sign the completed documents, swear to the truth and accuracy of their contents, and pay a fee.

In some cases it may take more than two meetings to finalise the matter but once probate has been granted, the executor will find it easier to transfer funds from bank accounts into his or her own name. It is best for the executor to open a separate bank account for this purpose. The executor has further duties in making returns to the taxman and settling any tax claims outstanding or arising as a result of the will. This includes making income, probate and inheritance tax returns. Because of the tax implications it may be necessary to get tax clearance before withdrawing money from bank or other saving accounts. The following are the rules:

Tax clearance is not always needed to withdraw money from a deceased person's account.

In the case of a joint husband/wife account, a surviving spouse is not required to present a tax clearance no matter how large the estate but the financial institution may require sight of the death certificate and/or will depending on the type of account i.e. whether two signatures were needed for withdrawals.

Tax clearance is needed to access an account in the deceased's sole name or in the joint names of the deceased and someone other than a spouse where the account has more than £5,000 in it, but such a clearance is granted quickly by the Capital Taxes Branch, Revenue Commissioners, Dublin Castle. The financial institution may also have its own rules with regard to having sight of the will, death certificate or grant of probate. For more details on joint accounts see chapter 2, page 19.

If the executor is not the spouse of the deceased, he or she has to inform the spouse of their rights under the Succession Act, 1965. As outlined above these include the right to at least a third of the estate (if there are children) or a half (if there are no children), and the right to keep the house in which they are living, together with the household chattels, in satisfaction or part-satisfaction of his or her share. Records of all transactions should, of course, be kept as should the original will.

Work rights

Your rights as an employee

8.

The source of most family finance is wages and indeed most breadwinners spend almost a third of their lives on the job. Over recent years there has been a great deal of legislation giving workers minimum rights and protection in matters like hours of work, minimum notice, redundancy, holidays, discrimination, unfair dismissal, etc. The laws apply to both full time and part-time workers who meet certain service conditions.

Some employers try to reduce their exposure to the employment protection laws by either contracting out work to self-employed workers, or by hiring employees under contracts which effectively prevent them acquiring their full range of rights. To qualify for most employment rights, employees have to have a minimum amount of service. Workers may be prevented from building up the required service if they are hired on a contract basis for a fixed term or for a specific job. The distinction between such workers and employees may, in some cases, be very obvious but that's not always the case. There is plenty of room for dispute where there is no written contract.

Employers who require workers for specific periods or specific jobs may limit the period of employment by contract. The contract may specify either a fixed time period or may cover the completion of a specific job. Workers taken on under such contracts are employees but they may not qualify for rights under all of the employment protection Acts.

People working on fixed term contracts may be covered by some of the employment laws.

As a rule of thumb, however, the contract must be seen to have a purpose other than simply to allow the employer avoid unfair dismissal legislation. An amendment to the legislation introduced in 1993 specifically states that employers cannot avoid the Act by using fixed term contracts and that a break of less than three months between two consecutive contracts does not constitute a break in service. This may be true even for work of a seasonal nature. It may not be possible to prevent workers building up entitlements under the Unfair Dismissals and Redundancy Acts. The Employment Appeals Tribunal has upheld claims for continuity of service by seasonal workers who showed a pattern of such work over a number of years.

A contract worker, however, is not normally covered under the unfair dismissals legislation unless he or she did work other than that specified in the contract of employment.

While workers in large firms with union representation can be fairly certain that their entitlements are not allowed to go by default, non-union workers particularly in smaller firms may find that their employers, either by accident or design, fail to give them their full entitlements.

The following gives a brief guide to the more important legislative provisions. Explanatory leaflets may be obtained from the Department of Enterprise, Trade and Employment, Conditions of Employment Section, Dublin 4. The Department also gives further assistance and advice. In the case of disputes arising you can seek redress through a Rights Commissioner who can be contacted through the Department.

The rights of part-time workers under these labour laws should not be confused with social welfare entitlements. Part-time workers earning more than £30 a week have some cover under the PRSI system — including unemployment, sickness benefits and old-age pensions. These are detailed in chapter 12.

Redundancy entitlements

Despite Ireland's booming economy redundancy has been the fate of a significant number of workers in recent years and will remain a fact of life for years to come. Under the redundancy payment scheme and the Protection of Employment Act, an employer is required to give at least thirty days notice to the Minister of Labour of any intention to make collective redundancies. Workers are entitled to minimum notice and to minimum lump sum payments based on the number of years service with the firm.

Who is covered? The scheme covers employees who are in employment which is insurable for all benefits under the Social Welfare Acts or who were in such employment in the four years prior to redundancy; are between the ages of sixteen and sixty-six; and who are normally expected to work for at least eight hours a week for the same employer. Domestic servants and agricultural workers — who are not relatives and who do not reside with their employers — are also covered.

An employee becomes eligible for redundancy pay if he has been employed by the same employer for at least two years after attaining sixteen years of age and is dismissed as redundant, laid off, or kept on short-time at less than fifty per cent of normal time for four consecutive weeks or a total of six weeks in a period of thirteen weeks.

The lump sum: The lump sum is calculated as follows. It is paid by the employer who is partially reimbursed by the State:

- A half weeks pay for each year of continuous service between ages sixteen and forty-one.
- One week's pay for each year of continuous service over the age of forty-one, and
- An additional amount of one week's pay.
- Income over £300 a week is disregarded in making the above calculation.

The number of years' service is calculated backwards from the date of dismissal with any remaining period of over twenty-six weeks regarded as a year. A period of under twenty-six weeks is disregarded. The same rule applies in working out the period over forty-one years of age.

As an example a worker earning £20,000 a year who had ten years service, five of them under the age of 41 would be entitled to eight and a half week's pay but the pay would only be calculated at the maximum rate of £300 a week. That works out at only £2,550 — not a lot after ten years service. That would be tax free but tax may be payable on any additional lump sum given by an employer. Where a company is not closing but rather cutting back on staff it has become common for employers to make redundancy payments well in excess of the statutory requirements — in some cases up to seven weeks pay for every year of service.

The employer can claim 60 per cent of the statutory lump sum from the Department of Enterprise, Trade and Employment provided two weeks' notice has been given.

Tax and the lump sum: The taxation on redundancy lump sums can be quite heavy. As mentioned above the statutory redundancy payment is not liable for tax. In addition at least £8,000 of any other extra redundancy payment is also tax-free.

That £8,000 is increased by £600 for each full year of service. That's the minimum entitlement. Another £4,000 may also be taken tax-free but that figure is reduced by the amount of any tax-free lump sum taken from a pension scheme. That's the lump sum received or that will eventually be received when the redundant worker retires. Any refund of pension contributions are treated separately and taxed at a flat 25 per cent.

The calculation of the actual exemption starts off at £12,000, plus £600 for each full year of service. The £12,000 figure is reduced by the amount of any other tax-free payments received or credited. That does not include refunds of pension contributions but it does include tax free lump sums from pension schemes. And it also includes a valuation put on any deferred payment from a pension scheme. In no case is the £12,000 reduced below £8,000.

To see how these calculations might work, let us first take the case of a man who is made redundant and leaves his pension contributions in the scheme as he is required to do. He has a right to a tax-free lump sum and a pension when he reaches retirement age. A valuation is put on that lump sum taking account of the amount that will be paid out and the number of years to go before it is paid.

Let's suppose that such a lump sum is valued at £3,500. The basic tax exemption on the redundancy lump sum of £12,000 would be reduced by that £3,500 to £8,500. If the value of the pension lump sum was £4,500, the exemption would only be reduced by £4,000 since in no case is it reduced below £8,000. That's on top, of course, of the £600 tax-free allowance for each year of service.

There is an alternative method of calculation which can give a high tax-free figure for workers with long service. It is up to the worker. He or she has the option of calculating the tax free

Workers with long service can get more of a lump sum tax free by opting for the Standard Capital Superannuation Benefit calculation.

lump sum on the following basis known as the Standard Capital Superannuation Benefit. The calculation is done as follows:

$$I \times \frac{N}{15} \text{ minus } P \qquad \text{where}$$

- **I** is average salary over the past three years
- **N** is the number of years service; and
- **P** is any tax-free lump sum paid, or due, from a pension scheme.

We can compare the two methods of calculation for a man whose average earnings over the last three years were £18,000 and who has thirty years service. For simplicity we can assume that there is no pension lump sum involved.

Using the Standard Capital Superannuation Benefit method we get a figure of £36,000 that can be taken tax-free. The average salary, £18,000 is multiplied by 30 giving £540,000 and dividing that by 15 gives £36,000. So using this method of calculation our example is entitled to get £36,000 of any lump sum tax free in addition, of course, to his statutory entitlement.

Using the other calculation of £12,000 plus £600 for every year of service gives a lower figure of £30,000. It would be made up of the basic £12,000 plus £18,000 (£600 for each of the 30 years service). So in this particular case it is clearly better to opt for the Standard Capital Superannuation method of calculation. But it all depends on the circumstances. It is important to do the sums for each case.

The tax on any remaining taxable lump sum can be worked out in two possible ways — the choice is up to the tax payer. Initially, any remaining taxable lump sum, after deducting the tax free element, is treated as income in the year in which it is received and taxed as such. This might be advantageous to someone being made redundant early in the tax year who does not expect to work during the rest of that year but the other alternative is usually better.

You can have your average tax rate over the past five years applied to any taxable lump sum.

Under the second alternative, tax is levied at the average rate you paid over the last five tax years. To work this out you take your taxable income for the five years. It is important to stress that it is your taxable income you take — that is gross income less tax allowances. You take that figure and divide by the actual tax paid. And that gives you the tax rate. A claim to have this average tax rate applied must be made to your tax office and if a refund is payable you normally have to wait until the end of the tax-year.

Tax in all these cases includes the health levy and PRSI where they are applicable.

Repayments from pension funds are taxed at a flat rate of 25 per cent but if the payment takes the form of a lump sum pension payment — rather than simply a refund of contributions — a tax free payment of up to $1\frac{1}{2}$ times final salary is possible. But relatively few pension schemes provide for such payments except perhaps in cases of disability. Twenty years service would be required to qualify for a tax free lump sum of $1\frac{1}{2}$ times salary from such a scheme.

A person who is laid off work because of a permanent disability can receive a lump sum entirely tax-free.

Holiday entitlement

Legal entitlement to paid holidays is provided in the Organisation of Working Time Act, 1997 which replaced an earlier 1973 Act. It covers all those working under a contract of employment or apprenticeship, employed through an employment agency, and most state employees other than the garda and defence forces. There is no qualifying period of service. All time worked qualifies for paid holiday time. The Act also provides for entitlements in respect of public holidays.

Holiday entitlement under the Act has been increasing on a phased basis to the level that applies during the 1999/2000 leave year. For the purpose of the Act a "leave year" means a year beginning on April 1.

For the 1999/2000 leave year the minimum entitlements are as follows:

- Four working weeks where the employee has worked at least 1,365 hours in the year — this method is not used where a worker changes jobs during the leave year.

- One-third of a working week per calendar month in which the employee has worked at least 117 hours.

- Eight per cent of the hours an employee works in a leave year subject to a maximum of four working weeks. In other words eight hours leave for every hundred hours or pro rata.

Some further points on this entitlement:

- If an employee on leave sends in a medical certificate stating that he or she is ill, the time covered by the certificate is not considered as leave.

- If board and/or lodgings is part of a workers remuneration, his holiday pay must include compensation for the loss of these during his annual leave.

- The employer determines when annual leave should be taken but he must give at least one month's notice to the employee or his trade union and the leave must be given either during the leave year or within six months after it ends.

- Holiday pay should be paid in advance at the normal weekly rate.

- After eight months work an employee is entitled to an unbroken period of two weeks holidays which may include public holidays. This entitlement may be ceded by mutual agreement. But it is illegal to pay an allowance in lieu of the minimum holiday entitlement unless a worker is actually leaving the job.

Most workers have an immediate entitlement to public holiday benefits. Part-time and casual workers must have worked at least 40 hours during the five weeks ending on the day before the public holiday.

The entitlement is to one of the following: a paid day off on the day, a paid day off within a month of the day, an additional day of annual leave, an additional day's pay. By law the decision on which compensation to give is up to the employer although that may be changed by mutual agreement. The level of compensation may also be increased, of course, by negotiation.

If an employee asks an employer within 21 days of a public holiday to nominate which of the above options he or she wants to apply and gets no response the worker is automatically entitled to take a paid day off on the public holiday.

There are normally nine public holidays: New Year's Day, St. Patrick's Day, Easter Monday, First Monday in May, First Monday in June, First Monday in August, Last Monday in October, Christmas Day, and St. Stephen's Day. New Year's Eve 1999 has been declared a special additional public holiday.

Working hours

The Organisation of Working Time Act which was passed into law during 1997 took effect from March 1, 1998. Subject to a wide range of exceptions the maximum working week is being reduced to 48 hours from the year 2000. Since March 1, 1998 the maximum has been 60 hours and that was reduced to 55 hours from March 1, 1999. The act doesn't apply to members of the defence force, the garda siochana, junior hospital doctors, transport employees, those working at sea, workers who control their own working hours, or family members working on a farm or in a private house.

The maximum working week may be averaged over twelve months where workers enter into a collective agreement approved by the Labour Court. In the case of seasonal workers it can be averaged over six months. In all other cases it can be averaged over four months.

Rest Periods

Since March 1, 1998 every worker is entitled to:

- An 11 hour rest period in every 24 hours.
- One period of 24 hours rest per week preceded by a daily rest period i.e. A total of 35 hours.
- Rest breaks of 15 minutes where up to four and a half hours have been worked or 30 minutes where up to six hours have been worked.

Night workers are defined as those who normally work at least three hours between midnight and 7 am the following day and who, during the year work, at least half of their hours during the night period. The 48 hour maximum working week came into effect for night workers from March 1, 1998. The hours are normally averaged over two months but may be averaged over a longer period laid down in a collective agreement approved by the Labour Court. For night workers whose jobs involve special hazards or heavy physical or mental strain an absolute limit of eight hours in a 24 hour period applies. Working time is net of breaks, on call or standby time.

Sunday work

Workers who don't already get special compensation for Sunday work are entitled to a Sunday premium equivalent to that applying to similar workers elsewhere. The premium payable should be based on the closest applicable collective agreement that applies in similar employment.

Zero hours on-call

Where a worker is requested to be available for work he or she is entitled to be paid for at least a quarter of the on-call hours even if not called upon to work subject to a payment for a maximum of fifteen hours.

So if a worker is required to be available for 48 hours a week, he or she is entitled to a minimum payment for twelve hours even if not required to work at all.

Unfair dismissal

The Unfair Dismissals Acts are aimed at protecting workers from being unfairly sacked by laying down criteria of what is unfair dismissal and providing an adjudication system for redressing such action. The Act applies to most workers who work for more than eight hours a week and who have at least a year's continuous service with the same employer. It does not cover those who have passed retiring age or those excluded from the redundancy payments scheme because of age. Neither does it cover people working for a close relative and living in the same house or farm, members of the defence force, gardaí, FÁS trainees, apprentices, or most State and local authority employees.

Normally it is up to the employer to prove that a dismissal is fair and justified on the basis of the capability, competence, or qualification of the worker for the work he was employed to do, conduct, redundancy, or the fact that continuation of employment would contravene another statutory requirement.

Dismissals are deemed to be definitely unfair if it is shown that they result from the worker's trade union membership or activities outside working hours or within working hours if normally permitted by the employer, race, religion, politics, pregnancy or related matters such as breastfeeding, membership of the travelling community, the exercise or proposed excise of rights to maternity, adoptive or parental leave, age, or unfair selection for redundancy.

The normal requirement of having a year's service does not apply in cases involving trade union membership or activities, pregnancy or related matters, and maternity or adoptive leave.

To take action against unfair dismissal, the worker should seek redress within six months. This may be done by contacting a Rights Commissioner, through the Department of Labour, phone (01) 6765861, or by writing to the Employment Appeals Tribunal, Davitt House, Dublin 4. The time limit can be extended to twelve months but only in exceptional circumstances

Where it is decided that the dismissal is unfair, the Commissioner or Tribunal can order any of the following: reinstatement in the old job, re-engagement in the old job, or in a suitable alternative, or financial compensation up to a maximum of two years pay.

Cases taken on the grounds of gender discrimination can be taken directly to the Circuit Court where there is no limit on the compensation that can be awarded.

Minimum notice

Any worker who has completed at least thirteen weeks continuous employment with the one employer is entitled to receive minimum notice of dismissal. The notice depends on the length of service as outlined in the table below. An employee who has worked for over thirteen weeks is required to give at least one week's notice of leaving the job to his employer.

Minimum notice entitlement	
13 weeks to two years	one week
Two to five years	two weeks
Five to ten years	four weeks
Ten to fifteen years	six weeks
Over fifteen years	eight weeks

Equality rights

The Employment Equality Act that came into force in October 1999 greatly extended the definition of discrimination in the workplace. Previous legislation outlawed discrimination on the grounds of sex but now the law has been extended to include discrimination on the additional grounds of: marital status, family status, sexual orientation, religious belief, age, disability, race, or membership of the traveller community.

This new law applies only to discrimination within the workplace. Another bill currently before the Oireachtas, The Equal Status Bill 1999, will prohibit discrimination in the provision of services, etc. It is expected to be enacted during 2000.

Since 1974 employers have been required to pay men and women equal pay for equal work. And since 1977 it has been illegal to discriminate against a person of grounds of sex or marital status is respect of his or her conditions of employment, recruitment, training or promotion. But discrimination on other grounds had not been illegal except in the case of dismissal from a job. Now discrimination on any of the grounds mentioned above has been outlawed in the wider areas of pay, other conditions of employment, recruitment, training and/or promotion.

Discrimination by employers is outlawed, as is discrimination in collective agreements, in advertisements, by employment agencies, in vocational training or by bodies such as trade unions and professional or trade organisations.

Harassment in the workplace is also outlawed by the Act. That includes sexual harassment and harassment related to any of the other grounds for discrimination. Harassment is defined as any act or conduct that is unwelcomed and offensive, humiliating or intimidating including spoken words, gestures, or the production, display or circulation of written material or pictures.

The obligation is on employers to take all "reasonable" steps to ensure that harassment doesn't take place.

There are some exceptions allowed for in the Act.

Sexual discrimination is allowed where the sex of the employee is an essential part of the job in areas such as acting or modelling for an artist. It is also allowed in the case of some foreign postings to areas where women, for instance, might not be accepted locally in certain jobs.

Discrimination in the provision of childbirth facilities or in the employment of care workers is also allowed, as is positive discrimination to maintain a desirable gender balance in the garda and prison services.

Discrimination on the grounds of age is outlawed for all those between 18 and 65 years of age. Age related pay is to be phased out over three years. An employer may discriminate against an elderly worker in relation to training if it can be shown that the cost of the training would not be recouped before the worker retires.

There is an important exception in the case of disability. An employer may discriminate against a disabled person if the cost of ensuring equal treatment is anything other than nominal. The original Bill enacted in 1997 was found to be unconstitutional because it required employers to bear greater than nominal cost in providing facilities for the disabled.

Another exception allows for discrimination on religious grounds in education and medical institutions where the discrimination is required to maintain a religious ethos. For public service jobs it is also permissible to require proficiency in the Irish language, residency in Ireland and/or Irish citizenship.

The Act also allows employers to discrimination in a positive fashion. It allows for actions specifically geared towards employing people over 50 years of age, people with disabilities, and members of the traveller community. The old 1977 Act allowed employers to discriminate against men by providing special training for women. That exemption has now been extended to include other measures or actions aimed at promoting equal opportunities for women in terms of recruitment and promotion.

Sexual harassment is not the only form of harassment outlawed by law,

Having laws that outlaw discrimination doesn't, of course, ensure that discrimination will be abolished. Equal pay for women wasn't achieved overnight following the enactment of the equal pay laws in 1974. Indeed some would claim that it hasn't yet been achieved. This new Act will help more women to achieve equal pay. To qualify for equal pay under the 1974 Act it was necessary to show that someone doing equal work was being paid more by the same or associate employer in the same locality. That requirement with regard to the same locality has been removed.

An Equality Authority has replaced the old Employment Equality Agency. This new body doesn't rule on equality issues but its job is to work towards the elimination of discrimination and the promotion of equality of opportunity in employment on all of the nine discriminatory grounds covered by the Act.

So the first port of call for people with a grievance should be the Equality Authority. It can be contacted at 1890 245545. It can help individuals and groups to make their case and get redress. A person who believes that he or she has been discriminated against has the right to seek and get information necessary in drawing up a case from the supposed discriminator. Most cases will go to a newly appointed Director of Equality Investigations who can award pay arrears for up to three years in equal pay cases and compensation of up to two years pay or £10,000 in other cases.

Dismissal cases can be referred directly to the Labour Court. To comply with a recent judgement of the European Court of Justice, cases involving discrimination on the grounds of gender can go straight to the Circuit Court with no limit on the compensation that can be awarded.

The Equality Authority will be drawing up codes of practice for employers. While not having the force of law a failure to comply with these codes will be taken into account in deciding a case.

Maternity leave

The basic entitlement is to fourteen weeks paid leave and four weeks unpaid leave. Normally at least four weeks is taken before the birth and at least four weeks after. The other six weeks are taken at the discretion of the worker — either before or after. Four weeks notice must be given of the intention to take maternity leave and two weeks notice must be given of your intention to return to work. The worker continues to earn holiday entitlement including bank holiday entitlements, during the period of paid leave.

An adopting parent is also entitled to ten weeks leave during which a social welfare payment can be claimed and a further four weeks leave without payment. The adopting parent is usually a woman but a man can qualify in certain circumstances where his partner has died or where the child is being placed solely in his care. The conditions as to notice etc. are similar to those applying to maternity leave.

Parental leave

Since December 3, 1998 parents of children born on or after June 3, 1996 are entitled to take a total of fourteen weeks leave before each child is five years old. That five year rule is modified in the case of an adopted child. The leave is unpaid but the worker retains employment rights and is entitled to return to the same job under the same contract of employment unless the employer can show that it is not "reasonably practical". In such a case the worker is entitled to suitable alternative employment.

Existing social welfare rights are also protected by the granting of credited PRSI contributions during the period of leave. The employee, who must have at least one years service must give six weeks notice of taking the leave and the employer has the right to postpone it where it would have an adverse impact on the business.

Emergency time off

Employees are entitled under the 1998 Parental Leave Act to limited time off for family emergencies resulting from an accident or illness. The entitlement is to paid leave unlike parental leave which is unpaid. The two are completely separate although provided for under the same Act.

Emergency leave can consist of one or more working days subject to a maximum of three days in each twelve months or 5 days in 36 months. The employee must show that because of an injury to or illness of a family member his or her presence is indispensably required.

Terms of employment

All employees are entitled to get a written statement of the terms and conditions of employment within two months of starting a job. Those who were in jobs before the Act came into effect on May 16, 1994 are entitled to a statement within two weeks of requesting it. The statement should include a job description, expected duration if temporary, starting date, hours of work, details of pay, overtime, bonus and holiday entitlements, and details of sick pay and pension arrangements.

Seeking redress

Trade union members can refer disputes over any of their employment rights to their union representation but those who are not in trade unions have to seek redress themselves. Further information on entitlements can be got from:-

- **The Department of Enterprise, Trade and Employment Information Unit,
  Davitt House,
  65 Adelaide Road,
  Dublin, 2   Telephone (01) 6312121 or 1890 220 222**

The Employment Equality Agency will provide assistance in cases of discrimination. It can be contacted at

- **Employment Equality Agency,
  36 Upper Mount Street,
  Dublin, 2   Telephone (01) 6624577**

Other disputes can be referred to the Rights Commissioner Service of the Labour Relations Commission at

- **Rights Commissioner Service
  Labour Relations Commission,**

Tom Johnson House,
Haddington Road,
Dublin, 4   Telephone (01) 6609662

Assistance on matters of discrimination can be obtained from

● **Equality Authority**
  Clonmel Street
  Dublin, 2   Telephone (1890) 245545

Insurance

Your guide to home insurance

9.

PROTECTING your assets involves more than simply picking the right investment. The single largest asset owned by most people is a house or apartment. Fire, burglary, accident, or even storm damage can, and does, result in substantial losses every day of the week. It is up to the individual to decide whether he wants to bear the full risk of such losses himself or spread it around by taking out insurance. For this is what insurance does — spreads the risk. A large number of people pay a small premium so that the few who actually suffer loss can be reimbursed. And you could be one of the few.

It's well worth taking a fresh look at your house insurance every now and then looking at the options and in particular at the value you have put on the building itself. The cost of reinstating a house after a fire or similar disaster has jumped by over 25 per cent in eighteen months according to the Society of Chartered Surveyors. Its latest guidelines for valuing a house for insurance purposes summarised in the accompanying table relate to July 1999.

Building costs, however, haven't been rising as fast as house prices so it still costs far less to reinstate a house than buy a new one. Many people are undoubtedly under insured but if you base your insurance value on the market value of your home then you are likely to be over insured and that's just a waste of money. You'll pay higher premiums but that won't entitle you to make higher claims.

You need to go for the happy medium. There is no benefit in being over insured and if you are under insured any claim you make may be subject to an averaging clause. That means that

Valuing your house for insurance

The Society of Chartered Surveyors, 5, Wilton Place, Dublin, 2 issues annual guidelines for valuing houses for insurance purposes. Copies are free on request but please enclose a stamped address envelope. The following is a summary of their 1999 figures. They are designed to cover rebuilding costs including site clearance.

House type		Dublin	Cork	Galway
Terraced —	2 bedroom 750 sq. ft.	£94.25 sq. ft.	£85.00 sq. ft.	£81.50 sq. ft.
	3 bedroom 1,023 sq. ft.	£89.75 sq. ft.	£80.00 sq. ft.	£76.50 sq. ft.
Semi —	3 bedroom 1,023 sq. ft.	£91.00 sq. ft.	£81.50 sq. ft.	£77.50 sq. ft.
	4 bedroom 1,270 sq. ft.	£86.5 sq. ft.	£76.00 sq. ft.	£72.50 sq. ft.
Detached —	4 bedroom 1,270 sq. ft.	£87.25 sq. ft.	£78.50 sq. ft.	£75.00 sq. ft.
Bungalow —	4 bedrooms 1,572 sq. ft.	£86.00 sq. ft.	£77.75 sq. ft.	£73.50 sq. ft.
Garage: Single attached garage £7,500, double detached garage £13,500.				

the compensation paid will be scaled down in proportion to the degree of under insurance.

Suppose for instance, that £100,000 is the true cost of reinstating your home in the event of it being a total write off after a fire. If you only have it insured for £50,000 then you are only half insured and the insurance company can reduce any claim in half. So a claim for £20,000 would be cut down to £10,000. In practice this scaling down of claims is only likely to arise if you are very clearly underinsured.

The figures compiled by the Society of Chartered Surveyors can help you ensure that you are adequately insured without being over insured. They apply to normal estate type houses built since the 1960s with standard fixtures and fittings. The valuations need to be increased to cover top quality fitted kitchens, built-in-wardrobes etc.

In the case of older houses or those with unusual once-off designs it's as well to get some professional advice on reinstatement costs. Don't rely on the market value. It is seldom, if ever, a good guide to valuation for insurance purposes particularly at present where house prices have soared ahead of building costs. According to figures issued by the Department of the Environment, the average new house price has jumped by 111 per cent between 1991 and 1999. In other words they have more than doubled – a 100 per cent increase is a doubling. But house building costs, according to the Department rose by only 26 per cent over the same period. The figures from the Society of Chartered Surveyors indicate a far steeper increase in costs.

The sharper increase in the Society's figures undoubtedly reflects the fact that they are considering the cost of once-off jobs. And those costs include an element of profit for the contractor, architect, and surveyor involved. The Department's figures on the other hand only reflect trends on the costs of materials and wages.

But from both sets of figures it is clear that the market price is not a good guide to valuing your house for insurance purposes. Take the example of a four-bedroomed semi-detached house in Cork comprising 1,200 square feet. Using the figures in the table the insurance value to be put on such a house is £91,200. Add in a further £7,500 for a single garage and the value is still below £100,000. It is very unlikely that you could buy such a house for that price. Indeed the market value could well be £200,000, even more in some areas.

You can do your own figures using the guideline costs in the table. Ensuring that you are not over insuring your home is the first step to saving money. Another is to shop around for your insurance. Insurance companies aren't all the same. Even on buildings insurance the cover can vary significantly and so can the cost per £1,000 of valuation.

Sample quotes sought in a survey by the Consumer Association of Ireland revealed differences of almost 40 per cent between the dearest and the cheapest insurer. Greater differences undoubtedly arise in some circumstances. Discounts can make a big difference where they apply and not all companies are the same.

Most, but not all, give discounts for smoke detectors and alarms. Senior citizens can also claim discounts from some insurers. 'Senior' can mean over 50 in some cases and over 55 in others. A couple of insurers also give discounts to people who also insure their cars with them.

So it pays to shop around or get a broker to do it for you. Don't forget, of course, that there are some companies that don't deal through brokers. You need to check them out yourself. And

You should reassess your insurance needs at each renewal and increase your valuation if appropriate.

The house itself

make sure your home is adequately insured but don't be scared by the spiralling rise in house prices to over insure it.

There are four general areas of risk which the average householder should consider covering by insurance. These are:

Damage or loss of the house itself. Damage or loss of contents — furniture, etc. Liability for damage to third parties arising out of defects in the building. All risks insurance for specific items, i.e. jewellery, etc. Very often all four types of risk can be covered by the one general policy, although individual policies covering any one type can be taken out.

For the sake of the relatively small premium involved it is not worth taking the risk of not insuring your house. If the house is rented, check whether or not you are liable for insuring it. With a short lease you possibly are not. With a long lease you may be. If you are buying a house with a mortgage, the bank or building society will require you to insure the house and in some cases will have done it for you. Given the recent sharp rise in house prices the initial purchase price may be significantly in excess of the reinstatement cost. The price paid includes a premium for the desirability of the area, etc. so the reinstatement value for insurance purposes may be a good deal less. While there is a chance that you will be tempted to over-value the house for insurance purposes there is also the risk of undervaluing.

The cost of insuring a house is about 15p or 16p for every £100 valuation. So the insurance on a house estimated to cost £90,000 to rebuild would be about £140 a year — a relatively small sum for the peace of mind such an insurance provides. Remember it insures you against a possible loss of £90,000. But the amount of cover you get depends on the policy. What some companies include as standard, others charge extra for. The usual policy will cover damage to the house itself, the garage and certain outbuildings, together with walls, gates and fences. It may also cover damage to fixtures and fittings such as washbasins, toilets, pipes and water tanks. Most policies cover loss or damage caused by:

Fire, explosion, lightning, thunderbolt, falling aircraft or other aerial devices: They exclude damage caused by supersonic bangs.

Storm damage: In many cases damage caused by flood, frost, subsidence or landslide are not covered. Storm damage to fences and gates or damage to television aerials may also be excluded.

Burglary, housebreaking or any attempt there at: The buildings policy simply covers damage to the house itself — not the contents. The cover does not apply if the house is left unfurnished, or, even if furnished, is left uninhabited for more than a set period. If you are leaving your house vacant it is best to check with the insurance company to ensure that you are covered. If you are leaving it unfurnished you will have to take out a special policy.

Bursting or overflowing of water tanks or pipes: Again it is usual to exclude some small part of any claim under this heading — the first £50 say — and the conditions on leaving the house vacant are the same as above.

Impact: Damage caused by impact with the buildings, walls, gates, fences of any road vehicle, horses or cattle not belonging to or under the control of yourself or your family.

Loss of rent: If the house is left uninhabitable you are usually covered in this regard up to a set percentage of the sum insured on the building — often 10 per cent.

Liability to Public: If you are proved liable for damages caused to another person by an accident which occurred on your property, the normal building policy will provide cover up to about £500,000.

It is possible to extend the normal policy to cover damage to underground water pipes running between your house and the boundary of your land, damage to radio and television aerials, breakage of glass, etc. It is too late finding out what is and is not covered when an accident occurs. So when you are taking out insurance you should read the proposal form carefully to see what risks are excluded and decide whether or not you want extra cover. It is a good idea to look at your insurance policies at least once a year, preferably long before the renewal date so as to give yourself ample time to shop around for a better deal.

Premiums for house contents insurance vary greatly depending on where the house is, the company providing the cover and the type of cover given. Many companies give discounts

Read the proposal form and the policy carefully to discover just what's covered and what's not.

House contents

where the occupants are over a certain age, for being in a neighbourhood watch scheme, or for having an approved alarm system. A discount may also be available if you agree to pay the first part of any claim yourself.

One of the main reasons for the increased cost of house insurance is the increased risk of loss. So can you afford not to be insured or to underestimate the value of your house contents? If the contents of your house are not insured, you may be running a serious risk of loss — tot up the value of the contents of your kitchen for instance. Could you afford to replace them yourself? If it would impose an undue burden, then you would do well to be insured.

Do not assume that you are insured just because the mortgage lender looks after your insurance. It is normally only interested in having the buildings insured. Insuring the contents is generally left up to yourself. The normal contents policy covers loss arising from the same causes as the building policy. Extras which may be included as standard in some policies include:

Tenant's liability to landlord: Useful if you are in a rented house, this clause provides cover for damage caused to fittings, etc., for which the tenant may have to reimburse the landlord.

Employer's liability: This covers claims by people employed to work in the house – anything from full-time domestic staff to tradesmen, etc., who may be doing repairs about the house.

Liability to third parties: This provides cover for claims arising from accidents occurring in or about the house to visitors or their property.

Most policies also include provision for replacing items on a new for old basis provided it is not more than (usually) five years old. Suppose, for instance, your cooker gets burnt it will be replaced with a new cooker of the same type. Some companies, however, only provide this as an extra, so check.

There can be some important exclusions which need to be borne in mind. There may only be limited cover for loss or damage to articles temporarily removed from the house. Usually if the value of any one article — a piece of jewellery for instance — is more than 5 per cent of the total sum insured, a special policy will be required. Cash and bank notes are often only covered to a maximum of 5 per cent of the total value insured. But there may be an even more onerous money limit, as low as £25. Usually the following items are not covered at all: deeds, bonds, bills of exchange, promissory notes, cheques, securities for money, stamps, documents of any kind, manuscripts, medals, coins, motor vehicles and accessories, and livestock (other than horses).

Some insurers offer discounts for homes with alarms but be careful before applying for such a discount. There may be a condition attached that the alarm is always switched on when there is no-one is the house. If the policy does contain such a condition then you may not be insured at all if you forget to turn on the alarm. Most companies now have what is known as a "best endeavour" clause rather than a complete exclusion clause so that you are covered as long as you did not blatantly refuse to turn on the alarm. But before looking for a discount or accepting one make sure that onerous conditions do not apply.

Personal liability

Most buildings and contents insurance policies provide cover up to perhaps £500,000 against claims arising from accidents to third parties in or about the house. This is adequate to cover most eventualities, but you may consider it worthwhile to extend the cover to provide for the possibility that you, or a member of the family, will be found liable for damage outside the house. Such policies provide for claims of personal negligence for events occurring outside of business activities or motor driving — an injured golf caddie for instance. It should be possible to get cover of up to £100,000 for an annual premium as low as £1.

All risks

As mentioned above, the normal policy on house contents does not provide cover for articles whose value represents more than 5 per cent of the total sum insured. So if you have a valuable piece of jewellery, a camera or a painting, you may find that you are not covered for its loss. If you have such valuable items, an all-risks policy is worth having. Usually a valuation certificate is required for each article worth more than £100. Rates vary considerably and range upwards of £1 a year for every £100 insured — a lot more for bicycles. Some insurance companies have a minimum premium as high as £10 a year.

Pensions

Planning for retirement

10.

Planning for retirement involves much more than arranging an adequate pension but given that this book is about finance that is the only aspect of retirement considered in this chapter. The law relating to personal pension plans was changed radically during 1999. Tax relief can now be claimed on a larger proportion of income put into a pension fund and there is much more flexibility in how the accumulated pension fund is used on retirement.

These changes only apply to self-employed people, directors of family companies and employees who are not members of company pension schemes. But further changes are in the offing. It is proposed to introduce new laws during 2000 to provide the framework for simple low-cost individual retirement savings accounts. The idea will be to encourage workers who are not in pension schemes to save for retirement in their own personal pension savings accounts. There will be the carrot of tax relief on every penny saved and the schemes will be a lot more flexible than those currently available. They may also be open to the stay-at-home spouses of employees. It is expected that the set-up costs will be relatively low and the level of contribution will be variable allowing the maximum flexibility.

The aim, of course, is to encourage as many people as possible to make financial provision for retirement as a supplement to social welfare pensions.

Less than half of the work force — about 550,000 people — are in company or industry pension schemes in Ireland and the percentage is much smaller in some sectors. Only 19 per cent of the 125,400 at work in the distribution sector, for instance, are in a company scheme. The majority of self-employed workers

Rights under the Pensions Act

The Pensions Act 1991 provides pension scheme members with a wide range of rights and protections. Members are entitled to elect their own representatives to the board of trustees and to access information about the scheme. The following is a brief summary of the main provisions of the 1991 Act.

Preserved pensions:

A pension fund member with over five years qualifying service is entitled to a preserved pension if he leaves the job. The value of that pension will be based on entitlements built up since January 1991 and will be revalued each year. The value will go up by the rate of inflation or 4 per cent a year whichever is the lower figure.

The law says nothing about contributions made prior to January 1, 1991. So failing any agreement to the contrary between worker and employer they will continue to be treated as they were in the past according to the rules of the scheme. With most schemes that means that a worker who is changing jobs and who has been five years in his company's pension scheme is entitled to a refund of the contributions he made prior to January 1, 1991 plus a preserved (deferred) pension which rises in line with inflation up to at most 4 per cent a year. The preserved pension may be transferred into a new pension scheme or into an approved pension bond.

Information entitlements:

Members of pension schemes are entitled to the following information: basic information about the scheme's benefits, contributions etc.; copies of the trust deed and rules of the scheme; an annual statement showing the individual's current entitlements; an annual report giving audited accounts; an actuarial valuation of the scheme; and an investment report. Some of that information must be given automatically to members, prospective members and their trade unions. All of it must be available at least on request. Actuarial reports are not needed for defined contribution schemes.

Adequate funding

Annual actuarial funding certificates have to be submitted each year to The Pensions Board. That certificate must show that the contributions being made are enough to cover the entitlements being built up from January 1, 1991 onwards. Any shortfall in respect of prior years has to be outlined but the funds have until the year 2001 to make it up.

Trustees:

Members in schemes covering more than 50 people are entitled to elect at least two of the trustees. At least 15 per cent of members or a trade union must request that right.

Pensions Board:

The Pensions Board can be contacted at Holbrook House, Holles Street, Dublin, 2. Phone (01) 6762622 don't make any pension provision for themselves either. Only about 12 per cent of farmers and 39 per cent of the self-employed outside farming have pension schemes.

While many workers have some pension cover through a spouse's scheme it is clear that a very big proportion are building up no pension rights other than the basic social welfare entitlements. People seem to have a blind spot with regard to pensions preferring not to think too much about the long-term future, post-retirement. Even those in pension schemes very often pay scant attention to them, although for many years now they have been entitled to elect trustees to their schemes and have access to a wide range of detailed information.

But no law can fully protect pension scheme members. They must make use of the safeguards, keep themselves informed, and also ensure that their scheme is adequate to their needs. The law does not impose any minimum levels of benefits. So the existence of protective legislation does not provide an excuse for forgetting about your pension entitlements or lack of them. Pension scheme members have had the right to elect at least two of the scheme's trustees. That's an important right which should be fully utilised and members should ensure that the trustees elected take the job seriously.

Scheme members have the right to elect pension fund trustees. It's a right that should be exercised.

On an individual basis there is a clear need to think about retirement from an early age and to ensure that provision is being made for those years in so far as it is possible. Social welfare will provide a floor but the benefits from a company or private pension scheme can mean the difference between hand to mouth existence and a fuller life. The average person retiring at age 65 will live another 15 years and, of course, the tendency is for people to retire earlier.

Securing an adequate pension doesn't come cheap. It has been estimated that a man would need to invest 15 per cent of his income into a pension fund from the age of twenty in order to fund a civil service type pension at age 65. If he wanted to retire at 60 he'd need to invest 19 per cent of his income each year and he'd need to invest 23 per cent of income if he wanted to start drawing his pension at age 55. A woman would need to invest more since women tend to live longer than men.

Retirement is a major watershed in life and most of the financial decisions made during your working years should be made with at least half an eye on those later years. There is no need to become paranoid about it, but the post-retirement years should be kept in mind from very early on in one's working life. Individual circumstances obviously differ a great deal. For many, job-linked pension schemes will prove adequate. For others — such as the self-employed, including farmers — there may be a hope that the future will take care of itself. In this chapter we will just look at some of the questions which you should be asking yourself.

For those in pension schemes

Pension schemes are normally imposed on employees by their employers and all too often the provisions are not examined too closely. Trade unionists are, thankfully, beginning to wake up to the inadequacies of some pension schemes, and there are signs that a more questioning attitude is asserting itself. In some cases trade unions or staff associations have their own experts — or else have access to experts — who can ensure that every worker knows what his or her entitlements are, and — perhaps more importantly — what the shortcomings may be.

Most company pension schemes that have been in existence for some time are of the "defined benefit" type. The level of benefit is laid out in the rules — for instance, one-sixtieth of final salary for every year of service. Usually the workers' contributions are fixed while the employer's contribution is open ended. The employer puts in whatever else is necessary to ensure that the promised benefits are paid. The legislation requires employers to show each year that they are adequately funding the scheme.

Most pension schemes set up in recent years are "defined contribution" schemes where both worker and employer contributions are fixed — say as a percentage of payroll. Pensions are determined by what those invested contributions will buy when the worker retires. So the pension level is not guaranteed and the employer is not faced with an open-ended commitment as in the case of a "defined benefit" scheme. Employers have a great incentive to switch to defined contribution schemes.

Few company pension schemes provide the maximum possible benefits so they are open to improvement.

Whatever the type of pension scheme the Revenue Commissioners set maximum pension levels which may be provided if the contributions are to qualify for tax relief. With defined contribution schemes they estimate the likely level of benefit which the fixed contributions will provide given assumptions about investment returns etc.

The Revenue Commissioners' maximum pension levels don't pose a problem for most schemes. They allow benefits well in excess of what the majority of scheme provide. The pension may be equal to two-thirds of final salary index-linked to wages. There may also be provision for widow's and dependant's pensions. One and a half times final salary may usually be taken as a tax-free lump sum on retirement — it is less for people with very short service. The two-thirds pension may be in addition to a social welfare pension.

So how far does your pension scheme fall short of those maximum benefit levels? With a defined contribution scheme you have to not only look at the forecast pension level but also at the assumptions on which those forecasts are based. The following are some of the more pertinent questions which should be asked:

- **Will the pension provided be adequate?** Normally schemes provide one-sixtieth of final salary for each year of service up to a maximum of two-thirds of final salary. Some schemes give one-eightieth and provide for a maximum pension of one-half of final salary. Very often there is a reduction in those levels to take account of a social welfare pension. It is up to the individual to decide what is adequate.

- **Is there provision for increases in the pension to allow for inflation after retirement?** Too few pension schemes provide for inflation. The cost of such a provision is high - contributions would have to be increased by about one-fifth to allow for an annual increase of two and a half per cent in the pension. But it's better to pay now to make some provision for inflation than to see your fixed pension dwindle in value as the years go by. There is little that can be done at that late stage.

- **Is there provision for a widow's or widower's pension should the pensioner die?** Again too often pensions die with the pensioner and no provision is made for widows or widowers. It is true that a pensioner can often provide for such an eventuality by surrendering part of his own pension on retirement. But this can be costly. Assuming both husband and wife are 65 years of age, the husband might have to accept a reduction of a pound a week in his pension in order to provide his widow with a pension of £2 a week after his death. If she were five years older than he, the reduction of £1 would buy her a pension of about £2.50 — again, of course, only payable after his death.

But it's hard to decide to give up part of your pension when you retire to provide for an eventuality that you hope will never happen. Most people turn the hope into a belief and do nothing. But the worst sometimes happens. The message is that it's better to have the provision for widows and widowers built into a scheme from the start.

Getting an employer to pay more into the pension scheme can be better than a pay rise since the contributions go into the fund tax-free.

• **Are the pension rights transferable from one job to another?** This is certainly the case in respect of contributions made after 1991 but the pensions legislation that came into force then does not apply to previous contributions. Pension rights built up after January 1, 1991 have to be preserved and may be switched to another scheme or into a personal pensions bond but there is no such legal requirement in respect of contributions made prior to that. — see details on page 168.

For contributions prior to 1991 most pension schemes only provide two options for a worker changing jobs. He can take a return of his own contributions less 25 per cent tax but, if he does, he loses out on the return made on that money over the years and on the contributions made by the employer. Alternatively, he can opt for a deferred pension based on present salary levels and service to be paid when he is 65 years of age. But unless he is close to 65, he loses out badly.

It is possible for trustees to change the rules to provide similar flexibility in respect of those earlier contributions and that is an improvement worth looking for.

• **Is there any provision for a continuation of salary in the event of long-term disability?** This is another feature missing from many pension schemes. While it is not directly connected with retirement, it is something worth looking for in order to provide some insurance against the imposition of an early retirement because of some disability.

The next step is to decide whether or not your pension scheme is adequate for your needs. If not, you may be able to do something about it. There are, in fact, a wide range of options from getting the scheme improved to setting up your own scheme.

Pension scheme inadequate?

Having got the answers to each of those questions above you can then decide what to do about it. It is no harm to also have a check on the funding of the scheme. Under the new laws both annual reports and less frequent actuarial reports will have to be made available to members. The better fund managers and trustees have been doing this for years. Both reports are worth looking at. Annual reports show flows of cash in and out of the fund and the value of its investments. They are strictly factual. Actuarial reports go further and try to calculate whether sufficient contributions are being made to meet the likely future liabilities of the fund. The actuary will make assumptions about the future: trends in wages, retirements, investment returns etc. The report may need expert analysis — a deficit, for instance, may not be something to be unduly concerned about if it arose because of recent improvements to the scheme or because the scheme is relatively young and, of course, provided steps are being taken to eliminate it.

Having got the relevant information it is up to you to decide whether your potential pension is going to be adequate or not. It is very much a personal decision.

If it is not, you are faced with two obvious options:

- You can campaign for an improvement in your company pension scheme, or

- You can start saving to ensure a better income for yourself when you retire.

Let us have a look at both of those in turn.

Improving company schemes

If the company pension scheme does not provide the maximum benefits allowed by the Revenue rules, it is possible to fund for an improvement and still have the contributions allowed for tax relief. But getting extra benefits obviously imposes an additional cost and that cost will have to be borne either by the employee or the employer. There may be circumstances where a pension fund is in surplus and additional pension rights could be given without any increase in the contributions. But usually companies use such surpluses either to reduce their own contributions to the fund or else pay *ad hoc* increases to those already out on pension. In every case, the provision of extra benefits costs someone money. It involves paying more into the fund than would otherwise be the case.

In many cases employees took a very short-sighted approach when the social welfare scheme was extended under PRSI to practically all private sector employees. Instead of continuing to contribute at the old rate into the company pension scheme, they accepted a reduction in the company scheme as an offset against the new social welfare entitlement. Instead of a possible two-thirds pension from the company scheme PLUS a social welfare pension they accepted that the company pension would be reduced by the amount of any social welfare pension. As a result they saved money — their contributions to the company pension scheme were reduced. But the company usually cut its contributions too, so the employees actually lost out. And even the savings they made in their own contributions were not all that large since they had, of course, been getting full tax relief on every penny they put into the pension scheme.

So for every 78p saved by a worker on the standard tax rate of 22p, there was a full £1 less going into the fund on his behalf and possibly another £1 less going in from the company side. For a saving of 78p, he or she was losing perhaps £2 worth of pension benefits. The situation was even worse for those paying tax at higher rates. This highlights one area where action could be taken to try and improve pension entitlements. Anyone who did accept that type of deal when PRSI came in for non-manual workers might now try to reverse the decision and go back to getting an increased pension entitlement.

An examination of the maximum benefits allowed by the Revenue rules will highlight other areas in which improved pension benefits might be sought. At the present time, the indexation of pensions may be considered less important than it was in the past but it may also be less costly to fund — there are a number of investments at present which can guarantee a return above the rate of inflation.

But there are other areas to look out for:

- Widows' and widowers' pensions — does your scheme provide such pensions automatically or is it necessary to accept a reduced pension in order to ensure that provision is made for a surviving spouse?

- Does the scheme provide for a pension of two-thirds of final salary, not including the social welfare pension?

- How many years service are necessary to qualify for a full pension? Many schemes provide for one-sixtieth of final pay for each year of service up to a maximum of forty-sixtieths (two-thirds). There is no reason, except cost, why a scheme should not provide a full pension of two-thirds final pay available after thirty years service (thirty forty-fifths).

There is no reason, except cost, why a scheme should not provide a full pension of two-thirds final pay available after thirty years service.

- Are you allowed to work on beyond retirement age if that will enable you to increase your pension i.e. because of an impending pay increase?

- What is "final remuneration" under the scheme? Is it an average of the few final years or the actual final year or can the retiring person opt to take the most favourable of the last few years. The difference can be significant in terms of pension entitlement.

- Are the death-in-service benefits up to the maximum allowed?

- Is there an income continuance scheme included?

These are all areas where improvements might usefully be sought. If they can be campaigned for on a joint basis through trade union negotiations, then well and good. But if that is not possible, there is usually provision for individuals to buy extra benefits in the pension scheme by making their own voluntary contributions.

Check list of possible pension scheme improvements.

Voluntary contributions (AVCs)

Most pension schemes allow members to make additional voluntary contributions in order to increase their potential benefits. The contributions need not go into the company's own pension funds but may be accumulated on the side under the control of the individual. The funds are, however, subject to the same restrictions as to access etc. as other pension funds. The individual cannot normally benefit from them until reaching normal retirement age.

Let us look at the options open to someone wishing to make voluntary contributions. The money may be put into the existing company pension fund or, as mentioned above, it may be put into a wide range of funds set up by the various life assurance companies. With some schemes it is possible to buy extra year's service at fixed rates of contributions. In that way there is a certainty about the extra pensions being subscribed for. Most private schemes allow members to either contribute more money to the existing pension fund or, alternatively, to set up a separate scheme of their own piggybacked onto the company scheme.

There is no single best answer. There are pros and cons for both options. Contributing to a personal scheme involves set-up and on going administrative costs that may be avoided by contributing extra money into the company scheme. But having a personal scheme provides some extra flexibility, in particular in the choice of investment fund. The worker can pick his own fund from a long list of unit linked investments; guaranteed endowment funds; or fixed interest deposit funds. The difference between them is the degree of risk and the potential return.

Unit linked funds possibly offer the chance of the highest return but they also contain the greatest element of risk. Unit fund values can move down as well as up. Endowment funds usually offer a guaranteed minimum return plus the promises of bonuses — just like with-profit endowment assurance policies. Deposit funds retain the investment in fixed interest deposits getting whatever the going rate of return is. There is no risk of the value going down but it may fail to keep pace with inflation. The choice is up to the individual — a good managed unit-linked fund which has performed well in the past is possibly the best compromise for most. There is some risk of a downturn in values but over the long term the chances are that such an investment will at least keep pace with inflation — particularly since the returns within the fund are tax-free. That is one of the tax concessions accorded to pension funds.

Care must be taken in choosing the best fund for your extra pension contributions.

Many schemes will allow the investor to switch into a safer deposit fund at any time and this can be particularly advantageous getting near to retirement age. The great trouble with unit linked funds is that they may be in the doldrums at the very time they are due to mature for you — at retirement age. If there is the facility to switch, however, one can keep an eye on things for a few years prior to retirement. If it seems that investments generally are heading for a downturn, it will then be possible to switch into the fixed-interest fund — in other words get out as close to the top as possible. Whoever sells you the plan, and benefits from the commission, ought to be on hand at that stage to advise on what best to do.

There can be no rule of thumb on what extra payments into a pension fund will buy in terms of extra benefits. It depends on the performance of the investment and on annuity rates at the time of retiring. What happens is that the sum built up may be used to buy a pension at pension age. How much pension it buys will depend on interest rates at that time.

The Revenue Commissioners' rules require that additional voluntary contributions should be made on a regular basis — once started the intention should be to continue them. But it is flexible in this regard if a problem arises as a result of illness or reduced earnings. It is also possible to make sizeable voluntary contributions in the years prior to retirement.

Making additional voluntary contributions may enable you to get a higher tax-free lump sum on retirement but not always. There is a maximum lump sum entitlement of one-and-a-half times final remuneration — lower if you have less than twenty years service. Making extra voluntary contributions will not increase that maximum. So if your existing contributions will enable you to get that maximum, no amount of additional contributions will increase your lump sum entitlement — they will have to be used to buy extra pension benefits.

Part-time workers

Part-time workers don't have any automatic right to join company pension schemes. The European Court of Justice ruled late in 1994 that workers could not be precluded from schemes on the grounds of sex. But it is still perfectly legal to deny pension rights to part-time workers where there is no question of sexual discrimination.

But even without any legal requirement there is likely to be growing pressure to include part-time workers in company schemes if for no other reason than the sharp increase in the number of part-time workers employed. But there is no easy way of extending pensions schemes to include part-time workers on an equal basis with full-time staff.

Most schemes currently limit entry to full-time permanent employees. There is no difficulty in changing the full-time requirement but there is a need to define "permanent". Having got over that hurdle, the larger question is how to calculate actual pension benefits in a defined benefit scheme.

In such schemes full-time workers normally get one-sixtieth of their final pay for each year of service. And there is no great problem extending that to part-timers either on the basis of their actual pay or by calculating service on the basis of equivalent full years. So a part-time worker who was with the firm 40 years and is on £6,000 a year would get a pension of £4,000 i.e. forty/sixtieths (two-thirds) of £6,000. A full time employee on £12,000 would get a pension of £8,000 assuming the same service.

That seems fair enough but problems can arise where social welfare benefits are taken into account, as they are in most schemes. Normally the company pensions is effectively reduced to take account of the State social welfare pensions. Should an equivalent reduction be taken from a part-timers pension or should the reduction be on some pro-rata basis. There is no easy formula to ensure equality in all cases.

The same sort of problem arises with regard to disability benefits (income continuance schemes). These are normally underwritten by insurance and the insurance companies insist on limiting benefits. A common maximum benefit is two-thirds of salary less twice the State disability benefit for a single person. Applying this formula to low-paid part-time workers could result in no benefit being payable or, at most, a very small one.

Pensions and marital breakdown

The rights of spouses to benefits from a pension scheme are not defined in any law. But the laws covering judicial separation and divorce allow the courts to make orders allocating such benefits between spouses in the event of separation or divorce. So part or all of the pension rights of one spouse may be allocated to the other even though he or she had not made any financial contribution to it. The actual application of these powers depend on the courts and individual circumstances. All pension rights are covered from both defined contribution and defined benefit company schemes, personal pension plans and State schemes.

Pensions for the self-employed

The self-employed are just as eligible for tax relief on pension contributions as the employed individual. It is simply a matter of organising their own personal pension scheme and there is no shortage of schemes tailor-made by the various assurance companies for this purpose. A personal pension scheme is an attractive way of saving for retirement since the contributions qualify for tax relief and no tax is payable on the gains made within the fund. There are some offsetting drawbacks, however, in that the money is tied up.

There is a limit on the percentage of income that can qualify for tax relief when put into a personal pension fund. Those limits were raised from April 1999. For the 1998/99 tax year relief could be claimed on up to 15 per cent of income for those under 55 years of age and 20 per cent for those over that age. Since 1999 the limits are as follows:

Employees in small businesses

Only about one-in-ten small firms have pension schemes for their staff and even a smaller number of sole traders make pension provisions for their workers. Sole traders are people who operate a business on their own account without having established a company. They are self-employed but very often they also employ others. If they want to make some pension provision for those workers they can either pay them extra and let them take out their own private pension plans, or else they can set up their own executive plan. That second option can be the most tax efficient even where the employee actually pays the lion's share of the contribution.

Tax relief is only given on contributions to an executive scheme where the employer pays at least one-sixth of the overall cost. That may simply be the cost of the life assurance attaching to the pension scheme.

The employer gets the tax relief on his or her own contributions but in addition doesn't have to pay PRSI on the employees contribution. The worker also saves PRSI on his or her own contributions. Contributions to a private scheme have to be made out of income after PRSI is deducted.

Let's take an example. Joe's a publican with one full-time worker, his son Sean who is paid £15,000 a year. Joe is already making some pension provision for himself and wants to start making early provision for his son. He wants £2,000 to go into the fund at the lowest possible net cost.

He could give Sean a pay rise and let him put the £2,000 into the pension fund. He'd get tax relief on it so the after tax cost would be £1,040. If Sean put the full £2,000 into a pension fund the tax relief would offset the tax which would otherwise be due. So there would be no tax implications for him. But there are PRSI implications.

Between them they'd have to pay 18.75 per cent of the £2,000 in PRSI — the 6.75 per cent employee rate and the 12 per cent employer rate. So the PRSI cost would be £365.

That can be saved if instead of giving the money to Sean, Joe paid the money directly into an executive pension scheme.

Age	Limit
up to 30	15%
30 but less than 40	20%
40 but less than 50	25%
50 and over	30%

The maximum income taken into account is £200,000 a year. If more than the maximum contribution is paid in during any year, then the excess may be carried forward and claimed in future years if the contribution falls below the threshold. It is also possible to backdate the relief to prior years for which tax assessments have not become final.

The tax relief is a very valuable concession. For someone paying tax at 44p in the pound that means that a net payment of 56p will buy a full £1 worth of benefit — less commission and charges, of course. As mentioned above there is the additional tax advantage in that the money in the pension fund accumulates entirely tax free and up to a quarter of the fund available on retirement can be taken in the form of a tax free lump sum.

The tax concessions make personal pension schemes a very attractive way of saving for retirement. There is, however, one major drawback — the fact that the money in the fund cannot normally be drawn out before age 60. That can be a good thing in that it may protect your savings against your temptations but it may not seem that way if you badly need the money to save your business from impending doom.

In the past there was another drawback in that while up to 25 per cent of the accumulated fund could be taken as a tax-free lump sum on retirement, the remainder could not be touched. Some of it could be used to buy life insurance but the bulk of it had to be used to buy a pension. That requirement no longer applies to the self-employed, directors of family companies and employees who are not members of an occupational pension scheme.

In what follows, we are considering a self-employed person acting as a sole trader. A person working for their own company is in a more advantageous position on the pension front. While such a person may consider himself to be self-employed, he is actually an employee — the company is a legal entity of itself. As an employee, he can be a member of a company pension scheme. And it can be a special top hat scheme for managers and/or directors, or even a special scheme specifically for the managing director.

So while the self-employed person may not normally be granted tax relief on contributions of above a certain percentage of income, there is no absolute limit on the amount a company may claim in tax relief on contributions it pays into a pension scheme for employees. The only limit is that the pen-

Self-employed — picking the right pension

Someone shopping for a pension plan has at least decided what they need. That's a start. The next step is to decide how to satisfy that need. The need is to provide income during retirement. The way to satisfy that need is to invest money in a pension fund. It is, of course, possible to save for retirement in various other ways but the pension fund route offers the advantages of significant tax relief. The downside is that the money becomes inaccessible until retirement age.

Once the decision has been made to invest in a pension plan it's a matter of picking the best plan. That varies with the individual. The following are the basic choices which have to be made. There is no single right answer. A lot depends on the individual and there is an element of luck involved as well.

Personal pension or company pension?

Where the self-employed person works for his or her own company there are advantages in having the company set up the scheme. The net cost is likely to be lower and the restriction on the size of contributions which qualify for tax relief is less onerous. It can be worthwhile setting up a company simply for this purpose but that has other implications. The choice may be particularly important for someone trying to fund a pension fairly late in life. Professional advice is advisable.

Regular premium or lump sum?

Many personal pension plans now allow the flexibility to alter contribution levels from year to year and they also spread the setup costs over the life of the plan. That flexibility can be very important to someone whose income may fluctuate. An alternative is to make annual lump sum contributions into a pension fund. Each investment is a separate transaction. The lump sums may go into different funds or even different companies. On retirement they are simply brought together to buy a pension. The advantage is flexibility. The disadvantage is that it is all too easy to forget the initial good intentions and fail to make the investment each year. With a regular contribution plan there is some degree of compulsion.

Company and type of fund?

The final decision is where to actually invest your money. There are many companies and a wide range of funds to consider. Professional advice is well worthwhile. The investment performance of the fund can make a very significant difference to the size of pension you eventually enjoy. Past trends may, or may not, be a good guide to likely future performance. With-profits funds offer a more secure return than unit-linked options in bad times but in the good times the return on unit funds can be significantly higher. Work out your own approach to risk. Take advice, and make your choice.

sion benefits from such a scheme must not exceed the very generous upper limits detailed earlier in the chapter.

As outlined above a director of a family company who controls more than 20 per cent of the voting rights of the company (what are known as proprietary directors) may claim tax relief on their own pension contributions up to the levels listed above but within a company scheme there is nothing to stop their companies claiming tax relief on a higher level of contribution.

So there can be advantages in working for your own company rather than operating as a sole trader i.e. chargeable to income tax under schedule "D". The pluses and minuses involved go beyond the scope of this book, however, since they include many factors apart altogether from the benefits in the form of extra tax relief on pension contributions. The advantages on this front are likely to be particularly attractive to someone coming close to retirement with no provision for pension benefits but all the pluses and minuses need to be considered and professional advice sought.

It can be better for a self-employed person to make pension contributions through his or her own company rather than as a sole trader.

But let us have a look at the rules as they apply to the self-employed. As always, it is necessary to get a couple of definitions straight. The most important is that of "net relevant earnings". This is basically earned self-employed income calculated on much the same basis as it is for the taxman. It is net of losses and capital allowances and of any payments such as interest on which tax relief is given but before deducting other tax allowances.

The other definition of importance is that for normal retirement age. In general it must be between the age of 60 and 70 but it may be as early as 50 or as late as 80 for occupations where such early or late retirement "is customary".

So a professional footballer might get away with a scheme which provided a pension at age 35. The Revenue have accepted that brass instrumentalists can retire at 55 while for other musicians the normal retirement age should remain at 60. It is hard to think of any job other than farming where retirement at age 80 might be considered customary but maybe there are others. In order to get tax relief the pension scheme must be approved by the Revenue Commissioners. And to be approved it has to meet certain conditions. These were eased significantly from April 1999.

In the past the money accumulated in a personal pension fund had to be used mainly to buy a life annuity. A quarter of the fund could be taken as a tax-free lump sum but the rest could not be touched. It had to be used to provide an income for life. That's no longer the case.

The pensioner now has much more control over his or her pension fund deciding how it is invested and how it is drawn down. The options available to retirees have been greatly widened. Those who wish to can still buy an annuity but they have the option of retaining control over their funds.

A quarter of the fund can still be taken tax-free on retirement. But the remainder doesn't have to be used to buy a pension. It has to be invested in an Approved Retirement Fund (ARF) but it remains the property of the pensioner and apart from a requirement of keeping a minimum of £50,000 in an Approved Minimum Retirement Fund (AMRF) until age 75 pensioners can draw down the money as they like. Anything left in the fund on death becomes part of the deceased person's estate.

There are practically no restrictions on how the money in an ARF can be invested.

The requirement to keep £50,000 in an AMRF until age 75 doesn't apply if the pensioner has another income of at least £10,000 a year. Any money not required to be kept in a fund can be drawn down. The only disincentive against drawing down too much, too quickly, is that money taken out of the fund is subject to income tax in the normal way.

In the past at least a part, and maybe all, of a pension died with the pensioner. Provision could be made for a reduced survivor's pension for a spouse and/or dependent children after the death of the pensioner but in the end there was nothing left for the pensioner's estate except, perhaps, from life insurance paid for by accepting a reduced pension.

But under the new rules any money left in the pension fund become part of the deceased person's estate. A spouse inheriting is not liable for any tax. In other cases liability for income tax, inheritance tax or both can arise — depending on the individual circumstances. But the rules are far from onerous. For instance children inheriting after the death of both father and mother are liable for tax at no more that 25 per cent.

Tax of pension funds (ARF/AMRF) on death

ON DEATH OF HOLDER

ARF inherited by	Income tax due	Capital acquisitions tax due
Surviving spouse	No tax on the transfer to an ARF in the spouses name	No
Children (under 21)	No tax due	Yes — subject to normal thresholds
Children 21 and over	Yes at 44 per cent	No
Others	Yes at 44 per cent	No

ON DEATH OF SURVIVING SPOUSE

	Income tax due	Capital acquisitions tax due
Children (under 21)	No	Yes — subject to normal thresholds
Children (over 21)	Yes at 25 per cent	No
Others	Yes at 25 per cent	Yes — subject to normal thresholds

PRSI and the self employed

Self-employed people with a total income of over £2,500 in a tax year are liable to pay social insurance contributions. People who have been told in writing by the Revenue Commissioners that they do not need to make a return of income for tax purposes are liable for a flat rate payment of £124 a year. Other self-employed people pay at a rate of 5 per cent on income between £1,040 and the ceiling level — £26,500 in the 2000/1001 tax year and £25,400 in the 1999/2000 tax year. PRSI is paid with income tax.

Those not liable for tax get special books and can make payments — through instalments — at any post office. It is important to make the payments in full since the rules state that if the annual payment is even a pound short, no contributions are credited while if they are correct or over, a full 52 weekly contributions are credited for the relevant year.

It is important to register with the Department of Social Welfare. There is a form to fill out. Even if you have not filled out a form you are still liable to pay PRSI. The registration only ensures that it gets credited in the right way. Benefits from the scheme are significant.

Self-employed, Class "S", contributions do not, of course, provide unemployment benefits. What is provided for is old age, widow's and orphans' pensions. Three years contributions are sufficient to provide widow's and orphan's cover while eligibility for an old age pension requires ten years contributions.

Up to April 1999 self-employed people who were over 56 years of age in 1988 and who had no previous PRSI or social welfare contributions were unable to built up sufficient contributions to qualify for an old age pension since ten years of contributions were required and contributions have to stop at age 66. Since April 1999 those with between five and ten years contributions will qualify for a 50 per cent pro-rata contributory old age pension.

Some self-employed people were already paying PRSI as voluntary contributors before 1988. They include people who became ineligible for normal full rate PRSI and opted to continue paying on a voluntary basis in order to maintain certain benefits. They retain eligibility for the extra benefits conferred by voluntary contributions. These include retirement pensions — which start at 65 whereas the old age pension starts at age 66 — and a death grant.

Queries with regard to PRSI for the self-employed should be addressed to the Self-Employed Section of the Department of Social Welfare at Aras Mhic Dhiarmada, Dublin 1, phone (01) 8740100.

Consumers

Consumers — their rights

Consumer protection in the financial services area remains in a state of flux at the beginning of 2000. It has been decided to establish a new regulatory authority to oversee the entire sector but the process of setting it up has taken far longer than expected. Consumers, however, continue to enjoy a wide range of protections in the financial and other areas as a result of very significant changes in the laws over recent years. There is also a means of redress through the Small Claims Courts which have been extended throughout the country. The maximum amount which can be claimed is £1,000.

In the financial area there are ombudsmen to adjudicate on disputes involving lending institutions and insurance companies. The Central Bank oversees the activities of financial advisers not already covered by the various consumer protection measures dealing with insurance. The Consumer Credit Act provides protection against unscrupulous lenders while new regulations to be introduced during 2000 will make it compulsory for life insurance companies and intermediaries to give consumers more information on the costs involved in taking out their products.

All of these add to the growing body of protective measures introduced partly as a result of EC membership. Some have the backing of law while in other cases professional bodies have been encouraged by the threat of legislation to adopt their own voluntary codes of conduct.

One of the voluntary schemes led to the appointment of the Ombudsman for Credit Institutions. The office was established and is funded by banks and building societies but the Ombuds-

Credit institutions

man can make awards of up to £30,000 to individuals who are found to have a legitimate complaint against one of the financial institutions involved. They have a vested interest in allowing him his independence and making the system work. The Government has the power to appoint its own ombudsman but it prefers the self-policing method as long as it works — it's cheaper for one thing.

Before going to the ombudsman you must first make a complaint to the company itself. All the banks and building societies have designated managers to deal with complaints. Obviously you should try to sort out any problem at local level first, then take it to the head office of the bank or building society. If you are still not satisfied, you can then take the matter to the ombudsman. He is unlikely to look at a complaint unless it has been though the complaints procedures of the institutions involved.

He is open to complaints from individuals, organisations and sole traders. He will also consider complaints from companies so long as their annual turnover is under £250,000. He can't consider matters of bank policy. For instance he will not adjudicate on a complaint about the general level of bank charges. But he can, of course, deal with a complaint about the application of those charges in an individual case.

All licensed banks and the two remaining building societies are party to the ombudsman system together with the State owned ACCBank and ICCBank.

Insurance

There is also an Insurance Ombudsman who deals with disputes between private policyholders and insurance companies. She can deal with cases involving amounts of up to £100,000 and the insurance companies have agreed in advance to be bound by her decisions. Individuals, however, are not so bound. They can reject her decision and seek redress elsewhere, through the courts, for instance. As with the Ombudsman for Credit Institutions the dispute has to be initially processed through the insurance company itself and it is only when the company admits that the matter has reached an impasse, that the ombudsman will get involved. All companies providing life assurance in Ireland and about 90 per cent of the general insurance companies participate in the scheme.

Where to complain

INSURANCE	Brokers	Paul Carty National Director, Irish Brokers Association, 87, Merrion Square, Dublin, 2.
	Companies	Irish Insurance Federation, Russell Court, St. Stephen's Green, Dublin, 2.
	Overall	Department of Enterprise and Employment, Kildare Street, Dublin, 2. Insurance Ombudsman, 32 Upper Merrion Street, Dublin, 2.
FINANCIAL INTERMEDIARIES		Central Bank of Ireland, Dame Street, Dublin, 2. Department of Enterprise and Employment, Kildare Street, Dublin, 2.
BANKS/BUILDING SOCIETIES		Ombudsman for Credit Institutions, 8, Adelaide Court, Adelaide Road, Dublin, 2.
DATA PROTECTION		Data Protection Commissioner, Block 4, Irish Life Centre, Talbot Street, Dublin, 1.
SOLICITORS		The Law Society, Blackhall Place, Dublin, 7. Independent Adjudicator of the Law Society, 26/27 Upper Pembroke Street, Dublin, 2.
EUROPEAN UNION		The European Ombudsman 1, avenue du President Robert Schuman B.P. 403 F - 67001 Strasbourg Cedex
ESB		ESB Customer Complaints Commissioner, 39 Merrion Square, Dublin, 2.

Before reaching the Ombudsman, disputes may go through a number of channels. The industry has adopted codes of conduct and implemented some self-policing machinery. The Department of Enterprise and Employment retains a large degree of discretion and is the ultimate overseeing authority but it has encouraged the establishment of self-policing bodies for insurance brokers; other insurance intermediaries; and the insurance companies themselves.

- **Brokers:** In most cases the consumer's first point of contact with the insurance industry is through an intermediary — a broker or agent. If there is cause for complaint and it cannot be sorted out between the customer and the intermediary, then there are a number of further steps which can be taken. Where you go depends on the sort of complaint and on the type of intermediary.

  Let us first look at a complaint about the service of the actual intermediary — for instance a belief that misleading claims were made when a policy was sold, or that a broker did not give really independent advice. It is important to distinguish the type of intermediary involved.

  The word "broker" now has a definite meaning. To ensure that he or she can give independent advice, a "broker" must be able to sell the products of at least five insurance companies and that cannot be made up of a mixture of life and general insurance companies. In addition there are "agents" who represent four or less companies and "tied agents" who only sell the products of one company.

  If the intermediary is a broker and he is a member of the Irish Brokers Association (IBA) you can complain to it. The IBA was formed out of a merger between the two organisations, NIIBA and the CIB. It has agreed complaints procedures with the Department of Enterprise and Employment. The first complaint should be to the broker, then to the IBA. But if you think that the complaint is not being adequately dealt with, you can appeal to the Department itself. (All the addresses are given on the previous page.)

- **Agents:** Those brokers who are not members of either organisation, and all agents are subject to no overseeing body other than the Department. So when a complaint is not dealt with at local level that must be the first port of call.

- **Companies:** In many cases, of course, the complaint will arise over the actual product sold — over the policy itself rather than the choice of policy. In such cases the insurance company must have a role to play and complaints can, of course, be taken directly to the insurance companies. Where satisfaction cannot be reached with the company itself, complaints can be brought to their self-policing organisation, the Irish Insurance Federation.

Like the brokers' organisation it is funded and controlled by the companies themselves so it cannot be said to be completely independent, but the industry, both companies and brokers, has a vested interest in seeing that complaints are properly dealt with, and that abuses are kept to the minimum. In all cases a final appeal can be made to the Department of Enterprise and Employment.

Under the Investor Compensation Act 1998 investors who lose as a result of fraud or liquidation may claim compensation for 90 per cent of any loss up to a maximum payment of £15,500. The claim is made to the Investor Compensation Company which was set up under the Act.

Financial advisers

There are many savings and investment products which are not linked to insurance. Financial advisers or brokers who take deposits, sell shares, or act as intermediaries for various types of non-insurance linked investments such as unit trusts and BES schemes are not regulated under the insurance schemes outlined above at least not when they are selling such products. The regulatory authority in such cases is the Central Bank so advisers who deal in both insurance-linked and non-insurance linked products may be answerable to two regulatory authorities – the Central Bank and the Department of Enterprise and Employment.

The Central Bank runs a LoCall phone service at 1890 200 469 for consumers who want to check the status of an individual or company claiming to be a registered financial adviser.

The whole regulatory system is in the melting pot at the beginning of 2000 and may well change during the year.

Solicitors

Solicitors are members of the Law Society of Ireland and it is to that body that complaints should first be directed after, of course, they have first been made to the individual concerned. The Law Society has its own complaints procedures. Com-

Going to Court need only cost you £6

Have you ever bought faulty goods or paid for less than adequate service? Who hasn't? Complaints often go unheeded. So what else can you do? Did you know that you can go to court for only £6. That's the cost of taking an action in the Small Claims Courts which have been operating throughout the country since 1994. Demand for the service has been growing but at a slow enough pace. Just over 2,700 claims were processed last year. In the majority of those the claimant got some redress.

Unfortunately winning the case is only half the problem. Collecting the actual awards has sometimes been a problem. A survey by the Consumers Association a couple of years ago found that only about two-thirds of consumers got their awards while the other third reported difficulties. However, the Small Claims procedure is always worth a try. The most you can lose is £6 and some of your time.

There is a limit to the size and type of claim covered by the scheme. The maximum amount that can be claimed is £1,000 and the dispute must relate to the purchase of goods or services for private use from someone selling them in the course of business. Also covered are claims for minor damage to privately owned property and the non-return of rent deposits. Precluded are claims for accidents, damages or for the recovery of payments under a loan or hire purchase agreement.

So how do you go about making a claim?

The scheme is administered by the Small Claims Registrar at local District Court Offices throughout the country. You can look up the address and telephone number in the telephone directory. The first approach is to the Registrar. He or she will provide help in drawing up a statement of claim. There's a special form to make the job relatively easy. The non-refundable fee of £6 is payable at this stage.

A copy of the claim is sent to the person against whom it is made — the respondent — and he or she has fifteen days to reply. If no answer is received the claim is automatically treated as undisputed and the District Court will make an order for the amount claimed to be paid within a stipulated time.

plaints may be referred to the Disciplinary Tribunal of the High Court or, in the case of excessive fees, to the Taxing Master, at the Four Courts, Dublin, 7.

Where a complainant is dissatisfied with the manner in which the Law Society has dealt with a complaint he or she may refer it to the Independent Adjudicator of the Law Society whose role is to ensure that complaints about the conduct of a solicitor are dealt with fairly and impartially by the Law Society.

If the claim is disputed the Registrar will try to reach an agreed settlement between the parties at an informal meeting. It is held in private. Both parties may be asked to outline the facts of the case and they may be asked questions by the Registrar.

His aim is not to make a judgement but rather to reach an agreed settlement. Either side can bring forward witnesses or present expert reports. But the parties have to pay for these themselves.

If the Registrar fails to get a settlement agreed, the matter is referred to the District Court and is heard before a judge. The hearing may not be in private and will, of course, be more formal. The parties may be asked to answer questions on oath. The Registrar attends the Court hearing to outline the facts as he has ascertained them.

There is provision for witnesses to be summoned to appear before either the Registrar or the Court. The Registrar will help in issuing the summons but it is up to the individual re-questing the witness to pay any expenses involved. There is nothing to stop either party hiring a solicitor to represent them but the whole idea is to keep the cost down and there is no need for a solicitor. Having won an award the next problem is to get the payment and that unfortunately can sometimes prove difficult. Enforcement is far from adequate. A company may have closed. The person may have no assets or they may just refuse to pay.

Many people have won cases to no avail. The Consumer Association surveyed 470 people. One third of those who won awards had still to receive them a year later. However the scheme had worked well for the other two-thirds. Of the 2,749 applications made last year, some 1,430 were settled by the Registrar. A further 234 cases went by default to the claimants because the claims went unanswered. Of 647 cases actually heard by a judge, decrees in favour of the claimants were made in 380.

People who don't get their awards can go back to the Small Claims Registrar and have the matter passed to a sheriff or county registrar for collection. But even that is not a sure fire way of getting the money. Not all the decrees passed to sheriffs for collection are enforced. Still most claimants win something. For £6 its worth a try.

In all cases the first complaint is made to the Law Society. The Adjudicator only considers the Society's handling of a complaint against the solicitor, not the actual complaint itself. The Adjudicator cannot award compensation and cannot consider any matters which have been dealt with by the Society's Compensation Fund Committee, the Disciplinary Tribunal of the High Court or the Taxing Master.

Complaints have to be made in writing and should include a copy of the Society's decision and confirmation that the subject matter of the complaint has not already been considered by the Disciplinary Tribunal of the High Court. For the address see the table on page 189.

Access to personal files

Under the Data Protection Act individuals have a right of access to most personal files relating to themselves held on computer by companies and other organisations. Most public sector organisations, financial institutions, providers of credit ratings, holders of direct mail lists, and those who keep sensitive information with regard to such things as racial origin, political or other beliefs etc. are required to register with the Data Protection Commissioner.

That register is open to the public and contains details of the type of information held. The right of access covers not only the files of those companies and organisations required to register but anybody with personal information on file. The individual has a right, first of all, to be told what sort of information is kept on file — in response to a written enquiry, and then to see the files relating to him or herself.

The holder of the files has duties with regard to maintaining the accuracy of the data, not keeping more data than is necessary for the specified purpose, nor keeping it for longer than necessary. He also has to take adequate measures to keep the files secure. There are certain files exempt from the requirement. These include police and prison files.

Your first approach should be to the person or organisation you think is holding files on you. You should write to them on the following lines —

"Please send me a copy of any information you keep on file about me. I am making this request under the Data Protection Act."

You should give any information which might help the individual or organisation to identify you. You should get the information within forty days and you may be asked to pay up to £5. If you experience any difficulty or if you want to see the register of data holders you can contact the Data Protection Commissioner at Block 4, Irish Life Centre, Talbot Street, Dublin, 1, phone (01) 6748544.

If the information on file is wrong you have, of course, the right to have it corrected and you may have the right to have information completely erased. Corrections must be made to factually wrong data but you have no right to have opinions changed. If, for instance a school is keeping assessments of its pupils on computer, the individual has a right of access to the data and could have actual markings changed if they were wrong. But there is no right to have teachers' opinions with regard to ability etc. changed.

Where information is being unnecessarily kept, there is a right to have it erased. As mentioned above the holder of data must have a stated reason for holding it. If the information held is not necessary for that purpose, then you can have it erased. For instance, information on a person's religious beliefs may be appropriate to personal files held by a hospital, but would be unnecessary to the files of a finance company.

There are a lot of files out there that may be worth looking at and checking. Your employer may have some files. So too might your trade union. Some schools have switched over to keeping files on computer. They might all be worth looking at. Then, of course, there are the banks and other financial institutions that maintain credit ratings. They are certainly worth checking if you have had any difficulty getting approval for a loan.

Holders of data have to exercise great care in how they gather and keep it. The data must be obtained fairly, it must be accurate, and it must be kept up to date. It must also only be used for a stated purpose. The purpose for holding the data has to be stated in advance and data said to be kept for one purpose cannot be used for another. The information kept must be adequate for the purpose; it must be relevant and not excessive. It must be erased when it is no longer needed for its stated purpose.

These requirements mean that a holder of personal files needs to ensure that they are kept secure. Even leaving on a computer with someone's personal data up on the screen would breach the requirements of the Act if a person passing by might be able to read it. In the same way a print out of computer files left lying around for someone to see would breach the security requirements of the Act. The holder of the data must take steps to prevent unauthorised access or alteration, disclosure or destruction of the data.

And it is not only fines under the Act that the holder of data has to fear. A person who suffers loss or damage as a result of a lack of care or unauthorised disclosure etc. can always sue.

Freedom of Information Act

The Freedom of Information Act came into force in 1998 and provides wide ranging rights to access information held by public bodies. It doesn't apply to private companies or organisations. It has a role in consumer protection in so far as all citizens are consumers of many state services. In this regard an individual has a right to access his or own personal files and to have them amended where they are incomplete, incorrect or misleading.

There is also a right to access official files dating back to April 21, 1998 when the Act came into force. That date restriction does not apply to personal files.

To get access to the information you are looking for you should write to the head of the relevant government department or organisation saying that you are making the request under the Freedom of Information Act.

Decisions to refuse access to information can be appealed to the Information Commissioner, Kevin Murphy, at 18, Lower Leeson Street, Dublin, 2, phone (01) 6785222.

Office of the Ombudsman

The Ombudsman, Kevin Murphy, who is also Information Commissioner investigates complaints from individuals about government departments, local authorities, health boards and the postal services. The office is independent of government and has powers to inspect files, require officials to give information, and make recommendations for redress including compensation.

While he has no power to force acceptance of his recommendations, if they are not accepted and acted upon he can report the fact to the Dáil and Seanad. Up to this all of his recommendations have been accepted.

Complaints should be made in writing to his office at 18, Lower Leeson Street, Dublin, 2, phone (01) 6785222, within a year of the action or lack of action complained of.

Credit ratings

The Irish Credit Bureau, of which most of the leading finance houses are members, provides members of the public with details of their personal credit rating as shown on the Bureau's books. It has been doing this since before the enactment of the Data Protection legislation. The information provided includes the name of the company which registered the information, the relevant account number and what is called the "conduct grading" of the account — likely to be only one word "satisfactory" or "unsatisfactory".

The members of the Finance Houses Association who use the Bureau are: AIB, ACCBank, AIB Finance & Leasing, Anglo Irish Bank Corporation, Bank of Ireland Finance, Bank of Ireland, Beneficial Bank, Bord Gais Finance Limited, BNP Capital Finance Limited, EBS Building Society, Equity Bank Limited, First Active, Friends First Finance, Ford Credit Europe, ICC Finance, ICS Building Society, Irish Life Finance, Irish Life Homeloans, Irish Nationwide Building Society, Irish Permanent, Irish Permanent Finance, Lombard & Ulster Banking, MBNA International Bank, National Credit Finance Limited, National Irish Bank, National Irish Investment Bank, Premier Banking Limited, TSB Bank, Smurfit Finance, Western Finance Company, and GE Woodchester Bank.

The Bureau can be contacted at Newstead House, Newstead, Clonskeagh, Dublin, 14. If you are finding difficulty in getting loan finance and you have no idea why, then you should contact the Bureau as well as your bank and ask for details of the information they have on you. Mistakes have been made. The Ombudsman for the Financial Institutions granted an award for damages to a man who had been refused business loans as a result of a mistake in the information held on a bank's files. The fact that he had paid off a loan early was mistakenly entered as something else on his file and he was effectively blacklisted. So it can happen.

ESB complaints

The ESB has its own ombudsman type operation to deal with complaints that cannot be resolved by their own internal procedures. The ESB Customers Complaints Commissioner has the power to issue binding recommendations to ESB Customer Services and may recommend that the company follow a particular course of action or make an ex-gratia payment. Before going to the commissioner with a complaint it is necessary to have exhausted all of the ESB's internal procedures.

There is no cost involved to the complaining consumer and he or she can reject any recommendation and pursue other remedies such as taking the matter to court. See page189 for details of how to contact the commissioner.

Consumer Credit

The Consumer Credit Act which was passed into law in 1995 is designed to provide a range of protection for borrowers. Its provisions have been coming into force under various Ministerial Orders. Consumers have been slow enough to view loans as a service which the lender is only too anxious to sell. Banks, building societies, finance houses, moneylenders, and pawnbrokers all make their money by lending money. For many years lenders were so pleased at even being considered for a loan that they seldom looked too closely at the cost and even less seldom shopped around for the best possible deal.

That has changed. Credit is more easily available. Consumers are better informed. There is growing competition among lenders. But there are still difficulties.

- Competition can only work if the consumer has the information needed to compare products. That information on costs and conditions has not always been easily accessible in clear terms.

- The fine print in some contracts has clearly favoured the lender and the borrower may not have the knowledge or the bargaining power to reject the onerous terms. Very often the borrower doesn't know that conditions exist until he or she runs foul of them.

- Concerns have been expressed in the past at some of the methods used to enforce loan agreements — calling at the borrower's workplace, for instance.

The Consumer Credit Act tackles those difficulties curtailing the rights of lenders and enhancing the rights of borrowers. It is a wide ranging piece of legislation and its full implications will take time to emerge. The Director of Consumer Affairs has responsibility for overseeing its operation and he also takes on a price-control task over bank and building society charges.

Let's have a look at some of the provisions:

- **Information:** All loan agreements will have to be written in plain language and contain a minimum amount of information on interest rates, charges, repayments, what happens in the event of a default etc. If there are two possible meanings to any clause the Courts will have to favour the one most beneficial to the borrower. That provision applies to all consumer agreements under a different Act which ensures that the Courts will not uphold "unfair conditions". A condition will be considered to be "unfair" if contrary to the requirement of good faith, it causes a significant imbalance in the parties' rights and obligations under the contract to the detriment of the consumer.

The borrower must also be given time to read and understand the agreement.

- **Refused a loan:** A person who is refused a loan will have the right to request and get information including the name and address of "any single person" from whom the lender sought information on the financial standing of the would-be borrower. The request has to be made within 28 days of the refusal and the lender has 14 days to comply.

  One lawyer has suggested that the wording of the Act would allow the lender to only supply one name even when more than one person was contacted. That advice may be taken on board by some financial institutions, so it is worth remembering and checking should you have a need to use these new rights of disclosure.

- **Interest Rates:** The only interest rates which can be quoted in advertisements and agreements will be annual percentage rates worked out under a fixed formula so that the consumer can compare rates on a like with-like-basis. A provision of the Act, which doesn't apply to bank or building society loans, allows the borrower to apply to the Circuit Court claiming that the terms of an agreement are "excessive". The Court will take all the circumstances into account including "the age, business competence and level of literacy and numeracy of the consumer".The Court can effectively rewrite the agreement reducing or eliminating further repayments.

- **Cooling-off Period:** All loan agreements with the exception of housing loans, credit cards and overdrafts must allow for a ten day cooling-off period during which the consumer can withdraw from it. But the borrower can waive that right.

- **Early Repayment:** The borrower must be compensated for making an early repayment of the loan. The formula on which such compensation is based will have to be agreed by the Central Bank or the Director of Consumer Affairs. The same compensation will have to apply where the borrower is forced to pay off the loan early because of some condition of the loan.

- **Enforcement:** The lender is barred from contacting a consumer at his or her place of work except in some cases where the borrower has a live-in job. Any contact at home, by phone or personally, has to be between 9 in the morning and 9 in the evening although the wording of the Act would seem to allow calls to be made before 9 am on a Monday morning. The Act reads "between 9 o'clock in the evening on any week day and 9 o'clock on the following day". The lender has to give ten days notice in writing of any action he wants to take under the agreement. It has to detail the action and the date on or after it is intended to take that action. Where the action has been prompted by a breach of the agreement on the part of the borrower no action can be taken for 21 days. If the borrower gets back on track within that time period the lender must not include any reference to it in the customer's credit record.

• **Lender's Liability:** A lender may be liable to make good any defect of goods or services bought with a loan. In certain circumstances where the loan is arranged through the supplier and the money is paid directly to the supplier of the goods or services the lender can become liable. The customer will first have to pursue his or her rights against the supplier of the goods or services but where that fails the claim can then be pursued against the lender.

Switching house insurance

Mortgage lenders often suggest that borrowers take out house insurance with a particular company or even from one of a group of companies but they cannot force a borrower to do so. However they can require that insurance be taken out and they may impose a charge if the insurance is taken out with a company other than one of those recommended. Taking out house insurance through a building society or bank, of course, need not be a bad thing. Some societies offer very attractive house insurance packages which are cheaper in many cases than can be obtained elsewhere. These are usually not available through insurance brokers but it is worth checking them out to see how your society's policy compares with other policies.

Insurance — right to cancel

Under a voluntary agreement entered into by the life assurance companies, people buying regular premium savings and investment type policies are sent a letter outlining details of the policy; warning them that it is a long-term contract and that they stand to lose if they cancel it in the early years; and telling them that they have fifteen days to withdraw from the policy without loss. The insurance cover under the policy remains intact during this cooling-off period. New regulations to be made in 2000 are likely to make that voluntary agreement compulsory. They will also require disclosure of additional information on setup costs, commission levels, the investment returns required to meet specific funding targets, and the impact of lower than expected investment returns.

Broker charges

Some insurance brokers charge clients a fee in addition to the commission they get on general insurance. Those charges must be itemised on the bill. The level of commissions on general insurance was controlled by the Department of Enterprise but that control was lifted during 1999 and there is no requirement to disclose details of the commission being paid to the broker or agent. Up to 1998 the life insurance companies operated a voluntary agreement on maximum commission levels payable to brokers. But this was found to be in breach of competition law. As outlined above it is expected that during 2000 the Department of Enterprise and Employment will bring in new regulations requiring the disclosure of commission levels.

Deposit insurance

Bank and building society deposits have always been relatively safe but there is also some guarantee against loss. Both groupings now have guarantee schemes which provide some measure of protection against loss in the event of a bank or building society failure. In such an event depositors are guaranteed to get back 80 per cent of the first £5,000 on deposit; 70 per cent of the next £5,000 and 50 per cent of the next £5,000. So someone with £15,000 on deposit would get back at least £10,000.

European Union

The European Ombudsman investigates complaints about maladministration by Institutions and bodies of the European Community. These include the Commission, the European Parliament, the Committee of Regions, the European Investment Bank, and the European Investment Fund. You don't have to have been individually affected by the maladministration, but you must first contact the institution or body concerned to inform it of your complaint. A letter of complaint is sufficient.

Complaints should be made in writing. There is a standard form which may be used if you like. You can get a copy from the Ombudsman's office — see page 189 for the address. The Ombudsman tries to find a mutually acceptable solution to the complaint. He can recommend how it might be solved. If the recommendation is not accepted, the Ombudsman can make a special report about the case to the European Parliament.

Goods and services

Consumer protection in the supply of good and services is provided by an 1980 Act which updated a lot of earlier legislation. The one main drawback is that the consumer's final redress must be through the courts. If the retailer, shopkeeper, or what have you, refuses to rectify a claim, the final judgment on who is right has to be made in court. The Small Claims Court offers a low cost route where the amount involved is less than £1,000.

The Act provided for the establishment of the office of Director of Consumer Affairs. She can investigate various practices and take direct action against traders who do not comply with the general provisions of the Act. But she has not really got a role in dealing with specific individual complaints. The office operates a helpline at (01) 4025555. Give them a ring if you need some advice on consumer affairs.

The provisions of the Act are mainly related to dealings between a trader and an end-consumer of a product or service. Some of the protections do not apply to deals between two traders — a retailer and wholesaler, for instance so a consumer may not be covered by the full Act if he does a deal at a "trade price".

When something goes wrong it is almost always the retailer who is, in law, responsible for putting things right. It is he who sold the goods and it is between him and the consumer that the contract was made — a contract for sale, remember, need not be in writing. Even if the manufacturer provides a guarantee against defect in the product it is still the retailer who is responsible to see that things are put right. There are five general areas of protection given to the consumer under the Act.

Your contract is almost always with the seller not the manufacturer although it can often be better to seek redress from the manufacturer.

- **The goods sold must be made of "merchantable quality".** The goods must be capable of being used for the purpose for which they are normally sold. It does not matter if the retailer did not know about the fault. He has a responsibility to the consumer but if there are defects he may cover himself by pointing them out. Goods marked "seconds" or "slightly defective", for instance, would not be expected to be of top quality. The buyer also has responsibilities — he or she is expected to have examined the goods and have no complaint if the defects could reasonably have been noticed before purchase.

- **The goods must be fit for their intended purpose.** In some cases the purpose is obvious but in other cases the consumer may be relying on the retailer for advice and he is expected to have some skill in this matter. If he says the product or service will do the job, or serve the purpose, then you have a claim against him if it turns out otherwise.

- **The goods must be as described.** Goods can be described in advertisements, pictures, or orally by the salesman and if these descriptions are not in keeping with the truth, then the purchaser has a claim for redress. The trader may also be liable for criminal prosecution under the 1978 Consumer Information Act.

- **The goods must conform with the sample.** This provision applies when the consumer buys on the basis of seeing a sample of the goods.

- **The trader can be assumed to be able to pass ownership.** This is a difficult area of law but, in general, the trader is assumed to be able to pass ownership of the goods to the purchaser. If, for instance, there is an unpaid hire purchase debt on the goods and the hire purchase company comes looking for them, the buyer may have a claim against the seller.

These rights are enshrined in the Act and in general, the trader cannot limit them. If a consumer has a valid complaint, then in general, he has a right to get his money back. He may, in some cases, be entitled to compensation and, indeed, may have a claim against the manufacturer if the goods are so defective that they cause damage. But that is another area of law. Retailers cannot rely on such notices as "no exchange", "no money refunded", "returned goods only exchanged for credit notes", or "no liability accepted for faulty goods". Indeed such notices are illegal under the Act.

If a contract is unfair it is unenforceable even if it is graced with the consumer's signature and had been read and freely entered into. The law no longer assumes that the consumer is a completely free agent. That was made very evident in regulations introduced by the government at the beginning of 1995 to comply with an EU directive. The regulations apply to contracts entered into by personal consumers with suppliers of goods or services and they greatly enhance the rights of consumers. A consumer cannot be assumed to have signed his or her rights away just because of a signature on a practically un-

If you have a complaint, your claim is against the retailer. It is his responsibility to see that matters are corrected. If you fail to get redress you could try the Small Claims courts.

Unfair consumer contracts

intelligible contract written in legalese and produced in small fine print. That doesn't mean that contracts can be signed with impunity and repudiated afterwards. The old adage of *caveat emptor* (let the buyer beware) still applies to some extent.

The regulations don't apply to core provisions of a contract such as the price or other terms that were individually negotiated with the consumer. They are aimed more at the type of standard clause often written into contracts to protect the seller or supplier without providing any benefit to the consumer - the type of clause included in the fine print and imposed on the consumer in a take-it or leave-it fashion. Such clauses are not automatically unfair and unenforceable. Only a court can decide that but the regulations lay down guidelines.

They require all consumer contracts to be written in plain and intelligible language. Consumers must be given a reasonable opportunity to read the contract and fully understand what's involved. Any term that allows the supplier to hold onto a deposit if the consumer pulls out of the deal must be matched by a similar clause providing equal compensation for the consumer if the supplier fails to deliver. An individual consumer may go to court to have a clause in a contract declared unfair. This may arise where a consumer is looking for compensation and the supplier is relying on the fine print of a contract to avoid payment. Alternatively the unfairness of a contract may be used by a consumer as a defence against a seller or supplier who is looking for extra payment.

So how does a Court decide whether or not a clause in a consumer contract is unfair? It has to take a range of factors into account including the balance between supplier and consumer in terms of rights and obligations and the strength of the consumer's bargaining position. A contract that imposes severe sanctions on a consumer for late payment, for instance, without imposing similar penalties on the supplier for late delivery might well be considered unfair, for instance.

Very few cases have come before the courts in Ireland but during 1999 Justice Con O'Leary in the Cork District Court declared that a clause in a home purchase contract was unfair to the buyer. The clause required payments to be made in stages while an apartment was being built. While not ruling against such stage payments in general Justice O'Leary found one particular clause in the contract to be unfair. It required the pur-

Consumers are not necessarily bound by clauses in contracts that are considered unfair.

chaser to pay a percentage of the agreed purchase price at the plastering stage. This meant in Justice O'Leary's view that he was required to pay 90 per cent of the purchase price before 90 per cent of the work had been completed. That was unfair he decided.

In each case the final decision is up to the courts so it can be expensive finding out. But as outlined on page 192 the Small Claims' Courts provide access to legal redress for claims up to £1,000 for a flat fee of £6. So if you are being held to a clause in a consumer contract that you believe to be unfair and you are willing to cap your claim at no more than £1,000 then the Small Claims' Courts are worth a try. There's little to lose.

The Director of Consumer Affairs also has a role in enforcing the regulations but not in individual cases. Hers is a more general role in that she can apply to the High Court for an order prohibiting the continued use of an unfair clause in a contract.

Using your rights

It is one thing having new consumer rights, it may be another thing altogether using them. The consumer may have a claim against the trader but how does he get redress, and what form will this redress take. The Office of Consumer Affairs has suggested the following guidelines:

- If the goods are incapable of doing what they are supposed to do from the very beginning, it is likely that the consumer is entitled to a full refund, and may refuse all offers of repair, replacement, or adjustment.

- If goods are not as described, the consumer is not bound to accept them. This is an important provision since it can be difficult for a retailer to claim that even a minor instance of false description was not important.

- The consumer's right to reject goods could be lost if he does not act promptly on discovering the cause of complaint. It could also be affected if he altered the goods or if he does anything which implies that he has accepted them.

- If the goods have been used for some time before the fault is detected, a repair may be all that the consumer can expect but the repair should be a permanent one which restores the goods to the quality that they should have been when sold allowing, of course, for wear and tear.

- If the consumer is entitled to his money back, a credit note is never good enough.

Social Welfare

Social welfare entitlements 12.

A full explanation of the workings of the social welfare system would require a book in itself, and, even then, it would not be complete since there are grey areas which are left to the discretion of the officials in the Department. A booklet giving a fuller summary of the system "Guide to Social Welfare Services" is available from Information Service, Department of Social, Community and Family Affairs, Aras Mhic Dhiarmada, Dublin 1, while information and advice can be obtained from local social welfare offices and local Citizens Information Centres throughout the country. A full list of these information centres is available free of charge and post-free from the National Social Services Board, Floor 7, Hume House, Ballsbridge, Dublin, 4 Tel: (01) 605 9000. Information on policy formulation, guidelines and the procedures for determining entitlement to the various payments can be accessed on the Department's internet website at www.dscfa.ie Everyone has a right to this information under the Freedom of Information Act. If you haven't got access to the internet you can request the information at any social welfare office. In this short chapter only a small number of topics are covered. But first a brief overview of the system.

Basically there are two types of social welfare payments — benefits and social assistance/allowances. Entitlement to benefits is based on meeting certain PRSI contribution requirements and also meeting some other conditions such as being unemployed, over 65 or widowed etc. The self-employed have been covered by PRSI since 1988 and most workers earning £30 or more a week are also covered. This £30 rule replaced the old rule which laid down that it was necessary to work more than 18 hours a week to come into the PRSI net.

A private sector employee is not liable for PRSI on the first £100 of weekly earnings. Also from April 2000 those earning less than £226 in any week are exempt from the health levy of 2 per cent. That was increased from the £217 which applied during the 1999/00 tax year. Most public servants pay a lower rate of contribution and are entitled to fewer benefits but since April 1995 new entrants to the public service are paying full rate PRSI and gaining entitlement to the full range of benefits. Public servants paying PRSI at the lower rate are exempt from paying it on the first £20 a week.

Entitlement to any social welfare *benefit* is not normally affected by the claimant's means. Entitlement to social *assistance*, on the other hand, is not based on any contribution requirement but on the basis of a means test. An example of the difference between the two is that the contributory old age pension is a benefit — there is no means test — while the non-contributory old age pension is a form of social assistance subject to a means test.

Part-time workers

Part-time workers who earn £30 a week or more are eligible for a wide range of PRSI benefits.

Part-time workers who earn £30 a week or more are covered for all social welfare benefits including unemployment benefit, disability benefit and invalidity pensions. As with full-time workers, there is no PRSI on the first £100 earned each week. Those earning less than £226 in any week are not liable for the 2 per cent health levy.

To be eligible for benefits part-time workers need to have worked for 39 weeks in insurable employment and also have 39 contributions paid or credited in the relevant contribution year. The same 39 contributions may satisfy both conditions. Having satisfied these contribution conditions part-time workers are entitled to the same PRSI benefits as full time workers but unemployment and disability benefits may be paid at reduced rates. Those benefits are paid on a pro-rata basis depending on the part-timer's weekly earnings during a specified tax-year. For those claiming in 2000 the relevant tax-year is 1998/99.

Contributory old age pension

In order to qualify for a contributory old age pension, it is necessary to have a minimum annual average of contributions either paid or credited over a specified number of years. The number of years can, however, differ with the individual — a fact which can result in some anomalies. A man who paid contributions for only three years could get a full old age pension while someone who paid for over ten years can find himself on a reduced pension or even ineligible for any pension. But let us look at the conditions in detail. To be eligible the claimant must:

- Have an average of at least 10 contributions either paid or credited for each year between the date he or she first entered insurable employment and the end of the contribution year prior to reaching age 66. Up to 2000 pre-1953 contributions were disregarded but that is being changed in the 2000 Social Welfare Act. So people who did not qualify in the past because of that disregard should reapply during 2000. An average of 48 contributions a year is required to qualify for a full pension while an average of 10 will be enough for a 'reduced' pension provided they have a minimum of 260 paid contributions. Those with an average of 15 to 19 contributions a year qualify for a pension of 75 per cent of the maximum rate while those with between 10 and 14 contributions qualify for a pension of 50 per cent of the maximum rate. Those with between 20 and 23 get about 92 per cent; those with between 24 and 35 get about 94 per cent and those with between 36 and 47 get about 97 per cent.

- Those seeking a standard pension only need to have worked for three years in insurable employment for which contributions have been paid at any time during their lives — a total of 156 paid contributions. This requirement could always be met by contributions prior to 1953. It is intended to increase the requirement to 260 by the year 2002 for all claimants and to 520 by the year 2012.

In assessing a claim the Department first looks at the insurance record back to 1979 and if the claimant qualifies for a full pension on that basis they do not look back any further. If the claimant does not qualify for a full pension on the basis of his or her contributions from 1979, then the rules above are applied.

Full rate PRSI became compulsory for most private sector workers from April 1974. Before that, non-manual workers earning above fixed income levels did not have to pay social insurance. If they did not make voluntary contributions they ended up with a gap in their contribution record. Since October 1988 those who re-entered insurance on April 1, 1974 have been given reduced rate pensions provided they had a minimum yearly average of at least 5 contributions. For those eligible, an average of 5 to 9 contributions provides a pension of a quarter of the reduced rate; 10 to 14 provides a half pension; and 15 to 19 a three-quarters pension. The people eligible under

In assessing a claim for a contributory old age pension the Department initially looks at the records only as far back as 1979.

this concession are those who did not stamp cards prior to 1974 because they were in white-collar jobs and went above the income levels at which social welfare contributions were compulsory. A similar scheme exists for people who stopped paying full rate PRSI because they went into public service jobs.

Means tests

Broadly your entitlement to social assistance as opposed to benefits is determined by whatever means you have. There are other conditions as well but once you meet those your entitlement and maybe the size of the payment is determined by your means. If you have some cash income, savings, or, in some cases, if you are living with people who have an income, you may be considered ineligible for social welfare payments, or entitled only to a reduced payment. Your means are taken as including the following:

- Any cash income.
- The value of property personally used, such as a farm but not including the applicant's own home.
- The notional income from savings and investments.

In the case of unemployment assistance, the value of any benefit or privilege enjoyed — such as board and lodgings in a parent's house — is also taken into account.

None of these are as clear cut as they seem. And the same criteria are not used for all entitlements. Claimants for unemployment assistance have their means calculated as follows:

Cash income may seem clear cut, but the Social Welfare Act requires the means test officer to assess the income which the applicant for unemployment assistance "may reasonably expect to receive" in the coming year — not his means in the past year, you will note. Income which an applicant may earn from self employment is also included.

If the officer finds it impossible to make an estimate of likely income in the coming year, he may take the income in the year just past as the means. The Department says that in estimating earnings "particular attention is paid to the availability of opportunities for self-employment in the particular case."

Income from any of the following is not taken into account: supplementary welfare allowance; rent allowance; pensions

Pensions, savings and means tests

Capital is taken into account in calculating the means of claimants for social welfare assistance. Capital in this context includes savings, investments and the cash value of property owned by the claimant but not used personally i.e. a second house which is, or could be, let to provide an income.

The rules for calculating means attributable to such capital in respect of claimants for the Old Age Non-contributory Pension, Blind Pension, Widow(er)'s Non-contributory Pension, and Carer's Allowance are being changed from October 2000 to the following:

The first £10,000 is ignored.

The weekly value of the next £10,000 (from £10,000 to £20,000) is assessed at £1 per £1,000.

The weekly value of the next £10,000 (from £20,000 to £30,00) is assessed at £2 per £1,000.

The weekly value of capital over £30,000 is assessed at £4 per £1,000.

So the annual means of someone with £50,000 in savings is assessed as follows:

The first £10,000 is ignored leaving £40,000. £10,000 of that is assessed at £1 per £1,000, another £10,000 at £2 per £1,000 and the final £20,000 at £4 per £1,000. That adds up to £70 of weekly means.

An individual can have capital of up to £16,000 and still qualify for a non-contributory old age pension or a blind pension. A couple can have £32,000. Above those levels and the pension is progressively reduced. With capital above £42,000 an individual ceases to qualify for a pension. It's £84,000 in the case of a couple.

and allowances in respect of the War of Independence; the first £80 a year of other army pensions or allowances.

A married applicant whose spouse is working can still claim an allowance for a qualified adult in respect of the spouse provided his or her earnings do not exceed £135 a week gross. A full dependant's allowance is paid if the income is below £70 a week. Above that and the benefit is progressively reduced. It is totally withdrawn for those with income over £135 a week. That tapering off of the qualified adult benefit is extended to recipients of Old Age Contributory Pensions from April 2000. The income of the spouse may be taken into account in deciding eligibility. The spouse is allowed a set sum for personal and

From April 2000 the benefit in respect of adult dependents of Contributory Old Age Pensions will be reduced if their income is above £70 a week.

travelling expenses, and the balance is then treated as the income of the applicant in assessing his or her means.

Farm income is combined with any off-farm income. The on-farm income is based on a cash basis. It's the actual profit made from farming i.e. cash receipts from headage etc. and the sale of livestock and produce minus expenses such as fertiliser, feed, vet fees etc.

The first £2,000 received under REPS and Special Area Conservation Schemes is disregarded and only half the remainder taken into account. So a £3,000 payment under REPS is assessed as means of £500 (£3,000 minus £2,000 divided by 2).

Only 60 per cent of the actual off-farm income from insurable employment of farmers with dependent children is assessed as means so a weekly wage of £100 would be assessed at £60. Where there are no dependent children the first £10 per day worked is disregarded.

If a spouse is in insurable employment the first £30 a week is disregarded if he or she works 1, 2, or 3 days a week. The first £45 if disregard if 4 or more days are worked. Self-employed income is assessed in full.

Those means test rules apply to Smallholders Assistance or the farmers' dole as it is often called. A new Farm Assist scheme introduced in April 1999 added two important additional concessions.

The first is that only 80 per cent of the actual on-farm income and income from other self-employment initially assessed is included in the means test calculation. So if a farmer is making £100 a week from his farm after expenses the means are assessed at £80.

A further £100 a year is disregarded for the first and second child and £200 for each child thereafter. So a farmer with four dependent children has assessed means reduced by £600 a year or £11.54 a week.

Savings and investments are also treated as means. The calculation is complicated. The first £2,000 is ignored, the next £20,000 is assessed as giving an income of 7.5 per cent and anything above £22,000 is assessed at the rate of 15 per cent. The same method is used in calculating a notional income from other assets, such as a second house. A similar notional income is calculated to arise from land or buildings owned by a farmer and not used in his own farm business. Such assets are assumed to be yielding some form of rent.

Board and lodgings is taken into account where a son or daughter is still living at home. The assessment of its value is a complicated process which involves taking into account the income of the entire household in which the applicant for unemployment assistance is living. The Department of Social Community and Family Affairs operates on the basis of guidelines looking at each case "on its merits". The following is how the calculations might be made in the case of an unemployed son or daughter.

A sum of £105 is deducted from the parents' net income (£95 in a single parent family). There is a further deduction to allow for rent or mortgage repayments and what is left is divided by the number of non-earning members in the household to arrive at the notional value of board and lodgings to the applicant for unemployment assistance. That figure is included in the calculation of his or her means. The maximum taken into account is 17 per cent of net family income. The minimum assessment for the value of board and lodgings in this case is £3.10 a week.

The minimum unemployment assistance payable to people living at home is £25 a week if the means assessed are only from the parents income.

Bereavement grant

A grant of £500 is payable on death subject to certain conditions. It is payable on the death of an insured person, the spouse of an insured person, a child under 18 (or under 22 if in full time education) where either parent or the person that the child normally lives with satisfied the PRSI contribution conditions, a contributory pensioner, the spouse of a contributory pensioner, the qualified adult dependant of a contributory pensioner, a qualified child, and an orphan in receipt of Orphan's Allowance.

Those paying PRSI at the full rate, the self-employed rate or the reduced rate applicable to some public servants can all qualify. The normal requirement is that at least 156 PRSI contributions have been paid since entry to employment.

A claim form can be obtained from any Social Welfare office or by phoning (043) 45211 or (01) 7043487.

In addition from December 1999 all widows and widowers with dependent children qualify for a grant of £1,000 on the death of a spouse irrespective of means or PRSI contributions.

Family income supplement

This scheme provides a supplementary benefit for families on low incomes. To be eligible it is necessary for one member of the family to be working for at least 19 hours a week and for the family income to fall below set levels depending on family size. If both partners are working their hours can be combined to make up the 19. It is also necessary for some member of the family to be entitled to the normal childrens' allowances i.e. Child Benefit. The aim of the scheme is to help families on low wages who might otherwise be better off on social welfare. Claiming the benefit does not affect eligibility for a medical card and it is tax free.

Family Income Supplement

To be eligible from May 2000 your net income must be less than the figure shown below. The payment is 60 per cent of the difference between your net income and the income in the table.

Family size	Family income must be below	Family size	Family income must be below
One child	£233	Five children	£318
Two children	£253	Six children	£338
Three children	£273	Seven children	£355
Four children	£293	Eight children	£372

The family income supplement payable is 60 per cent of the difference between actual income and the prescribed income given in the table. Actual income is defined as pay net of tax, PRSI and health levy. The figures in the table are those which apply from May 2000. The thresholds were £13 lower during the previous year. Once the actual income level is established the FIS payment remains unchanged for some time. It doesn't fluctuate up and down on a weekly basis according to the earned income in the previous week.

To qualify it is necessary to show that the employment will last at least three months. Job-sharers can qualify. The rate of payment is adjusted immediately on the birth of a child. Applications forms are available from social welfare offices or from: Social Welfare Services Office, Ballinalee Road, Longford.

Treatment benefits

Most private sector workers making PRSI contributions are entitled to at least some financial contribution towards the cost of dental, optical and aural services and appliances. There is no upper income limit. To qualify you have to meet certain contribution conditions. You must have paid PRSI classes A, E, H or P. Class A is the full rate paid by most private sector workers while Class H is paid by privates and NCOs in the defence forces. The number of contributions required depends on your age. .

Who qualifies?

If you are under 21 you need to have paid at least 39 PRSI contributions at some time or other. Credited contributions will not do

If you are aged between 21 and 25 you can qualify if: you have paid at least 39 contributions since first starting work; have at least 39 contributions paid or credited of which 13 must have been paid in the relevant tax-year which for applicants during 2000 is the 1998/99 tax-year or in either one of the two previous tax years, or any tax year subsequent to the relevant tax year.

If you are aged between 25 and 65 you can qualify if: you have worked and paid PRSI for at least five years — 260 paid contributions and have at least 39 contributions paid or credited in the relevant tax year of which 13 must be paid contributions on the basis listed above for 21 to 25 year olds.

If you are over 66 and were entitled to benefits when the changes were first introduced in 1992 you retain entitlement for life. Otherwise you need to have worked for five years paying PRSI and have 39 PRSI contributions paid or credited in either of the two tax years before reaching age 66. At least 13 of these must be paid contributions on the basis listed above for 21 to 25 year olds. The 13 week requirement does not apply to the long-term unemployed or those in receipt of Pre-Retirement Allowance; disability benefit for more than twelve months; invalidity pension, retirement pension or if you are over 55 and signing for credits or are on certain FÁS schemes.

What benefits?

If you get over all the contribution hurdles, what benefits do you get? They fall into three categories: dental; optical; and aural.

Dental: Routine preventative treatment is free — a yearly examination, scaling and polishing including mild gum treatments. You have to pay about 30 per cent of the cost of other procedures. That includes £9.75 for a back filling; £9.40 for a standard front filling; and £7.70 for normal extractions. A full set of dentures costs £129.80, a half-set £88.45, a partial set £64.85.

Optical: Eye tests are free but you should have prior approval. Otherwise you have to pay but can claim the cost back. Standard glasses are free while you pay £10.00 for a slightly better set or can get a benefit of £23.45 towards frames or contact lenses of your choice. If you need contact lenses for medical reasons you can get half the cost up to a maximum of £250.

Aural: You can claim for up to half the cost of a hearing aid up to £250 and half the cost of any repairs. Further information is available from The Social Welfare Services Office, Treatment Benefits Section, Letterkenny, Co. Donegal. You can phone Dublin (01) 8748444 (which gets you through to Donegal) or direct to Donegal (074) 25566.

Medical cards

Eligibility for medical cards is also normally based on the means of the applicant. If your income is below the guideline figure then you are entitled to a card. The table gives an indication of the guidelines that applied from March 1999. From March 1, 1999 the means test threshold for the over-70s was raised by a third as part of a promised doubling of that threshold over a three year period. The thresholds will be increased further in 2000 with extra large increases in the thresholds for the over 70s.

The allowances are added up. For instance if you are paying £21 for your house each week and are married with one child under 16 you could have an income of £154 a week and still be eligible for a Medical Card. That's made up of £5 in respect of the rent, £16 in respect of the child and £133 in respect of a married couple.

Medical card means test

	Up to 66	66 to 69	70 to 79	Over 80
Single — living alone	£92.00	£100.00	£133.00	£140.00
Single — living with family	£81.50	£86.50	£115.00	£120.00
Married couple	£133.00	£149.00	£199.00	£209.00
Allowance for child under 16	£16.00			
Allowance for other dependents	£17.50			
Allowances for outgoings on house	Excess over £16.00 a week			
Reasonable expenses necessarily incurred in traveling to work	Excess over £14.50 a week			

Farmers who don't produce accounts or a notice of tax assessment are assessed on a notional basis. An annual income is attributed to livestock and tillage according to a table prepared by Teagas. The following are indicative of the figures used although they can vary. The figures shown are those that applied in the Western Health Board area from February 8, 1999. You are entitled to ask for details of the method used to assess your means.

The means thresholds for medical cards are being raised significantly for the over 70s.

Dairy Cow	£340	**Suckler cow including calf**	£152
Calves 0-12 months	£32	**Calves 12 months and over**	£62
Sheep, lowland including lamb	£22	**Sheep, mountain**	£13
Pigs – sow with piglets	£20	**Sugar beet, per acre**	£176
Potatoes, per acre	£464	**Oats, per acre**	£55
Barley, per acre	£70	**Horse including foal**	£150

These are net figures after taking account of all input costs.

The dependants of people working in other EC countries are entitled to cards irrespective of means as are those drawing state pensions from other EC countries who are neither employed or self-employed in this country.

People are living longer thanks to improved living conditions and advances in medical science. One of the consequences is that an increasing number of elderly people find themselves in need of some nursing care — very often in a nursing home. The costs can easily exceed ability to pay so it is

Nursing home subvention

not surprising that the State, through the Health Boards, provides some assistance by way of subvention. But the payments are not made automatically. The person is initially assessed for "dependency" i.e. do they need nursing home care and to what degree? Secondly there is a means test which includes not only an assessment of the claimant's means but also the means of their sons and daughters.

There are some anomalies. For instance the means test treats cash differently than a house so that a person who sells their house may be excluded from a subvention to which they would otherwise have qualified.

Regulations on the payment of subventions towards the cost of nursing home care came into effect from September 1993. The rules are complicated but are better than the very confused situation which existed previously. Those already in nursing homes prior to that date continue to qualify for assistance under the old regulations but all new applicants are subject to the new assessments.

So let's have a look at how it works.

First there is the assessment of dependency. To get a subvention at all, the Health Board must be satisfied that you need nursing home care. There are three levels of dependency: medium, high and maximum. A person with medium dependency is likely to have impaired mobility requiring supervision or a walking aid. Someone with high dependency need not be bed bound but may have a combination of mental and physical disabilities. Maximum dependency would apply to someone requiring constant nursing care.

The maximum level of weekly subvention for the three categories are: medium, £70; high, £95; maximum, £120. These rates are reduced pound-for-pound where the person's means exceeds the amount of the non-contributory old age pension — £85.50 from May 2000.

So how does the means test work?

First the claimant's own income and assets are considered. The income is defined as actual income received during the twelve months prior to the application i.e. pensions, earnings, rents received, farm income etc. The income of a married or cohabiting person is taken as half the combined income of the couple.

On top of actual income a notional income is attributed to assets.

A principal residence is ignored provided it is being lived in by a dependent spouse or child, or a relative who is receiving Disability Allowance (formerly DPMA), a blind, disability or invalidity pension or a non-contributory old age pension.

Otherwise the house is assessed as providing an annual income of 5 per cent of its market value. So a house worth £60,000 is equivalent to an income of £3,000 a year (5 per cent of £60,000). That wouldn't be enough to exclude a person from a subvention but they would be excluded if they sold the house and had £60,000 in cash — see below.

Assets other than the principal residence are taken into account in a different way. These include other property, stocks, shares, business interests, life assurance policies, valuables held as investments, and any interest in land. Assets disposed of within the previous five years can also be taken into account. So giving away assets doesn't get around this. A life interest in a house transferred to someone else more than five years previously is disregarded.

A value is put on the assets, the first £6,000 is disregarded and the remainder assumed to be available to pay for nursing home costs during the first year. It's not the potential income from the savings but the savings themselves which are taken into account. At the end of each year the Health Board assesses the situation again.

Let's take an example.

Suppose the person has £8,000 in savings. Taking £6,000 from that leaves £2,000 to be taken into account. It's divided by 52 to give a weekly figure of £38.46. Let's assume also that the person has a net income of £90 a week between state and private pensions. Adding that to the notional amount available from the savings gives a notional weekly figure of £128.46. An amount equal to 120 per cent of the non-contributory old-age pension is disregarded — £94.20 — so that leaves £34.26 to be taken into account. The subvention is reduced by that amount. Let's assume that the person could qualify for the £120 subvention on the grounds of maximum dependency. They'd actually only get £85.74 (£120 minus £34.26).

EU entitlements

For information on benefits in other EU countries ask at your local Social Welfare office or write for leaflet SW59 from the Department of Social Community and Family Affairs, EIU Section, International Records, O'Connell Bridge House, Dublin, 2. Telephone (01) 8748444.

Up to January 1999 the income of sons and daughters was sometimes taken into account but this provision no longer applies.

Under EU regulations workers throughout the community enjoy some degree of transferability of social welfare benefits. Contributions in any member country can be taken into account in determining eligibility for benefits. That, at least, is the theory. But unfortunately it does not always work out like that. It is all too easy to lose out on benefits simply by not knowing, and not conforming with, the rules.

An Irish worker leaving a job in another EU country and coming straight home does not automatically qualify for unemployment benefit here. It doesn't matter how many social welfare contributions were paid abroad or how the job was left — voluntarily or otherwise. Someone coming straight home will not be entitled to draw unemployment benefit here unless he or she enters insurable employment in Ireland and has at least one weeks PRSI paid.

EU regulations do allow for contributions in other member countries to be taken into account in deciding eligibility for benefits. But there are rules to be complied with. It is not just a matter of adding up all the contributions and claiming the benefit in whatever country you like. That is certainly not the case with regard to unemployment benefit. Unless a person has initially registered as unemployed in the country in which they last worked. Having been registered as unemployed for four weeks, the person can then move to another EU country to look for work and continue to draw the benefit for up to three months while looking for work. At the end of the three months they either go back to the country they last worked in, or else the benefit runs out. Another alternative is to work even one week in Ireland and pay at least one PRSI contribution. That way Ireland becomes the last country worked in and unemployment benefit can be claimed here. In this case contributions both here and in other EU countries are taken into account in deciding eligibility.

The same type of rule applies to people leaving Ireland to look for work in other EU countries. If they are entitled to unemployment benefit in Ireland they can make arrangements to continue drawing that benefit abroad while they look for work.

There is an upper time limit of three months but shorter if the benefit would have run out in Ireland before then. If there is three months or more of benefit to run, then three months benefit can be paid abroad. The person has to be registered as unemployed here for four weeks prior to leaving the country. They should also register as unemployed as soon as possible in the country they go to. As long as they do this within seven days they should not be at the loss of any benefit.

It is, of course, important to let your local Social Welfare office know before you go. There are some forms to collect and bring with you. These give details of your insurance record and can save a lot of delay if you need to claim some benefit. People coming home from working in another EU country should make sure to get similar forms to bring with them. It is possible to get booklets on the social welfare systems which operate in other EU countries from the EU Office in Dublin. If you are going to work in another country of the European Union, it is no harm knowing how their systems work. It may be important to know because once you get a job there it is their social welfare system rather than the Irish one which will apply.

For booklets on the social welfare system in each country write to EC Commission Molesworth Street, Dublin, 2. Specify which country you are interested in.

Free travel

Free travel is available to the following: All those aged 66 years or over, residing permanently in the State; those receiving Invalidity Pensions from the State, those receiving a Disability Allowance, Blind Person's Pension, Carer's Allowance and people aged eighteen or over who are registered with the National Council for the Blind. Also entitled are people who have been getting an invalidity pension or benefit continuously for at least a year from another EU country or a country with which Ireland has a bilateral social security agreement.

All wheelchair users and blind people who are entitled to free travel are also entitled to a free travel companion pass as are those who are being cared for by someone in receipt of a carer's allowance. Anyone aged 75 or over who is medically assessed as unfit to travel alone is eligible for a free travel pass for a companion. The pass enables the holder to have any person aged 16 or over accompanying him or her free of charge on public transport. People who transfer from Invalidity Pension, Disability Allowance or Blind Person's Pension to another social welfare pension such as a widow's pension are entitled to keep their entitlement to the free schemes. Those receiving State pensions or allowances should receive their free travel

The free schemes are being extended to all people over 70 regardless of income or household composition from October 2000.

authorisation automatically. Others can get details and an application form from any Post Office. Someone travelling with a recipient of Disability Allowance or Blind Person's Pension is also entitled to free travel. All carers of people getting Constant Attendance or Prescribed Relative Allowance qualify for a Free Travel Pass in their own right.

Free gas or electricity

The following can qualify for a free electricity allowance or free natural or bottled gas: those over 66 receiving:

—   **pensions from the Department of Social, Community and Family Affairs;**
—   **social security pensions from other EC countries or from countries with which Ireland has a bilateral agreement;**
—   **any other social welfare payment;**
—   **an ordinary garda widow's pension from the Department of Justice;**
—   **pensioners who do not have social welfare pensions but whose total weekly income is not more than £30 above the Contributory Old Age Pension Rates of £89 under age 80 and £94 over 80 from June 1999 plus any appropriate allowances e.g. Living alone allowance.**

People under 66 years of age can qualify if they are in receipt of

—   **Invalidity Pension;**
—   **Blind Person's Pension;**
—   **Unemployability Supplement or Worker's Compensation Supplement;**
—   **Disability Allowance;**
—   **Disability Pension/Benefit (or equivalent) for at least twelve months from another EU country, or another country with which Ireland has a bilateral agreement.**

From October 2000 free electricity allowance and free television licences entitlement is being extended to people getting Carer's Allowance or caring for people getting Constant Attendance or Prescribed Relative Allowance.

The allowance covers the standing charge together with the cost of up to 200 units in each two-monthly billing period during the summer and 300 units during the winter. Up to 600 unused free units can be carried forward to the next billing period and unused daytime units can be offset against the cost of night-time units used for storage heaters etc. As an alternative the claimant can have a natural gas allowance of 322 kilowatt hours during each two-monthly summer billing period and 498 kilowatt hours during each winter billing period. Another alternative is to opt for fourteen bottled gas refills a year.

With some exceptions the applicant must be living alone or with a dependent spouse/partner; an invalid; dependent children under 18 or, if over, still at full time education; or, if the applicant is an invalid or infirm, one other person who provides care and attention for him/her. People over 75 years of age in receipt of a qualifying payments or who satisfy a means test are entitled to free electricity, natural gas, or bottled gas refill allowance no matter who lives with them. This is being extended to all people over 75 in 2000. Widows and widowers aged 60 to 65 whose late spouses had entitlement to free schemes retain that entitlement. Application forms can be obtained from any Post Office, Social Welfare Office, or direct from the Department.

Free TV licence

Anyone entitled to a free electricity or gas allowance is also entitled to a free colour TV licence. Those entitled can obtain their licence at any Post Office by presenting a recent ESB bill, showing the free electricity allowance.

Free telephone rental

Persons aged 66 or over who receive a "living alone" allowance in addition to their pension from the Department of Social, Community and Family Affairs, or who would be entitled to such an allowance but for the fact that they are living with one other person who is permanently incapacitated, are entitled to an allowance to cover the full cost of a telephone rental. The presence in the household of a child under 22 years of age or a carer who is in receipt of a carer's allowance does not affect eligibility to this concession. Since 1997 all pensioners over 75 are entitled to free telephone rental. Those in receipt of social security pensions from other EC countries or countries with which Ireland has a bilateral agreement may also qualify.

All carers getting Carer's Allowance and carers of people getting Constant Attendance or Prescribed Relative Allowance are entitled to free telephone rental allowance.

Tax system

Guide to the tax system 13.1

The tax code has been undergoing a major overhaul in recent years and additional far ranging changes will come into effect from April 2000. There's a further movement towards replacing tax allowances with tax credits. Many allowances are being increased but will in future only be allowed at the standard rate of tax and not at the higher rate. Income tax rates have been cut and the standard rate band widened for single and two-income married taxpayers but not for single income married taxpayers.

From April 2000 a single taxpayer with just personal and PAYE tax allowances will pay no tax on the first £110 of weekly income and will be able to earn £17,000 a year before moving onto the new top 44p tax rate.

A range of other tax changes were also unveiled in the December 1999 budget. Tax exemption limits for the over 65s were raised by £1,000 per individual. Many minor allowances were doubled but also standard rated so that those paying tax at the top rate get no additional benefit but those on the standard rate do. PRSI rates and the health levy rate remained unchanged but the thresholds were changed.

The overall impact of those basic changes in the income tax system will vary with the individual, but in broad terms the more you earn the more you gain. A single taxpayer on the average industrial wage of £17,000 will gain about £20. And two income married couples with incomes in excess of £28,000 will also gain significantly. A new standard rated allowance of £3,000 for the spouses of marrried one income families who work in the home and look after children, the aged or handicapped will be worth £660 in saved tax (3,000 x 22p).

Budget 2000 — summary of the main changes

INCOME TAX

Tax rates cut — 24p cut to 22p and 46p rate cut to 44p

Standard rated personal allowances increased

— by £1,000 to £9,400 for married couples;

— by £500 to £4,700 for single taxpayers;

Widowed additional allowance, age, blind person's, incapacitated child, dependent relative and widowed parent's bereavement allowances all doubled but restricted to the standard rate.

Standard rate tax band widened:

— from £14,000 to £17,000 for single taxpayers,

— from £28,000 to £34,000 for two-income married couples,

— the band remains unchanged for married couples with a single income.

New £3,000 allowance for the spouses of one income married taxpayers who work in the home and look after children, the aged or handicapped persons.

Tax exemption limits: Raised by £1,000 a year for single and widowed taxpayers aged over 65 and by £2,000 for married taxpayers either of whom is over 65.

Business use of cars: The threshold used for calculating capital allowances and expenses for the business use of cars was raised from £16,000 to £16,500 from December 1, 1999.

Mortgage interest relief: Disregard of £100 for a single taxpayer and £200 for a married couple that had been applied to non-first time buyers is abolished.

PRSI

— Payment ceiling raised by £1,100 to £26,500.

— Lower exemption limit for the health levy raised from £217 to £226.

CAPITAL ACQUISITIONS TAX

—With effect from December 1, 1999 family homes are exempt where recipient has lived in it for three years previously and retains it for six years after the transfer.

— Also with effect from December 1, 1999 the class 1 threshold is raised to £300,000, the Class 2 thresholds to £30,000 and the Class 3 threshold to £15,000.

— Liability for the tax previously arose where the disponer was domiciled in the State. In future the disponer must be resident in the State or, as before, the property is situated in the State.

PROBATE TAX

— The exemption threshold has been raised from £11,250 to £40,000 in respect of deaths occurring on or after December 1, 1999.

CAPITAL GAINS TAX

From December 1, 1999 the 20 per cent rate was extended to disposals of non-residential development land and the disposal of residential development land to connected persons. The ceiling on relief for the disposal of business assets by an individual over 55 was raised from £250,000 to £375,000 with effect from December 1, 1999.

The possibility of assessing the provision of a parking space as a taxable benefit-in-kind is still being considered as are new incentives to encourage profit sharing.

There were also major concessions on Capital Acquisitions Tax with the exemption of family homes in certain circumstances and a lifting of the tax exemption ceilings with a particularly significant rise in the exemption limit on gifts and inheritances to children.

A summary of these changes is given in the table on the opposite page and they are treated in more detail below.

Most people believe that they are paying too much tax — on the basis that any tax is too much. There are certainly many, many people paying more tax than they need to — simply because they don't claim all the allowances they're entitled to, or because they are not making use of every tax avoidance measure possible. Tax avoidance is no crime. It is simply using the tax system to the best advantage. It is tax evasion which is illegal.

The following are some ideas worth considering. Further details on each option are given later in this chapter or in chapter fourteen on page 271.

Reducing your tax bill

- Make sure that you are claiming all the allowances to which you are entitled. PAYE taxpayers are likely to lose rather than gain by not making an annual return. That is not always true but it generally is. Have you increased your claim for medical insurance in line with the premium increases? Have you a claim for medical expenses? A careful reading of the following pages could be worthwhile.

- Any individual can make up to £1,000 in tax-free capital gains in any one tax-year. Even with the tax rate reduced to 20 per cent that concession can save you £200. It's worth making use of by means of a "bed and breakfast" deal if you own shares. See page 259.

- If you are self-employed consider employing your children on a part-time basis. As a family you can save some tax that way. From April 2000 it may also be worthwhile formally employing a spouse. In the past there was no tax advantage in paying a spouse a wage even if he or she worked in the family business.

But that has changed with the introduction of a wider standard rate band for two income married couples. See page 272.

- Subject to certain generous limits there is full tax relief on pension contributions so, for the self-employed, a personal pensions scheme offers a particularly favourable way of saving for the future. No longer has the bulk of the accumulated fund to be used to buy an annuity on retirement. It will be worth taking a fresh look at pensions during 2000. Workers can also benefit by putting extra money into their own pension schemes. For details see chapter 10, page 167.

- Get some of your income by way of an approved profit sharing scheme negotiated with your employer. It is possible to get up to £10,000 tax free each year. New incentives may be introduced during 2000 but the existing schemes can be very attractive. For details see page 286.

- You can also get certain benefits from your employer tax free. They include a subsidised canteen, child minding facilities, some leisure facilities, and travel passes for a period of more than a month.

You will find other ideas throughout the book.

Pay As You Earn

The vast majority of income tax payers come under the Pay As You Earn scheme (PAYE). They have no alternative. With very few exceptions all employees come under the scheme which was initially sold on the basis that it spread income tax liability over the year. That saved taxpayers being faced with large bills once a year. That was the idea anyway. Of course, it also provides the exchequer with a nice even flow of revenue throughout the year. The tax year runs from April 6 to April 5 and it is your income during that period which dictates your liability to tax. PAYE is simply an administrative method of collecting that tax in easy stages during the year, once a week or once a month.

It is all too easy for PAYE taxpayers to be overtaxed. It is important to check that you are claiming all your allowances. You will not get them all automatically.

Employers have a legal obligation to stop tax on payments to employees and they do so on the basis of instructions given to them by the Revenue Commissioners. These instructions are summarised on your certificate of tax free allowances. A certificate should be sent to you before the start of the tax year. It will list the tax reliefs you have been allowed. Do not ignore it. The tax man can make mistakes and so can you. You may not have claimed all your allowances. Some allowances are given

Tax credits

While tax credits are still not formally in existence the standard rating of most allow-ances creates exactly the same impact. Mortgage interest relief and the relief on medical insurance premiums have been standard rated for some years and from April 1999 both the personal and PAYE allowances were standard rated. From April 2000 a range of other minor allowances will also be standard rated. The full changeover to tax credits will take place from April, 2001.

A tax allowance is a deduction from gross income. An increase in an allowance reduces taxable income and the resultant saving to the taxpayer depends on his or her top rate of tax. A taxable allowance of £1,000 reduces the taxpayer's taxable income by that amount. If he or she is paying tax at 22p in the pound the resultant tax savings is £220 (1,000 times 22p). But if he or she is paying tax at 44p in the pound the tax saving is £440 (1,000 times 44p).

A tax credit, on the other hand, is a deduction from tax liability. A tax allowance of £1,000 might be converted into a tax credit of £220 say. Such a tax credit would be of the same value to a standard rate taxpayer as an allowance of £1,000. Either cuts his or her tax bill by £220. But a taxpayer on the top rate of tax would need a tax credit of £440 to compensate for the loss of a £1,000 tax allowance.

To ensure that those paying tax at the standard rate did not lose out most of the allow-ances standard rated from April 2000 were doubled. For instance the incapacitated child allowance goes up from £800 to £1,600 from April 2000 but the increased allowance is only allowed at the standard rate. A top rate taxpayer benefiting from the allowance saved 800 times 46p or £368 in the 1999/2000 tax year. In the 2000/2001 tax year he or she will benefit to the tune of 1,600 times 22p or £352. The slight reduction in the benefit is due to the cut in the standard rate of tax.

A standard rate taxpayer benefits from the change. In 1999/2000 the relief was worth 800 times 24p or £192. That goes up to 1,600 times 22p or £352 in 2000/2001.

to you automatically but others you will not get unless you claim them. So check your allowances.

The check list of tax allowances on page 310 contains most of the concessions applicable to the average taxpayer. A fuller list starts on the next page. Check both. Details of the allowances for the five years up to and including 2000/2001 are also given on page 310. The table on page 245 is designed to help you to work out your annual tax liability in exactly the same way the taxman would work it out. It is done on an annual basis whereas the PAYE system is geared to collecting the tax due from your

If you have failed to claim your full allowances in the past you can claim rebates for up to at least six years.

pay packages over the course of the tax-year. It should ensure that your tax payments over the year add up to your full liability and no more. But in some circumstances it may result in you paying too much or too little. If it has taken too much, then you are due a rebate. If it has taken too little and the taxman finds out, you will swiftly get a demand for the difference. Your legal tax liability is worked out in the way outlined in the following table — how it is collected is simply an administrative matter. Some of the technicalities — in particular the matter of table allowances — are explained on page 231.

The tax on some income may not be collected under the PAYE system but your total taxable income is arrived at by deducting your allowances from your total gross income. Income includes all emoluments (pay) of any office or job including salaries; fees; wages; perquisites; profits; pensions; headage and other similar payments; most interest; and benefits-in-kind. Some of these may not be caught in the PAYE net but the tax liability is calculated in the same way. People who are part-time self-employed in addition to being in paid employment may be liable to pay tax on the self-employed income under what is known as schedule "D" which allows for the tax to be paid in one annual instalment — more about that later in the chapter. But the tax liability is calculated on the basis of your total income from all sources.

So what allowances can be claimed? The following apply to the 2000/2001 tax year. Rates for previous years are given in appendix 1 on page 310. Details of tax bands and rates for past years are given on page 308. Except where stated the allowances are standard-rated i.e. only allowed only at the standard rate of tax — see note on tax credits, page 229.

- **PERSONAL ALLOWANCES:**

Single person	**£4,700**
Married couple	**£9,400**
One parent taxpayer	**£9,400**

- **AGE ALLOWANCE**

If the taxpayer or his spouse is over, or will reach, the age of 65 during the tax year, the following extra allowances apply

Single or widowed	**£800**
Married couple	**£1,600**

Table Allowances

The PAYE tax scheme presents tax collectors with an administrative problem. The income tax code provides that the first portion of a person's income is free of tax. That is the portion covered by allowances. Then there is a portion subject to tax at 22p in the pound. For a single person that amounts to £17,000 in the 2000/2001 tax year. Any income over that is subject to tax at 44p in the pound.

But most taxpayers would find it hard to cope with a system which taxed them lightly at the beginning of the year and progressively raised the tax take as the year went by. To get over the problem employers are instructed to stop income tax at a constant rate throughout the year. The tax allowances are also spread evenly over the year so that each month the worker gets the benefit of one-twelfth of his total tax allowances for the year. The rate of tax applied to the remaining income is the top rate to which the tax-payer is expected to be liable.

If nothing else was done it is obvious that the tax-payer would end up paying too much tax. He will have got the benefit of all his tax allowances but he would have been paying tax at say 44p on all his taxable income rather than 22p on some of it and 44p on the balance. Taking the case of a single man the first £17,000 should be taxed at 22p. If taxed at 44p he will be overtaxed to the tune of 17,000 times 22p (44p minus 22p) or £3,740. The table allowances are designed to compensate for this. In the case of a single person paying tax at 44p in the pound the allowance must provide a tax saving of £3,740. Since he or she is paying tax at 44p in the pound he needs an extra allowance of £8,500. That will save him £8,500 times 44p which works out at £3,740. So what he loses one way he gains in another.

The table allowances are as follows:

	Table	1999/00 Rate	1999/00 Allowance	2000/01 Rate	2000/01 Allowance
Married	"S"	46p	£13,392		
One income	"S"	—	—	44p	£14,000
Two income	"S"	—	—	44p	£17,000*
Single/widowed					
With dependent child	"B"	46p	£6,696	44p	£10,075
Without dependent child	"B"	46p	£6,696	44p	£8,500[+]

* Only if both spouses have incomes in excess of £6,000. The allowance is reduced by £50 for every £100 the lower income falls below £6,000. [+] Single parents enjoy a wider standard rate band.

Low income exemption limits

People with incomes below certain exemption limits are taken out of the income tax net altogether, although they would otherwise be liable for some tax if the calculations were done in the normal way.

The table below gives the exemption limits for both the current and coming tax years. **It is important to remember that these are not allowances.** If your income is above the limits, then your tax liability is calculated in the normal way, except that those with incomes slightly above the limit are entitled to some marginal relief. The tax they pay will not amount to more than 40p of the difference between the exemption limit and their actual income. For example a married man aged 66 with an income of £15,100 i.e. £100 above the exemption limit, will pay £40 in tax. That would be 40 per cent of the £100.

The exemption limits shown below are increased by £450 for each of the first two dependent children and by £650 for each subsequent child. Since the tax authorities do not automatically know how many children a taxpayer has, since the general child tax allowance was abolished, it is important that taxpayers with children make a claim if their income is below or even marginally above the relevant exemption limit.

	1999/2000	2000/2001
Single and widowed	£4,100	£4,100
Married couples	£8,200	£8,200
Single and widowed 65 or over	£6,500	£7,500
Married, either spouse over 65	£13,000	£15,000

• CHILD ALLOWANCES:

There is an allowance of £1,600 in respect of an incapacitated child, although this is reduced if the amount spent in maintaining the child is actually less. The child must have become incapacitated before reaching 21 years of age, or while still receiving full-time education. There is no tax relief in respect of other children. But tax exemption limits are increased depending on the number of children in a family. This can benefit low income families — see page 215 for details.

- **DEPENDANT RELATIVE'S ALLOWANCE: £110.**

This allowance is granted for each relative of the taxpayer, or spouse, who is incapacitated, and, even if not incapacitated, the widowed mother or mother-in-law of the taxpayer. The allowance is also granted in respect of a son or daughter of the taxpayer who is resident with him, and on whose services he or his wife depend because of old age or illness. Although small, this allowance can be an important one to claim and it can be shared among a number of people in respect of the one person. For instance a number of children could claim it in respect of a father or mother. By doing that they can then claim tax relief on any contribution they make to the parent's medical expenses and that includes the cost of maintenance in a recognised nursing home or hospital. See page 300 for details of an alternative way of claming tax relief on such expenses. The allowance is reduced by £1 for every pound by which the dependant's income exceeds the maximum contributory old age pension rate for someone aged 80 or over and living alone — about £5,512.

Dependent Relative's Allowance, although small, can be important in claiming allowances for a dependent's medical expenses.

- **BLIND PERSON'S ALLOWANCE: £3,000.**

This allowance can be claimed where either the taxpayer or the taxpayer's spouse is blind. If both are blind the allowance is £6,000.

- **SPECIAL HOUSEKEEPER ALLOWANCE: £8,500.**
  — allowed at the top marginal rate.

This allowance is given to an incapacitated taxpayer who is employing a person to care for him or herself or for an incapacitated spouse. Since April 1999 it is also allowed where a family employs a carer to look after a totally incapacitated person. Family members contributing to the cost of the carer can share the allowance between them.

- **PAYE ALLOWANCE: £1,000**

This allowance is granted to all people liable to be taxed under the PAYE system. If a husband and wife are both wage-earning, there is a double allowance of £2,000. It is allowed to a child working full-time in a family firm but not to a spouse.

- **HEALTH INSURANCE:**

The allowance is granted on the amount paid in premiums during the previous year. It is granted in respect of insurance against the medical expenses of the taxpayer, spouse, child or other dependants.

- **HOME WORKING SPOUSE'S ALLOWANCE:** An allowance of £3,000 is to be introduced from April 2000 in respect of a taxpayer's spouse who works at home caring for children, the aged or the handicapped.

- **PERMANENT HEALTH BENEFIT SCHEMES:**

  The relief is allowed against premiums paid to insure income in the event of ill health or disability. It is limited to 10 per cent of the taxpayers income in the year of assessment. Benefit paid under the insurance policy are taxed as income.

- **MEDICAL EXPENSES:**
  — allowed at the top marginal rate.

  Full allowance is granted for most medical expenses paid by the taxpayer in respect of himself, his wife, or any other person for whom he claims tax allowances. The first £100 is disallowed (£200 for a family). Relief can either be claimed in the tax-year during which the payment was made or in the year in which it was incurred.

  Medical expenses in respect of the following are not allowed: normal childbirth; normal dental treatment; eye testing; or the supply of spectacles.

  Dental treatment which is not considered 'normal' in this context includes: crowns, veneers, tip replacing, gold posts, gold inlays, endodontics — root canal treatment, periodontal treatment, orthodontic treatment and the surgical extraction of impacted wisdom teeth. The tax relief is available on treatment performed outside the State provided, of course, the receipts are submitted.

  A person for whom a Dependent Relative's Allowance is given is considered part of a family for this purpose. This allowance can be shared among a number of people — see above. This means that a number of children, for instance, contributing to the medical expenses of a parent can all consider the parent to be part of their families for the purposes of a claim for relief under this heading.

  An alternative is for the children to covenant money to the parent who then uses the extra cash to pay for the medical or nursing home expenses. The parent then claims the tax relief.

Unlike the old type covenants to student children this type of covenant can still be tax efficient. See page 300. In certain cases — kidney patients and child oncology patients — the Revenue Commissioners accept the cost of travelling to and from treatment centres as legitimate medical expenses for the purpose of this relief. A rate of 25p a mile has been allowed since April 1997. Telephone costs and certain costs involved in home dialysis treatment is also allowed. Full details are available from the Revenue Commissioners' Information Office, Dublin Castle, phone (01) 8780000. The claim is made at the end of the tax year on the form MED 1 which can be obtained from the local tax office.

- ## PENSION CONTRIBUTIONS:

The contributions to an approved scheme are allowed in full subject normally to the following maximum percentages of income:

Age	Limit
up to 30	15 per cent
30 but less than 40	20 per cent
40 but less than 50	25 per cent
50 and over	30 per cent

Those percentages apply since April 1999. In the 1998/99 tax year the limits were 15 per cent of income for those under the age of 55 and on 20 per cent of income for those over 55. There is a cap of £200,000 on the income taken into account.

- ## YEAR OF MARRIAGE:

Married couples are taxed as single persons in the year that the marriage takes place. If they would have paid less tax as a married couple they can claim a rebate at the end of the tax year in respect of the proportion of the full tax year for which they were married. The various options facing married couples are considered in more detail in a separate section on page 279.

- ## INTEREST PAYMENTS:
Apart from the few exceptions mentioned below relief is only allowed in respect of the interest on loans taken out to buy, maintain, or improve the taxpayer's principal residence, the residence of a former or separated spouse, or the residence of a dependent relative (other than a child) who is living in the house rent free. There is an upper limit on eligible interest for first-time buyers during the first five years of a loan of £2,500

for single taxpayers; £5,000 for a married couples, widows and widowers. The limit for widowed taxpayers was £3,600 up to April 2000.

Other borrowers can claim relief on interest payments of up to £4,000 a year (married and widowed) and £2,000 (single/widowed). It is intended from April 2001 to grant this relief by way of deduction from the mortgage repayment. Taxpayers will get the relief by way of reduced repayments rather than through their pay packets.

Where a taxpayer moves house and there is a delay in selling the original house, both houses can be considered to be the sole or main residence for up to one year. And during that year the interest on any loan taken out to buy the new house is allowed for tax relief in addition to the tax relief on the old loan — the limit is doubled. Interest on loans taken out to pay death duties is allowed for tax relief without any restriction. And so too is interest on money borrowed to buy newly issued shares in one's own company. More information on this latter point is given in the section on reducing your tax bill on page 271. A more detailed treatment of mortgage interest relief with detailed examples and tables is given in chapter 6.3. starting on page 131.

This relief has been restricted to the standard rate since April 1997.

- **WIDOWS/WIDOWERS:**

An extra allowance of £1,500 in the year following bereavement for widows and widowers with dependent children, applied for the first time in 1990/91. It was increased to £5,000 from April 1998, reducing to £4,000 in the second year after bereavement, £3,000 the following year, then £2,000 and finally £1,000 in the fifth year reducing to nothing in the sixth year.Those figures are being doubled from April 2000 and the allowance standard rated.

- **RENT ALLOWANCE:**

This relief can be claimed by tenants living in private rented accommodation in respect of the rent paid. The maximum rent allowed for relief for those under 55 from April 2000 is:

Married	£1,500
Widowed person	£1,125
Single person	£750

Alternatively a taxpayer over 55 years of age living in rented accommodation can claim an allowance of up to £2,000 in respect of the rent paid. The maximum is £4,000 for a married couple and £3,000 for a widow or widower. The allowances were half those in the 1999/2000 tax year but the relief was allowed at the taxpayer's top marginal rate. The allowance cannot be claimed in respect of rent paid to local authority or on tenancies of fifty years or more.

- **EXPENSES:**

Allowance is also made for expenses incurred by the taxpayer in performing his job. In the case of a PAYE worker the expenses must have been wholly, exclusively, and necessarily incurred. The 'necessarily' criterion does not apply to the self-employed taxpayer. PAYE workers may claim relief against the expense of buying tools and special work clothes, for instance.

Travelling expenses to and from work are not allowed. Very often the Tax Inspector will agree a figure that can be claimed without any evidence of the expenses being incurred. But the taxpayer can claim more, provided he can justify the higher claim. The following table provides an insight into the level of agreed rates which may find favour with the Revenue. They are rates applicable to civil servants in 1999.

Civil Service Subsistence Rates

Rank	Night Allowances			Day Allowances	
	Normal	Reduced	Detention	10 hours or more	5 to 10 hours
Assistant principal	£73.18	£67.47	£36.59	£20.74	£8.46
Executive officer	£65.76	£56.25	£32.89	£20.74	£8.46
Clerical officer	£55.00	£45.51	£27.53	£20.74	£8.46
Clerical assistant	£47.58	£40.15	£23.79	£15.66	£7.74
Service grades	£38.98	£32.32	£19.47	£15.66	£7.74

The normal overnight rate applies for the first 14 nights, the reduced rate for the next fourteen and the detention rate for subsequent periods.

- **SERVICE CHARGES**

  While water charges have been abolished the tax relief on local authority service charges remain. The relief is given at the standard rate in respect of up to £150 of local authority service charges paid in full and on time. The relief is in respect of the charges paid during the previous year.

- **COLLEGE FEES:**

  Since April 1995 tax relief is allowed on fees paid for undergraduate study at an approved private third level college either on behalf of the taxpayer or on behalf of a dependent. The fees must not be recouped by grants or scholarships and the relief may not exceed the tax liability of the taxpayer. The relief is given only at the standard rate.

- **ALARMS FOR THE ELDERLY:**

  An allowance of up to £800 is granted in respect of the cost of alarms installed by a taxpayer over 65 living alone.

PRSI liabilities

Pay Related Social Insurance (PRSI) is every bit as much a tax on income as income tax itself. It is normally taken to include both the health and the employment and training levies but, in fact, they are three separate items. The rate of PRSI you pay depends on your job. Most people fall into one of three main categories: private sector employees; public sector employees; and the self-employed. Public servants recruited since April 6, 1995 pay PRSI at the full 4.5 per cent rate. The following table lists the position for 2000/2001.

PRSI and Levy Rates

PRSI	Private Sector	Public Sector	Self-employed
Rate	4.5%	0.9%	5%
Ceiling	£26,500	£26,500	£26,500
Exemptions	£100 a week	£20 a week	£1,040 a year
Levy			
Rate	2%	2%	2%
Ceiling	None	None	None

Those earning less than £30 a week are outside the PRSI net while those earning less than £226 in a particular week are not liable for the health levy in the 2000/2001 tax year.

The threshold was £217 in 1999/2000, £207 in 1998/99 and £197 in 1997/98 and applied to both the training and health levies. The training levy was abolished in April 1999.

The first £100 of weekly pay (£20 for public sector employees paying the lower rate PRSI) is exempt from PRSI. That exemption applies on a weekly basis while the ceiling for contributions is applied on an annual basis. Once earnings in a particular year go above the ceiling of £26,500 — £25,400 for 1999/2000 — PRSI is no longer stopped from the pay package and the exemption no longer applies. So someone earning say £53,000 a year will only get the benefit of the exemption for half the year — halfway through the year they'll have stopped paying PRSI so won't be able to benefit from the weekly exemption for the final six months.

Tax on social welfare

Many social welfare benefits have been taxable for years. But tax liability was extended to some short-term benefits — unemployment and disability benefits — from April 1994. A number of concessions were introduced subsequently. The first six days of disability benefit is not subject to tax. In addition the following exemptions apply:

- Child dependent additions to social welfare payments are not taxed.

- The unemployment benefit of systematic short-term workers is not taxed.

- The first £10 a week of unemployment benefit is disregarded for tax purposes.

Tax and the company car

A company car is a valuable addition to any remuneration package. On the basis of AA estimates it costs well over £6,000 a year to run an average sized car when depreciation, tax, insurance and all running costs are taken into account. That's a measure of what you save if the company provides you with a car and covers all the costs.

But a car is not one of those few benefits which an employer can provide tax-free to an employee. It is viewed as part of the recipient's salary — a Benefit in Kind (BIK) — and as such is

Reducing car benefit-in-kind

The options available for reducing the tax liability on a company car fall into a number of fairly obvious categories:

Reduce the price: The lower the original market price of the car the smaller will be the benefit in kind assessment. That boils down to a choice over the type of car you want and the status you attach to it. There is, however, one way of having your cake and eating it i.e. having a high status car and at the same time reducing your tax liability. That's by buying an old but good second hand car. Such cars are also attractive to people who want to buy their own and charge the company for the business milage done.

Pay some of the costs: Paying for all the petrol you use for the non-business milage done in the car reduces the initial assessment from 30 per cent to 26 per cent. On a £16,000 car that reduces the BIK assessment by £640 and the tax bill by £281 (assuming tax at 44p). That would buy you about 500 litres of petrol. Only you can say whether it's worth it. Similar type calculations can be done for the other items which reduce the assessment if you pay for them yourself.

Do more milage: If you're close to one of the thousand mile cut-off points it can obviously be worth while to move into the higher bracket. For instance if you do 19,001 business miles rather than 18,999 you cut the assessment by 20 per cent rather than 15 per cent. That can be a significant saving just for the sake of a few miles.

Use the car pool: There is no benefit in kind assessed if the company car you use is out of a car pool. But the Revenue apply very strict rules. The car must be made available to and used by more than one employee. The car must not normally be kept overnight at or close to any of the employees' homes. Any private use must be minimal and incidental to business use.

Charge milage: If you use your own car for business use you can, of course, claim a milage allowance from your employer. To escape Revenue displeasure the payment must be based on actual milage and an acceptable milage rate. The employer has to get Revenue approval not to deduct tax from the payments and while there is no definitive milage rate the Civil Service own rates provide an indication of what may be appropriate.

Use a van: If you have a company van rather than a company car somewhat more favourable rules apply to the calculation of benefit-in-kind. It's assessed on the annual value of the van which is defined as 12.5 per cent of its cost plus total running expenses. A portion of that is attributed to private milage in the ratio it bears to total milage.

subject to income tax. And you can forget about the AA estimates — the Revenue Commissioners have their own strict rules for putting a monetary value on your "perk".

But there are ways of reducing the tax liability or avoiding it altogether by buying your own car and charging the company a milage rate. Or if you don't claim a milage rate you can claim tax relief on the expense of running the car including an allowance for the capital cost of buying it. That approach is most often used by self-employed people but it can be used by employees — see page 253 See the table on the page opposite for some other options.

The maximum benefit assessed by the Revenue Commissioners is 30 per cent of the original market value of the car. The full 30 per cent is applied where the company bears all of the costs involved including petrol for your private use, insurance, tax, maintenance etc. The following reductions are made if you bear some of the costs yourself.

You supply petrol for your private use	4.5%
You pay for your own insurance	3%
You pay for all repairs and servicing	3%
You pay the road tax	1%

So you could get a reduction of 11.5 points i.e. to 18.5 per cent of the car's cost.

In addition there is a sliding scale applied depending on the amount of business milage you do. If you do more than 15,000 business miles in the car during the year there is a further reduction in the assessment on the basis of a sliding scale starting with a 2.5 per cent reduction if you do between 15,000 and 16,000 business miles and ranging upwards to a maximum reduction of 75 per cent if you do more than 30,000 business miles. Full details of the scale are given in appendix 2 on page 318.

A special 20 per cent relief from the tax was introduced in 1996. It's available to company representatives who spend at least 70 per cent of their working hours away from their place of business and who do at least 5,000 business miles a year. This is an alternative to the high mileage relief.

Let's have a look at an example of those calculations: Take the case of a salesman who does 19,500 business miles in the year.

He has a middle range car with an original market value of £16,000. He pays for his own insurance and road tax and also covers all the maintenance costs on the car while his employer supplies all the petrol even for personal use. The fact that he bears those costs himself reduces the initial assessment to 23 per cent of the £16,000. That works out at £3,680.

That's further reduced since the business milage is more than 15,000. On the basis of the sliding scale the reduction for 19,500 miles is 20 per cent. So the £3,680 is reduced by 20 per cent to give a final assessment of £2,944. That's the figure that's liable for tax.

At 44p in the £ that would amount to £1,295. It's painful but it may not be a high cost to pay for the benefit of a company car. Compare it with the depreciation costs on a £16,000 car you'd buy yourself. Without putting it on the road at all it must be costing at least £2,000 a year just by going down in value. In estimating motoring costs the AA assumes that cars have an economic life of eight years.

Calculating your tax liability

Calculating your total tax liability will be a lot easier from April 2001 when tax credits come in fully. However most allowances are already only allowed at the standard rate of tax. In other words each pound of allowance can only save you 22p of tax even if you are paying tax on the top slice of your income at 44p. The easiest way to do the calculations is to treat the standard rated tax allowances as if they were tax credits, which, in effect, they are. Each pound of standard rated allowance is worth so many times 22p in saved tax. An allowance of £1,000 is worth £220 in saved tax. There are two rates of tax 22p and 44p from April 2000. The 22p applies to the first slice of income as shown in the following table. Income above the threshold is taxed at 44p.

Category of taxpayer	Band at 22p
Single	£17,000
Married, one income	£28,000
Married, two income	£34,000
Single parents	£20,150

tax liability that way the actual net liability is arrived at by subtracting the value of the standard rated allowances. A very simple example would be a single taxpayer on £18,000 a year entitled to only the personal and PAYE allowances. First of all we ignore the allowances and calculate the tax due on the full £18,000. The sums work out like this.

£17,000 at 22p	£3,740	
£1,000 at 44p	£440	
Total	**£4,180**	

The personal allowance of £4,700 and the PAYE allowance of £1,000 are worth 5,700 times 22p or £1,254. So the actual tax due is £4,180 minus £1,254 or £2,926.

Let's have a look at a more detailed example. The calculations are shown in the table on page 244 overleaf. Mr. Murphy is married with two children — both still at school. He is going to earn £35,000 during the 2000/2001 tax year. In addition his company supplies him with a car which is valued as a benefit-in-kind. Mr. Murphy will pay £1,750 in interest on a house mortgage, and will be allowed that in full since it is below the upper limit of £4,000 for non-first time buyers. He paid £500 in VHI contributions during 1999/00. Relief on VHI is based on the previous year's premiums. He paid £1,200 into the company pension scheme. His mother-in-law is living with the family and has no means of her own so he gets an allowance of a lowly £220 in respect of a dependent relative. The calculations are shown in the table. In doing your own calculations you can use the form provided on page 245.

With the exception of an agreed expenses allowance of £100 all of Mr Murphy's tax allowances are standard rated. Since his wife has no income he is only allowed a standard rate band of £28,000. But they do benefit from the £3,000 home working spouse allowance. Mr. Murphy's total income tax liability is £6,497 for the year. The PAYE system will ensure that he pays that in weekly or monthly instalments over the period. It may be necessary to arrive at an estimate of the interest payments, but if there is any under or over payment of tax it can be sorted out in a balancing statement at the end of the year. These are not automatic so if you think you have been overtaxed it is important for you to claim.

While most taxpayers pay their tax weekly or monthly the tax liability is actually based on annual figures.

The Murphys — how they are taxed

GROSS PAY		£35,000
Plus Benefit-in-kind (company car)		£3,000
Less Pension contributions		£1,200
TOTAL		£36,800
Allowances at marginal rate i.e. agreed expenses		£100
Income after marginal rate allowances		**£36,700**
First £28,000 at 22p		£6,160
Remainder (£8,700) at 44p		£3,828
Tax before adjusting for standard rated allowances		**£9,988**
Standard rated allowances:		
Personal allowance	£8,400	
Home working spouse allowance	£3,000	
Allowable interest	£1,200	
VHI premiums	£500	
PAYE allowance	£1,000	
Dependent relative allowance	£220	
Total standard rated allowances	£15,870	
Tax credit for standard rated allowances — 15,870 @ 22p		£3,491
TOTAL TAX		£6,497

Doing your own sums

The pro-forma table and the Murphy example can help you to do your own sums. Even if you don't feel like getting the calculator out, at least have a look at the list of some allowances and reliefs which are commonly missed on page 246. All the figures for your own calculations can be obtained earlier in this chapter and/or by reference to Appendix 1 on page 308. Don't forget to include taxable benefits-in-kind. The private use of a car is not the only benefit-in-kind which may be valued and assessed as part of the taxpayer's income. Other such items include the provision of accommodation, entertainment, services or indeed any benefits or facilities supplied by the employer and not paid

Doing your own sums

The pro-forma table below can help you work out your liability in the same way as the Murphy's liability is calculated in the table on the opposite page. Details of all the tax allowances and bands are in Appendix 1 on page 308 and more details of the allowances are given earlier in this chapter starting on page 230. While tax credits have yet to be formally introduced the standard rated tax allowanxces can be treated as tax credits for the purposes of calculating total tax liability. The method of doing this can be seen in the table opposite. The total of all standard rated allowances is multiplied by 22p to give their value in reducing the tax liability.

GROSS PAY		
Plus Benefit-in-kind (company car etc.)		
Less Pension contributions		
TOTAL (*A*)		
Less	Allowances at marginal rate	
Total allowances at marginal rate (*B*)		
Income after marginal rate allowances (*A* minus *B*)		
First £28,000[1] (£17,000 single) at 22p		
Remainder (*A* minus £28,000[1] or £17,000 if single) at 44p		
Tax before adjusting for standard rated allowances (*C*)		
Standard rated allowances:		
Personal (£4,700 single £9,400 married)		
Allowable interest		
VHI premiums		
PAYE allowance (£1,000)		
Total standard rated allowances (*D*)		
Tax credit for standard rated allowances — (*D*) by 22p		
TOTAL TAX (*C* **minus** *D*)		

Note: 1. A two income married couple has a standard rate band of at least £28,000 but where both spouses have incomes of at least £6,000 the band is widened to £34,000. The band is £28,000 plus the income of the lower earner up to a maximum of £34,000. The band is £20,150 for one parent families.

Claiming back tax for previous years

Many people pay too much tax simply because they haven't claimed all of the allowances and reliefs to which they are entitled. But, if you have missed out, it is possible to go back at least six years with your claim. The following lists some of the allowances most often missed and details of how they have changed over the years. If you have a claim all you have to do is get some tax return forms from your tax office and fill them out in respect of each year. If you can only get forms for the current year don't be afraid to simply write in the relevant dates for past years.

Rent Allowance: A taxpayer over 55 years of age living in rented accommodation can claim an allowance of up to £2,000 in respect of the rent paid. The maximum is £4,000 for a married couple and £3,000 for a widow or widower. The allowance cannot be claimed in respect of rent paid to local authority or on tenancies of fifty years or more. Tenants under 55 can claim relief of up to £1,500 married, £1,125 widowed, or £750 single. The limits were lower before April 2000 but the relief is still worth claiming.

Medical insurance premiums: This allowance is granted on the amount paid in premiums during the previous year. It is granted in respect of insurance against medical expenses and for income continuance assurance in the event of ill-health.

Medical expenses: Full allowance is granted for most medical expenses paid by the taxpayer in respect of himself, his wife, or any other person for whom he claims tax allowances. The first £100 is disallowed (£200 for a family).

Expenses: Allowance is also made for expenses incurred by the taxpayer in performing his job. In the case of a PAYE payer the expenses must have been wholly, exclusively, and necessarily incurred. The "necessarily" criterion does not apply to the self-employed. The allowance can be given for tools and special work clothes.

for by the employee. It is even intended to do a value on a car park space supplied by an employer and tax it. There are some noteable exceptions, however. Childcare facilities supplied by an employer and at least partially managed by him are not treated as a taxable benefit.

Payments towards childcare expenses are taxable, however, although legitimate expenses wholly, exclusively and necessarily incurred in the performance of one's duties are not assessed for tax. Neither is the benefit of subsidised canteen meals.

Self-employed income

Income from self-employment is subject to a somewhat different tax regime than wages or salaries. The earnings are, of course subject to tax in just the same way as outlined in the previous section but it is collected in a different way and there are different rules with regard to allowable expenses and costs. Both of these differences are looked at in this section.

Some self-employed people are actually employees of their own companies. The company is considered to be a separate legal entity from the tax point of view. The owner is treated as an employee and taxed as such under the PAYE system although subject to certain restrictions aimed at preventing tax evasion. Here, however, we only consider the self-employed person not working for a company. Such a taxpayer has to calculate his or her own tax liability and pay a lump sum payment before November 1 each year. Detailed tax returns must be submitted by the end of January. The November payment is an estimated amount relating to the current tax year while the January return relates to the previous tax year.

Failure to make a full and true disclosure leaves the taxpayer liable not only for interest but also for a 10 per cent surcharge. That 10% surcharge can also be imposed when a return is not made by January 31. The original estimate of tax due, issued by the tax inspector in his "notice of preliminary tax", becomes immediately payable plus a 10 per cent surcharge but minus, of course, any tax already paid.

The annual tax return should be made on the normal tax form to which should be added summary accounts for the business. These accounts need not be all that elaborate. A single page is sufficient for a simple business. But, of course, the back-up receipts and invoices should be available in case the tax inspector wants to see them. Under the self-assessment system a proportion of all returns are examined in detail and the taxpayers involved may be subject to a revenue audit. Most are picked according to a number of unpublished criteria but some are simply picked at random. You can reduce your chances of being picked for an audit by explaining any peculiarities in your tax return — see page 249.

Self-employed income

The business accounts for the tax office need not be over elaborate but backup receipts and invoices etc. should be available if asked for.

So self-employed people do pay their tax somewhat later than employees who are subject to the PAYE system but the advantage is no longer as great as it used to be when tax was paid on a prior year basis and it does require some planning to maximise the cash flow benefits.

In particular the choice of accounting year can be important and so too can the calculation of the preliminary tax which is paid each November. To make the right choices it is important first to understand how the system works.

Self-employed taxpayers are required to pay tax in one lump sum before November 1 each year. It is an estimated amount based on a self-assessment of the tax which will eventually be payable for the current tax year. That tax is not necessarily based on the income during the normal April to April tax year but rather the accounting year which ends during the tax year. The choice of accounting year is up to the self-employed taxpayer.

That's easier to understand from an example. Many businesses operate on a calendar accounting year e.g. from January 1 to December 31. Let's take the case of such a business operated by Ms Murphy. This coming November 1, 2000 she will have to make a preliminary tax payment based on her assessment of the tax due on her 2000 calendar accounts.

Ten months of the year will have passed so she'll be paying the tax on ten months income in arrears and on two months in advance. It's actually a bit better than that because she won't have to submit a final tax return for the year until January 31, 2002. At that stage a final assessment of her tax liability will be made and she'll have a further month to pay any additional tax.

Underpaying preliminary tax can prove costly so it pays to take a bit of care in doing the calculations.

If the preliminary tax payments she makes this November is at least 90 per cent of the tax eventually found to be due, she'll suffer no interest or penalties. Another way of avoiding interest and penalties is to opt to pay a preliminary tax of at least 100 per cent of the previous year's tax liability (after adding back some extra relief such as BES). For a growing business that's usually a far better option.

The benefit, of course, is only in terms of cash flow. The full tax eventually has to be paid but it leaves extra money in the business for at least fourteen months.

Avoiding a tax audit

Most revenue audits are targeted. Some taxpayers are picked at random but the vast bulk – perhaps over 90 per cent – are picked because of their past record or because their tax returns trigger some alarm bells in the Revenue computers or the tax inspector's mind.

It is not too difficult to imagine the type of return which might trigger an audit. All you have to do is put yourself in the tax inspector's shoes and consider what he or she might be looking for. An irregular trading pattern, for instance, might be considered a bit strange and worthy of investigation. It might reflect tax evasion but it might also be due to the nature of the business, lost contracts, illness of key workers – any number of possible explanations.

If there is an explanation like that it is better to add a note to the VAT or other tax return. It might just offset an audit. The same is true of the other possible factors which might put a tax inspector wondering – factors like the following:

Low drawings: Where the amount of money drawn out of a business by the proprietor seems unduly low by reference to previous periods or by reference to realistic spending needs the inspector may wonder what is sustaining the taxpayer's lifestyle. If there is a legitimate explanation, make it in an addendum to your tax return.

Fluctuating turnover: This may, of itself raise questions in a tax inspector's mind unless the business is of an obvious seasonal nature. A change in the pattern is, of course, just as likely to prompt questions.

VAT: Discrepancies between VAT and income or corporation tax returns are very easily spotted now that the Revenue has encouraged a standardisation of tax periods. In small businesses particularly there can be a legitimate explanation. If there is it is better to make it before an audit is prompted than during the audit.

Careless returns: Sloppy VAT and PAYE returns will obviously raise a suspicion that accounting procedures are not all they should be.

For a growing business the choice of accounting year may also be important. Let's suppose Ms Murphy's business operated on a July 1 to June 30 accounting year. The tax paid in November 2000 will be based on the income generated during the accounting year from July 1999 to June 2000. If income is growing that has to be better than paying the tax on the basis of calendar year 1999 income.

But remember some of the cash flow benefits can be offset by delays in claiming allowances. And if you change your end of year accounting date the Revenue will go back a year and calculate what your liability would have been had you used the new accounting period during the previous year. You'll get an extra tax bill if the profits in that accounting period were in excess of the actual profits assessed.

That doesn't mean that it can't be worthwhile changing your accounting year or picking a favourable starting date for the business. But there's likely to be many other factors involved in that decision and the cash flow benefits don't accrue for a few years in any case because the tax liability during the early years of the business are subject to special rules.

The cost of capital items such as plant or office equipment is deducted from taxable income over seven years.

The profits assessed for the first tax year is the actual taxable income from the date of commencement to the following April 5. The profits assessed in the second year are those for the first twelve months of the business. It is only in the first year that the normal ongoing system starts to operate.

Let's take the example of someone who started a self-employed business during September 1999. In November 2000 they will calculate their preliminary tax on the profits made between September 1999 and April 5, 2000. In November 2001 they will pay preliminary tax on the basis of profits made during the twelve months from September 1999 to September 2000.

There are, of course, additional allowances which can be claimed by the self-employed. These are basically the costs of running the business. To be allowed as a tax deduction an employee must show that any expenses were incurred wholly, exclusively and necessarily for trade or professional purposes. The self-employed taxpayer has only to meet the "wholly and exclusively" requirements. He does not have to show that the expenses were necessarily incurred. That makes more expenses allowable.

The following are some of the more general possibilities.

- Wages paid to employees. See a later section for the benefits of formally paying wages to children who may be helping in the business.

- Rent paid for business premises is allowed but it may not be worthwhile claiming a notional rent allowance for a room in your private home even if it is used as an office. Instead you can claim for the cost of heating and lighting that room. Claiming for rent could result in part of your house being considered to be a commercial premises. That can have implications for local authority rates and capital gains tax. There is no capital gains tax on a principal residence but there could be a liability on a business premises. If it is only a matter of using one room as an office it is probably best just to claim tax relief on the "running cost" of the room — perhaps, in the case of a four bedroomed house, a seventh of your total household outgoings on heat and light.

- Repairs to premises and repairs to plant and machinery are allowable costs but not the cost of improvements or additions.

- Interest paid on business loans. Restrictions of the type applicable to mortgage interest relief on a home do not, of course, apply.

- The cost of advertising.

- Other business costs include travelling, stationery, telecommunications, postage etc. Receipts should, of course, be kept. Motoring expenses are considered in more detail below.

- Bad debts are also an allowable expense. That includes doubtful debts but the expense must relate to specific debts. It cannot simply be a global provision in the expectation that a certain proportion of bills will be unpaid.

- Allowance can also be claimed in respect of capital expenditure on plant and machinery used in the business. The cost of such items is written off at the rate of 15 per cent a year for six years with the remaining 10 per cent written off in the seventh year. For example if you buy a computer for use in the business for £2,000, you can claim £300 as a cost against earnings in each of the first six years and £200 in the seventh year. Different allowances are made in respect of motor cars. We'll look at those in some detail in the next section.

In addition to these business expenses the self-employed taxpayer who has no other income can also deduct the same personal allowances outlined above for the PAYE payer. The only exception is the PAYE allowance which the self-employed person cannot claim. The PAYE allowance is not available either for a spouse working for a self-employed taxpayer. It may be worthwhile formally employing a spouse in a family business to make use of the new wider lower rate tax band available to two income couples. The pros and cons are examined on page 272

The expense allowances will, of course, vary according to the type of business.

Income from rents

Income from the letting of flats, houses or other property is treated in the same way as the self-employed income mentioned above. It is added to the taxpayer's other income in arriving at his overall tax liability but it is not, of course, paid under the PAYE system. In assessing the taxable income from rents, the normal personal allowances are obtainable if they have not already been offset against other income and, in addition, the cost of the following may be deducted from the gross income before arriving at taxable income.

- Any rent payable by the taxpayer himself — i.e. ground rent on the premises.

- Any rates on the premises.

- The interest on borrowing used to acquire or improve residential property by non-owner-occupiers after April 23, 1998 is not allowed as a relief against rental income. If the property was acquired prior to that or contracts in writing were exchanged before that date and the transaction completed by March 31, 1998, then interest remains a deductable expense. On residential properties acquired before that date and on all non-residential property the interest on any money borrowed to buy the property or improve or repair it is allowable as a deduction from rental income for tax purposes. This interest relief is unlimited — not subject to the individual upper limit which applies to mortgage interest relief on a principal residence. In this case the interest is considered to be on business borrowings and is allowable in full against rental income.

- The cost of any goods or services which he provides to the tenants and which are not paid for separately from the rent. An example might be providing electric light in the hallways of flats.

- The cost of maintenance, repairs, insurance etc.

- Management costs i.e. cost of collecting rents, advertising for tenants etc.

- Wear and tear allowances on the cost of furniture and fittings at the rate of 15 per cent of the cost in each of the first six years and 10 per cent in the seventh year.

Where the costs exceed the income from the rental property, that loss is only allowed as an offset against future rental income. It cannot be used to reduce the tax due on PAYE earnings for instance.

Motor vehicles

A ny taxpayer, whether employed or self-employed, who uses his own motor car for business can claim for wear and tear on the car in addition to running expenses. It doesn't arise too often in the case of an employee since he or she is normally either supplied with a company car or has the expenses reimbursed by the employer. But self-employed taxpayers very often use their own cars.

There are restrictions on the amount which can be claimed but they have been eased over recent years. The calculations are based on the value of the car at the time of purchase subject to a maximum which was raised to £16,500 on December 1, 1999. It was £16,000 from December 2, 1998.

The wear and tear allowed each year is calculated at 20 per cent of the declining value of the car restricted by that initial maximum value. It is also reduced to allow for any private use of the car. A one-third private to two-thirds business is a generally accepted norm.

The following table provides an example of the calculation.

Capital allowances on a car

Cost	£18,000
Restricted to £16,000	£16,500
Allowance at 20 per cent (20 per cent of £16,500)	£3,300
Restricted for business use (2/3rds of £3,300)	£2,200
Allowance for year 1	**£2,200**
Written down value for year 2 (£16,500 minus £2,200)	£14,300
Allowance at 20 per cent (20 per cent of £14,300)	£2,860
Restricted for business use (2/3rds of £2,860)	£1,907
Allowance for year 2	**£1,907**

A somewhat similar restriction applies to running expenses although the calculation is a bit more complicated. In this case there are two restrictions applied. The running expenses are first of all restricted to business milage. That's obvious enough since tax relief cannot be claimed in relation to the private use of the car. The second restriction is aimed at reducing the relief available on more expensive cars. So the relief is restricted on the basis of the lowest of one of the following two calculations:

- A third of the amount by which the cost of the car exceeded £16,500.
- Business running costs multiplied by (cost of car minus £16,500) divided by cost of car.

The following is an example of how it works.

Allowable running costs

The following is based on a new car bought for £18,000 which is used one-third for personal purposes and two-thirds for business. It is assumed that total running costs for the year are £3,600. After allowing for the private usage it is necessary to calculate two possible restrictions on the allowable costs and apply the lowest of the two.

Total running costs	**£3,600**
Less: one third restriction for private use	£1,200
Business costs	**£2,400**
Restriction 1:	
One third of cost of car minus £16,500 (1/3rd of £1,500)	£500
Restriction 2:	
£2,400 multiplied by (£1,500/£18,000) — see text	£200
Restriction 2 is applied:	
Business Costs — from above	**£2,400**
Less restriction 2	£200
Allowable costs	**£2,200**

To be liable for tax in Ireland you need to be resident in Ireland or, in some cases, to have recently been resident in Ireland. The definition of "resident" is strictly defined in this context but it is a fairly liberal definition. For instance it is possible to be non-resident and still have a home in Ireland and there are tax concessions for people who spend as little as 90 days a year out of the country.

The tax position can be considered under three separate categories:

- Working abroad
- Non-resident
- Emigrants

An individual who works part of the year outside of Ireland and Britain may qualify for a tax relief whereby part of his or her income is treated as tax free. To be eligible it is necessary to:

Have worked abroad for 90 days during a twelve month period. The ninety days must include a consecutive period of at least fourteen days. A day is included in the calculation if the individual is abroad at the end of it and if, during it, he or she devoted a substantial amount of time to actual work rather than leisure or travel. Once qualified a proportion of the individual's income is treated as tax-free. The proportion is calculated on the basis of the number of days abroad minus 15 divided by 365 i.e.

$$\frac{\text{number of days minus fifteen}}{365}$$

Working abroad

A person is considered to be resident in Ireland for tax purposes if he or she is in the country for 183 days or more in a tax year; or is in the country for more than 30 days in that year and 280 days or more during that and the previous tax year.

You are counted as having spent a day in Ireland if you are in the country at the end of the day so you could, in fact, spend every day in Ireland provided you left the country every night.

Non-resident status

In broad terms that means that if you spend less than 30 days in the country during a tax year you are not considered to be resident for tax purposes. If you spend less than six months here you may qualify for non-residence status provided your combined time in the country over the current and previous tax years does not exceed 280 days.

As a non-resident you are not liable for income tax on earnings you make abroad. But for the first three years after becoming non-resident, you are liable for tax on income arising in Ireland, on capital gains and on investment income from any source. So if you go abroad for three years and save up your surplus income you may not be liable for Irish income tax on your earnings but you will still remain liable for tax for three years on the interest earned on your savings

Tax rebates for emigrants

People who leave a job in Ireland to emigrate may be entitled to a tax rebate but it has to be claimed. Such claims can be backdated for up to at least six years. The size of the rebate depends on a number of factors — most notably the date of leaving the Irish job. The potential refund is highest for those who leave jobs a few months into the tax year which begins on April 6. It is lowest for those who leave towards the very end of a tax year. If you leave just prior to April 5 there is unlikely to be any rebate entitlement at all.

The entitlement arises as a result of a special concession which has existed for many years although it was only formally written into law in the 1994 Finance Act. Basically it separates for tax purposes the Irish and overseas earnings of an emigrant in the year he or she leaves the country. It also operates in the year an emigrant returns to work in Ireland.

To be considered an emigrant for the purposes of this tax concession you need to spend at least one full tax year — from April 6 to the following April 5 — out of the country. Occasional visits home, of course, don't affect the entitlement.

Let's first see how it works, how you can go about claiming the rebate, and also look at how to time your return to Ireland to make the maximum use of the concession.

Normally an Irish resident is liable for tax in Ireland on their world-wide income and while the definition of "resident" for tax purposes was eased in the 1994 Finance Act most emigrants would be considered to be resident during the year they emigrated. So technically they should be liable for Irish tax not only on their earnings in Ireland before they leave but also on their earnings abroad during the remainder of the tax year while also paying tax in their new home.

They might, of course, be able to get some relief under a double taxation agreement between Ireland and their new host country. But that's complicated to say the least. But what's known as "The Split Year Rule" allows you to ignore all of that.

If you leave Ireland to work abroad and you stay abroad for at least the following tax year, then you are only liable to pay Irish tax on income earned in Ireland before you left.

A tax rebate may be due both in the year you leave and in the year you return.

There can be no disputing your claim if you have already stayed abroad for the full tax year. But you can make the claim even before you emigrate. The Revenue Commissioners may accept that you intend staying abroad if you have sold your house, for instance, or if you have evidence of taking a long-term job abroad.

So, how does the rebate arise?

Under the PAYE system your tax allowances are spread out equally over the full year. You are allowed a proportion of them for each week or month, depending on how you're paid. So if you leave a job and emigrate after say six months you will only have got the benefit of half of your tax allowances for the year. It's the other half that entitles you to the rebate.

Suppose, for instance, that you're single earning £20,000 a year. Your basic tax free allowances for the year total £5,700 just counting personal and PAYE allowances. Your allowances could be more if you include medical insurance and mortgage interest or rent. Six months into the tax year — by October 5 — you'll have earned £10,000 and have got the benefit of half of those tax free allowances or about £2,850. If you leave the job and emigrate at that stage you can claim the benefit of the other £2,850 of tax allowances. At 22p in the £ that's worth £627 of a rebate. Don't forget, of course, that there is the overriding condition that you are going to work outside the country for the whole of the following tax year.

The claim should be made to whatever tax office you dealt with prior to leaving Ireland. You will need to fill out a tax return for the year you left the country and possibly catch up on earlier years if you hadn't been making tax returns. Ideally you would have a copy of the P45 form you got from your Irish employer on leaving. That would show your earnings during the tax year up to the date you left and details of the tax stopped.

But the tax office should have that information if your previous employer has been making his returns.

Remember that the Revenue Commissioners will normally allow a back-claim for up to at least six years.

The size of a possible tax rebate is obviously not the only thing to be considered when planning a date for either emigrating from or returning to Ireland. But its a factor to be taken into account.

The point to remember is that you can earn up to your annual tax free allowance level without any liability for income tax. Since the annual tax free allowances for a single individual who is paying PAYE amount to £5,700 it follows that if a single person earns less than £5,700 in Ireland from the April 6 before he or she emigrates there is an entitlement to a full rebate of all the tax paid in that tax year i.e since April 6. A single person returning to Ireland can earn up to £5,700 between the date they return and the following April 5 and pay no tax on it.

For example if you return at Christmas, get a job and decide to stay, you can earn up to £5,700 between then and April 5 without incurring any tax liability. Remember though, that this only applies to those who have spent at least a full tax year abroad.

Even if you left Ireland six years ago you may still be due a rebate and it's not too late to claim.

If you buy an asset at one price and sell it at a higher price, you have made a capital gain and since April 6, 1974, most gains of this type are liable for tax. A number of changes to the tax rate were introduced late in 1997 and during 1998. The standard rate was reduced to 20 per cent from December 3, 1997 and a special 26p rate on disposals of shares in certain small to medium sized companies was abolished. Since April 23, 1998 the lower rate of 20 per cent applies to gains made from the disposal of serviced development land zoned residential. That special concessionary rate is to apply for four years before being increased to 60 per cent. The 20 per cent rate was extended to gains from other development land sales from December 1, 1999. With the exception of gains from the disposal of development lands, any gains arising simply from the effects of inflation are not liable for the tax.

An example will show how this indexation works. Suppose you bought an asset four years ago for £10,000 and have just sold it for £13,000. You have made a gain of £3,000 but the taxable gain is less because you are allowed to adjust the buying price upwards in line with the general rise in prices since you acquired the asset.

Capital gains

Let us suppose for this example that prices have risen by 10 per cent in the four years. The Revenue Commissioners actually publish their own index numbers to be used in this adjustment process — they are given in appendix 1 on page 308. But on the assumption of a 10 per cent rise in prices the relevant index number would be 1.1. Liability to capital gains tax is calculated like this:

Selling Price	**£13,000**
Adjusted buying price (£10,000 x 1.1)	**£11,000**
Taxable Gain	**£2,000**
Tax at 20 per cent	**£400**

If that was the only gain made during the year, there would be no tax payable since there is an exemption limit below which no tax is payable. The first £1,000 of gains made by an individ-

How Capital Gains Tax is calculated

The following calculation is based on an asset acquired for £4,000 during the tax year 1979/80 and sold during early in 2000 for £24,000. There were selling expenses of £600. The base purchase price is multiplied by the relevant index number i.e. 3.139. If the value of the asset simply rose in line with inflation it would have risen in value by 3.139 times. It is assumed that no other capital gains were made in the year.

Selling price	**£24,000**
Less selling expenses	£600
Adjusted selling price	£23,400
Adjusted purchase price (£4,000 x 3.139)	£12,556
Capital gain	**£10,844**
Less annual exemption	£1,000
Taxable gain	**£9,844**
Tax payable (at 20%)	**£1,969**

ual (£2,000 for a married couple) but it is not transferable between spouses.

You are also allowed to deduct from the price you get on disposing of the asset any cost involved in acquiring or selling the asset, and any expenditure wholly and exclusively incurred for the purpose of enhancing its value.

Making a gift of assets can be considered to be a disposal for tax purposes. Suppose you give a holiday home to a child. You will be considered to have disposed of the home at its current market value and your liability for capital gains tax will arise in exactly the same way as if you had sold it. The child might also, of course, have a liability for Capital Acquisitions Tax on the gift — see page 263. However where a liability to both Capital Gains Tax and Capital Acquisitions Tax arise on the same transaction one may be claimed as an offset against the other.

There are special concessions for business assets passing to a child on the retirement of a parent — see page 261. The transfer of assets on the death of the owner is not a disposal for tax purposes so no Capital Gains Tax liability arises. The person in-

Saving Capital Gains Tax on business assets

Business assets which have been held for ten years by an individual aged over 55 may be passed to a natural or adopted child without any liability for Capital Gains Tax. Child, in this case, is defined to include nephews or nieces who have worked full-time in the business for at least the previous five years. The child has to retain ownership of the assets for at least six years.

Shares in a family business may also qualify for this concession provided the person selling them or passing them on was a full-time director of the company for at least ten years including five years as a full-time working director.

Where the transfer is to someone other than a child the concessions are less generous. The seller has to be over 55 and no tax is payable provided the consideration is less than £375,000 (£250,000 prior to December 1, 1999). Where the sale is for more than £375,000 the maximum tax payable is set at half the proceeds from the sale minus £375,000. So the maximum tax payable on assets sold for £475,000 would be £50,000. There is, of course, no Capital Gains Tax payable on transfers between spouses.

Where tax liability arises it may be possible to defer it by investing in replacement assets. This 'roll-over' relief is allowed on business assets including plant, machinery, certain land, building and goodwill. The replacement assets must normally be acquired during the period starting one year before the sale of the old assets and three years after.

A similar relief is available on the disposal of shares in a trading company in which the seller held at least a 15 per cent voting stake and was a director employee for at least the three previous years. The money must be reinvested in new ordinary shares in an unquoted Irish company and a 15 per cent stake built up over three years — 5 per cent after one year. The individual must become a full time employee or director of the new company within a year.

A person who fails to meet the one year condition and pays the tax may have it refunded if he/she meets the conditions within three years.

heriting the assets is deemed to have acquired them at their market value on the date of the inheritance.

Exempt gains

The following gains are totally exempt from the tax:

- Gains from the sale of your principal residence including up to one acre of land. If the price you get is based on the development value of the land then you are liable for tax on the gain attributed to that development value.

- Gains on the sale of a residence, also including up to an acre of land, which you have been providing for the sole occupation of a dependent relative as his or her sole residence. Dependent relative in this regard includes any relative who because of incapacity or infirmity is not able to maintain him or herself. Also included is the widowed mother of either spouse who need not be incapacitated.

- Bonuses on Post Office or State savings schemes.

- Gains from the disposal of Government stocks.

- Gains from life assurance policies or deferred annuities.

- Gains from the disposal of a movable tangible asset worth £2,000 or less when sold.

- Gains on assets with a predictable life of under fifty years — a car, livestock etc.

- Gains from the disposal on retirement of a farm or business to a member of one's family.

- Winnings from lotteries, betting etc.

Rates of tax

From December 1, 1999 the standard rate of 20 per cent applies to all gains. The indexation mentioned above does not apply totally to development land. The original use value of the land may be indexed but not any development value. For example the indexation could be applied to the "agricultural use" value of the land but not to its higher value as building land.

Inheritance and gift taxes 13.5

There are two taxes which may be applied to inheritances — Capital Acquisitions Tax and Probate Tax. Both can be charged on the same estate but they are different taxes and are collected separately. Capital Acquisitions Tax may also be charged on gifts with all gifts and inheritances taken after December 1, 1988 — irrespective of the class of donor — added together to decide whether a threshold level has been reached. If so then tax becomes payable. The liability falls on the recipient. Gifts and inheritances totalling £1,000 or less in any tax year are ignored for tax purposes. That figure was £500 prior to December 2, 1998.

The impact of the tax on business assets has been greatly reduced in recent years and in the 1999 budget family homes were exempt subject to certain conditions. At the same time the threshold levels were significantly increased. The threshold for gifts or inheritances to children taken during 2000 is £300,000 (the same threshold applies to gifts or inheritances passing from children to parents); £30,000 for brothers, sisters, nieces, nephews and children of deceased children; and £15,000 for non and distant relatives. Spouses get inheritances and gifts tax free. There is a single tax rate of 20 per cent. Details of the earlier thresholds and rates are given in appendix 1 on page 314.

Let us have a look at an example. Suppose a man first got a gift of £10,000 during 1998 from a friend. He had received no other gifts or inheritances before that. The first £500 of that gift was exempt leaving £9,500. None of that was taxable at the time since it was below the relevant threshold. Suppose the man now gets an inheritance of £25,000 from an uncle. The relevant threshold in this case is £30,000. But the previous gift is also taken into account. This time the first £1,000 is exempt from tax leaving £24,000 to which is added the previous gift of £9,500 putting the total of taxable gifts and inheritances acquired by the man at £33,500. From that is deducted not the £30,000 threshold but rather the £24,000 which is all that was received. So all of the previous £9,500 becomes liable for tax. At 20 per cent it works out at £1,900.

Capital Acquisitions Tax

Family businesses

Concessions on the transfer of agricultural and business assets by way of gift or inheritance have been greatly extended in recent years and since January 23, 1997 the value of such assets is reduced by 90 per cent for tax purposes subject to certain conditions.

It's a very valuable concession. The main condition with regard to business assets is that they are held by the recipient for at least ten years after the transfer. If this requirement is breached within six years all of the tax concession is clawed back. If it is breached between six and ten years the relief is reduced and the difference clawed back. But the claw back is limited to the additional relief granted under the past two budgets.

The business concerned must be carried on wholly or mainly within the State but the definition of business assets is quite wide ranging. It includes property consisting of a business or an interest in a business; unquoted shares or securities of an Irish company subject to some restrictions; quoted shares or securities in an Irish company which were owned by the disponer before they became quoted; building, land and machinery owned by the disponer but used by a company controlled by him or her, or else used by a partnership in which he or she was a partner.

Businesses whose sole or main business is dealing in land, shares, securities etc. are not covered by the concession.

The business assets on which the concession is claimed must have been owned by the disponer or his/her spouse for at least five years prior to the transfer in the case of a gift, or for at least two years where the transfer results from the death of the disponer. So the business assets don't have to have been in the family for very long to qualify for the relief.

Concessions on the valuation of agricultural assets have been a feature of Capital Acquisitions Tax since it was first introduced. They have been greatly extended in recent years in line with similar concessions which now apply to business assets outside of farming.

Subject, as always, to some conditions agricultural assets are valued at only 10 per cent of their true market value in calculating liability for Capital Acquisitions Tax. That 90 per cent reduction has applied since January 23, 1997.

The reduction applies to farm assets transferred to a "farmer". The definition of farmer is important as is the definition of farm assets. Another important factor may be the "valuation date" for an inheritance i.e. the date on which the transfer is deemed to take place and on which the assets are valued.

Farm assets include: farm land, buildings and woodland, machinery, livestock and bloodstock. Money may also qualify so long as the transfer is conditional on it being invested into qualifying agricultural property and that that condition is met within two years. That latter concession widens the availability of the relief considerably. The donor doesn't have to have ever been a farmer or even to have owned farm assets.

But in all cases the recipient has to be a "farmer". However a "farmer" in this context doesn't even have to know the difference between a bull and a cow or be able to tell the difference between wheat and barley or silage and slurry. The sole requirement is that at least 80 per cent of his or her assets are farm assets. That requirement is measured after getting the inheritance or gift, or after complying with a requirement to buy such assets.

A "farmer" in this context doesn't even have to know the difference between a bull and a cow.

It is not too difficult to ensure that all the necessary conditions are complied with. But it is also all too easy to fail some of the tests through a lack of adequate planning.

A recipient of a farm inheritance could fail the 80 per cent test through owning a house or apartment in Dublin for instance. Where there is a danger of such a problem arising the will may be drawn up in such a way that the recipient has time to arrange his or her affairs after the death of the donor so that the 80 per cent rule is met by the time the farm assets are transferred.

For tax purposes assets need not necessarily transfer at the time of death or on the date probate or administration is granted.

As with business assets the agricultural assets transferred must be held for at least six years to avoid a claw back of the concessions. If the assets are disposed of, and not replaced, within six and ten years there is a partial claw back. After ten years there is no claw back.

Tax can also be reduced by ensuring that the maximum possible proportion of the assets being transferred consist of farm assets at the time of the gift or on the valuation date used for inheritance tax purposes. Crops in the ground are farm assets. Crops lifted are not. In the same way livestock are farm assets. The cash from their sale is not.

Other factors to consider are outlined on page 276. There are such a wide range of factors involved that careful planning is essential and professional advice advisable.

There is a further concession in respect of business property or shares in a company left or given to the child of a brother or sister. If the nephew or niece has spent five years working in the donor's business, the tax liability is calculated as if he or she were a child of the donor.

The requirement is that the nephew or niece have worked at least 24 hours a week at a place where the business is carried out, or a lower fifteen hours a week where there are no employees other than the person leaving the inheritance, or making the gift (the disponer), his or her spouse, and the recipient.

If the disponer is not domiciled in the State, or the proper law of the disposition is not Irish law, then the recipient is only liable for tax on that part of the gift or inheritance which is situated in Ireland.

Siblings living together

The 1999 budget exempted the family home from CAT subject to certain conditions. It must be the principal private residence of the disponer and/or the recipient and the recipient must have been living there for the three years prior to the transfer and not have an interest in any other residential property. The recipient must not dispose of the property for six years after the transfer.

This latest concessions supplants earlier more restrictive reliefs. Since April 1991 there has been a special relief for brothers/sisters over 55 years of age who have lived in the one house for at least five years ending on the date of death.

There is a special relief for brothers and sisters leaving a family home to the survivor.

The relief was increased in the 1994 budget allowing for the value of the house, or portion of the house, passing to the survivor from the deceased brother or sister to be reduced by 80 per cent for tax purposes subject to a maximum reduction of £150,000. For some years up to December 3, 1997 the reduction was 60 per cent or £80,000.

From that date a similar concession was available to nephews, nieces, and to brothers and sisters under 55 years of age. The relative inheriting the house must have lived in it for at least ten years prior to the death and not be the beneficial owner of any other house or part of any other house. The reduction in value for tax purposes is the same as for siblings over 55 i.e. 80 per cent or £150,000 whichever is the lesser.

Other exemptions

The owners of heritage houses or gardens can avoid Capital Acquisitions Tax liability on a transfer by gift or inheritance by allowing limited public access. Up to 1997 the house had to be open for 90 days a year including not less than 60 days during the summer. That has now been reduced to a total of 60 days of which at least 40 days must be during the summer months. While the number of days that the house or gardens have to be open has been reduced the conditions with regard to publicity have been tightened up. Full details of opening hours and admission prices must be notified to Bord Failte before January 1 each year.

A similar exemption from CAT applies to other assets of national, scientific, historic or artistic interest. This includes works of art, scientific collections, and libraries. In all cases the tax exemption may be lost if the assets are disposed of within six years of being transferred either by way of gift or inheritance.

Other assets which are exempt from CAT include: the first £1,000 received from any one disponer in any calendar year; charitable gifts or inheritance; pension and death in service benefits payable to an employee; certain compensation payments; reasonable payments received from a family member and used for support, maintenance or education; prizes and lottery winnings; and, of course, the proceeds of qualifying insurance policies taken out with a view to paying eventual CAT liabilities.

Probate tax

Probate Tax applies to the estates of people dying on or after June 17, 1993. While Capital Acquisitions Tax is payable by the recipients of inheritances or gifts, Probate Tax is charged on the value of the estate and is normally payable by the executor. All assets passing between spouses are exempt while the value of agricultural land is reduced by 30 per cent in assessing the tax. The tax is charged at the rate of 2 per cent on the value of the estate passing by will or, in the absence of a will, under an intestacy, after a death. Property passed at any time before death is not liable for the tax. So someone given warning of impending death can completely avoid the tax by passing over his or her property before death.

Where the estate is valued at £40,000 or less there is no tax payable. But once it is valued at more than £40,000 the whole estate is liable for tax at 2 per cent. There is marginal relief for estates valued at slightly above £40,000. The figure was £11,150 up to December 1, 1999.

Where there is no surviving spouse there is no tax payable on that share of a house left to a dependent child or relative normally residing in the house. A 'dependent' must not have an income in excess of £5,512 a year. That figure is equivalent to the contributory old age pension payable to someone over 80 living alone at the rates applying from May 2000.

The dependent does not have to be drawing such a pension. The requirement is that they have an income less than that figure or the equivalent figure at the time. There are also exemptions for property passing to charities, heritage property as defined for inheritance tax, and pension benefits.

Joint ownership

The tax should be paid within nine months of death if heavy interest penalties are not to be incurred.

There is no probate tax payable on property held in joint ownership if it automatically passes to the survivor without having to go through probate. That exemption does not exist in the case of Capital Acquisitions Tax. It is an important concession. But see page 19 for a note on joint bank accounts.

The tax will normally be paid by the executor of the will although the liability can pass to all the beneficiaries if the tax is not already paid by the time they get their share. Where no provision is made for the tax in the will, it is charged pro-rata on the taxable value of the individual legacies.

To get a grant of probate or letters of administration it is necessary to send an inland revenue affidavit to the Revenue Commissioners. This affidavit must be accompanied by a self-assessment Probate Tax Form together with the tax due.

If the tax is paid within nine months of the death, a discount of 1 per cent per month or part-month is allowed. After nine months a penalty of 1 per cent per month or part-month is payable up to a maximum of doubling the tax due. The Revenue Commissioners have been granted discretion to postpone the collection of the tax where there is a lack of ready cash to pay it. Probate tax is not allowed as a tax credit against inheritance tax but it is allowed as an expense.

Tax saving

Cutting your tax liability

14.

There is nothing that can be done to alter your basic tax allowances but it is possible to reduce your tax bill by making use of the many concessions and incentives available within our complicated tax system. It is not only the self-employed who can make use of these legal tax avoidance measures. At least some of them are available to the ordinary PAYE payer as well. This chapter outlines a number of ways of reducing tax liability in addition to detailing the tax position in some specific areas — such as separated couples. Many taxpayers can save tax by simply checking their income tax position and making up-to-date returns. A lot of allowances go unclaimed. Have a look at the panel on page 246.

Most income tax allowances are applied automatically but not all. If you do not make annual tax returns your certificate of tax free allowances will not take account of increased VHI or BUPA contributions, for instance. It is possible now to ask either company to automatically inform your tax office of the premiums you pay so that the relief is always up to date. Otherwise you have to make your claim for any increases.

There are other allowances which have to be claimed. Many PAYE workers are entitled to some small claim for expenses. Tax relief on medical expenses will only be given if claimed — see page 234. It is not too difficult to exceed the thresholds of £100 per individual, £200 for a family. You can claim for previous years too. Even PAYE workers can get some of their income tax free if they arrange things right. Other options range from subsidised canteen meals to leisure and childcare facilities provided by an employer. The following sections outline a few approaches which could save you some money.

Employing your child or spouse

Self-employed people may be able to cut their family tax bills by formally paying their children and, from April 2000, their spouse for work done in the business. In small family businesses it is not unusual for children and a spouse to do a significant amount of work. This must be particularly true of retail businesses or farms. But the type of business does not matter.

Employing your child

The tax saving in the case of a child arises from the fact that any individual can earn up to £5,700 a year free of tax in the 2000/2001 tax year. That figure is comprised of the personal tax allowance of £4,700 and the PAYE allowance of £1,000. In the case of a spouse the saving can arise from the fact that a two income couple benefits from an extra £6,000 standard rate tax band – £34,000 instead of the £28,000 that applies to a single income couple. So a self-employed couple with an income of over £28,000 can benefit from having two earnings. More about that later in this section but first the potential tax saving from employing a child.

As mentioned above a child can be paid up to £5,700 from the family business and not be liable for tax. If that payment reduces the father's taxable income by that amount, the family's overall position has improved. The child can get the money free of tax while the father would have had to pay tax at his highest marginal rate.

That is how the tax advantage arises, but remember that the child must be genuinely doing the work for which he or she is paid. And there are other factors to be considered. It is necessary for the proprietor of the business — the father or mother in this case — to register as an employer for PAYE and PRSI purposes. And it may be necessary to pay PRSI on the wages paid to the child — even though the income is too small to be liable for tax. These requirements need not be as onerous as they might seem. In most cases there will be very little paper work after the initial registration.

There is no clear cut guideline on liability for PRSI payments. In some cases PRSI may be payable on the money paid to the

A child who works in a family firm is entitled to get a wage from it and can earn up to £5,700 tax free.

child but, if it is, there could be an eventual benefit in the form of unemployment and pay related payments if you cease employing the child. The final decision rests with the Department of Social Welfare and it does not spell out in detail just who is liable for PRSI at the various rates. The following, however, is an outline of the factors it takes into account in making its decisions.

If the work is full time and there is a written or implied contract of employment, then the employee is liable for PRSI at the full rate. In deciding whether an implied contract exists the Department will take account of whether there are fixed hours involved and whether there is a fixed wage or salary.

A son living on a farm and helping his father is unlikely to be considered to have a contract of employment for instance. In this case the son would be classified as a Class K contributor and might be liable to pay the 2 per cent health levy. But they are not payable if the weekly income is less than £226— £217 a week in 1999/2000. Anyone earning less than those threshold levels of income is exempt from the levies.

Where a child is employed in a family business the work is likely to be part time and the question of whether there is a contract of employment or not may not be relevant. There are two classes of PRSI which may apply. Class M applies to employees under 16 years of age — they pay no PRSI. Close relatives working in a family business or farm are exempt from the requirements of the Protection of Young Persons (Employment) Act 1996 provided the health and safety of the young person is not put at risk.

That exception apart the general minimum age for a regular job is 16 but a 14 year old may be employed on light work outside of school term-time subject to a maximum of 35 hours a week on holiday work or 40 hours on work experience. A 15 year old may be employed for eight hours a week during school-term. Class J may apply to children over 16 earning less than £30 a week. In this case, the employer pays $\frac{1}{2}$ per cent on all income.

Anyone intending to employ someone at more than £6 a week or £26 a month must register as an employer. You write to your local tax office for a form CC151. Once completed the tax man will take it from there. It is not too complicated and the savings can be worthwhile.

Employing a spouse

There is no tax advantage in a PAYE taxpayer employing a spouse, as a housekeeper for instance, since the wages paid would have to come out of the after tax income of the taxpayer. The couple could end up paying more tax. That remains the case after the 1999 budget but the proposed widening of the standard rate tax band for two-income couples from April 2000 may make it worthwhile for a self-employed taxpayer to formally employ a spouse and pay him or her an income. The spouse, of course, needs to be actually working in the business and have a total income – earned and unearned – of less than £6,000. The joint income of the couple needs to be at least £28,000. The maximum tax saving is £1,320.

In the past there was no financial sense in formally employing a spouse in a family business yet many spouses actually do a significant amount of work in such businesses. The farmer's wife is an obvious example. There was no sense in a farmer putting his wife on the payroll since her income would simply be jointly assessed with his. She could benefit from no additional tax allowances in her own right. A spouse can't benefit from the PAYE allowance.

From April 2000 a two income family can benefit from a £34,000 standard rate band as opposed to the £28,000 band available to a single income family. That can be financially worthwhile to employ a spouse since to fully benefit from that wider band each spouse must have an income of at least £6,000. No one spouse can use more than £28,000 of the band.

Let's a a look at an example.

Tom is a self-employed businessman who is going to earn a £38,000 in the 2000/2001 tax year. His wife is not formally employed but she does a fair amount of office work, keeping books, answering phones etc. If Tom doesn't employ his wife his income tax liability works out as follows:

Taxable Income	**£38,000**
£28,000 at 22p in £	£6,160
£10,000 at 44p in £	£4,400
Total Tax	**£10,560**

That liability will be reduced as a result of personal allowances etc. but they are the same in each case so they can be ignored for the sake of the example.

If Tom formally employs his wife and pays her £6,000 the tax works out as follows:

Tom		Mary	
Taxable income	£32,000	Taxable income	£6,000
£28,000 at 22p	£6,160	£6,000 at 22p	£1,320
£4,000 at 44p	£1,760		
Total tax	**£7,920**		**£1,320**

A grand total of £9,240 – a saving of £1,320 on the situation that would apply if Mary wasn't formally employed. That savings would be partially eroded – to the tune of £660 – if Tom and Mary were entitled to the £3,000 home working spouse's allowance.

There is possibly no additional PRSI implication. Employed spouses come under Class K where the only payment is the Health Levy and the first £226 a week is exempt. There could be a small savings there since Tom would be paying the 2 per cent levy on the top slice of his income. So if he kept the £6,000 he'd be paying the levy whereas in Mary's hands it is likely to be exempt.

The above is based on the announcements made in the 2000 budget. The detailed legislation will be contained in the 2000 Finance Bill and there is a possiblity of change in the 2000 Social Welfare Bill.

Reducing inheritance taxes

The 2000 budget greatly eased the burden of Capital Acquisitions Tax particularly on gifts and inheritances received from parents. But the tax can still hit relatively small gifts and inheritances from more distant relatives and friends. In certain circumstances there is no tax payable by a person inheriting a family home and similar reliefs apply to business and farm assets provided certain conditions are met. It is possible to save a lot of tax by meeting the relevant conditions.

A person can receive any amount from a spouse without tax liability while, from December 1, 1999 a child can receive up to £300,000 from a parent or grandparent before coming into the tax net. But the tax thresholds for gifts or inheritances from more distant relatives are much lower and because of low marriage rates in the past particularly in some rural areas it is not uncommon for people to receive inheritances from sisters, brothers, uncles, aunts or cousins. The tax on such inheritances can be quite steep. But it can be reduced, or eliminated, by a little advance planning.

Careful advance planning is needed to reduce inheritance taxes but such planning can be very worthwhile.

Reducing inheritance taxes

The calculation of Capital Acquisitions Tax liability is fairly complex with all gifts and inheritances received since June 2, 1982 taken into account in calculating the tax due on any fresh inheritance. It is detailed on page 238.

There are only three threshold levels: the £300,000 for transfers from parents or grandparents if a parent is already dead; £30,000 for transfers from brothers, sisters, aunts, and uncles; and £15,000 for transfers from anyone else. But that does not mean that you can receive £300,000 from a parent and then £30,000 from a sister all tax free.

In broad terms once you have received £15,000 from a parent or anyone else, then any inheritance from a cousin is going to be fully taxable. In the same way someone who has received £15,000 from a cousin will find at least part of a subsequent inheritance from a parent liable for tax. Tax is levied at a flat 20 per cent. It can be argued that this is only right given that inheritances are unearned windfalls, but then no-one likes paying tax if there are ways of avoiding it, and there are some. Each individual case will vary. But there are a number of ways of reducing tax liability by planning the transfer. The following are some points worth considering:

- The liability for CAT is on the recipient, so the wider an estate is spread the lower the tax is likely to be. For instance an uncle wishing to leave his assets to a nephew can reduce the tax payable by leaving it to the nephew and his children. Suppose he wants to leave £40,000 to the nephew. If the nephew has not received any gift or inheritance before the first £30,000 would be tax free and the other £10,000 would be subject to tax — at 20 per cent the tax would be £2,000.

  It could be totally avoided if the will left the £40,000 divided between the nephew and his two children. The nephew could be left £25,000 and the rest divided among the children. Each would be below the recipient's individual threshold. It is true that any subsequent gifts or inheritances received would move them into the tax net that much more quickly because of the fact that past inheritance are taken into account. But the tax is being delayed, perhaps for a very long time.

  CAT liability can be reduced by leaving an estate to as many people as possible i.e. instead of just leaving it to children, dividing it among children and grandchildren.

  The high £300,000 threshold applies not only to transfers from parents to children but also transfers in the reverse direction. This can provide a way of reducing the tax liability in those unfortunate cases where an unmarried child is facing an untimely death. He or she may wish to leave the estate to a brother or sister who would only be entitled to a £30,000 tax threshold. The tax liability can be greatly reduced by passing the inheritance back to a parent who could then give it to a brother or sister.

- Full details of the exemption of the "family home" from CAT were not released with the December 1999 budget but it applied from December 1 and some conditions were outlined. The house has to be the principal private residence of the disponer and/or the recipient. The recipient must have been living there for at least three years before the transfer and retain ownership of the home for six years after. He or she must not have an interest in any other residential property. Those conditions, and maybe some others, will be outlined in the 2000 Finance Bill. Some planning may be required to ensure that they are met.

- A gift or inheritance can be disclaimed — in other words refused. That right may be used to refuse tax liability in some circumstances. Suppose a parent leaves a house between a sister and brother. Let's assume that neither has been living in the home and therefore don't qualify for the tax exemption related to the family home. But let's further assume that it has been agreed that the sister will actually get it for various family reasons. Ideally the will should have been changed but it wasn't. Neither might be liable for tax on the inheritance of half a house and whatever other assets were in the estate. The tax threshold is £300,000. But if the brother who inherits half the house subsequently gives it to the sister a sizeable tax liability could arise since the tax threshold is only £30,000 and, of course, the sister would already have received an inheritance of half of the house from the parent. But that tax liability can be avoided by the brother disclaiming the inheritance so that the sister inherits the full house directly from the parent.

- There are concessions for agricultural land and the recipient does not have to be a farmer provided that after the inheritance, farm assets comprise at least 80 per cent of his or her total assets. The actual assets left do not have to be farm assets either. It could comprise money with an instruction to buy farm assets with it.

- There can be an advantage in making provision in a will for the transfer of assets to be delayed for some weeks after death to allow the recipient some time to arrange his or her affairs. This could be important in meeting the 80 per cent agricultural assets rule, for instance, allowing for the disposal of some assets. The fact that a principal resident is included in total assets can make the 80 per cent rule hard to meet in some circumstances.

- Gifts made at least two years before death are liable for tax at only three quarters of the full CAT tax rates. But the tax has to be paid earlier so that the advantage may be eroded by the loss of interest on that part of the estate. Another possible disadvantage is that a gift may be considered a disposal for Capital Gains Tax purposes so that the giver may become liable for Capital Gains Tax just as if the asset had been sold. A transfer on death doesn't give rise to Capital Gains Tax.

- Probate tax can be avoided by holding property in joint ownership with the person who you wish to have it after your death. In such a case the survivor automatically gets sole ownership of the property without it having to go through probate.

These are just some suggestions. Careful planning is obviously important since each individual case is different.

Tax and marriage

Married couples have a constitutional right to be taxed no more harshly than two single individuals would be. That was the ruling of the Supreme Court back in 1980— it still stands. Since then that right has been written into the tax code. Where a husband and wife are both income earners, they can opt to be taxed as if they were two single people. But unfortunately there is seldom, if ever, any monetary advantage in so doing. It can have relevance where the couple are separated but otherwise it is hard to envisage a situation where a married couple would be jointly better off opting for single assessment. That is not going to change with the phased introduction of individualised standard rate bands. As a first step towards this a two-income couple can benefit from up to a £34,000 standard rate band during 2000/2001 while a single income couple can benefit at most to £28,000. It has yet to be tested whether a single income married couple have a right to be taxed no more harshly than a two income couple.

When it comes to deciding how they would like to be taxed there are, in fact, three options facing two income married couples. If they do nothing, they will be automatically taken to have opted for joint assessment. And neither of the other options can result in their joint tax bill being reduced. By opting for separate assessment, however, it is possible to divide the tax burden more equally between them. Opting for single assessment may achieve exactly the same end, but it could result in their overall tax bill being higher.

Let's look at each of the options in turn.

Married couples can end up paying less tax than two single people but not if they opt for single assessment.

Joint assessment

This is how most married couples are taxed. It was the only option open to them before the Supreme Court ruling in the Murphy case and the majority of couples have stuck with it.

The highest earner will automatically get the benefit of the bulk of the couple's joint tax free allowances. A spouse will only get his or her own PAYE allowance — £1,000 this year. That only applies, of course, if the lower earning spouse is wage earning and not working in the family company. The PRSI allowance is only given to those paying PRSI at the top rate.

The lower earner also gets the benefit of the table allowances if his or her income is high enough. These are not really allowances at all but simply an administrative device for ensuring that the tax burden is spread fairly evenly over the year as a whole. Instead of having the first portion of taxable income taxed at 22p in the £ before moving onto the higher rate of 44p, the system arranges for the highest rate to apply for the full year. The table allowance is then given to compensate for the over-taxation which would otherwise occur. The tendency to overtax by applying a 44p rate instead of a 22p rate for instance is exactly offset by providing the additional 'table' tax free allowance.

Under joint assessment, the couple is still legally taxed as one unit. And indeed either spouse can be nominated as the accountable person for tax purposes. The important point is that concessions not used by one spouse can be transferred to the other. This is the important point. The true legal liability for tax is worked out at the end of a tax year by way of a balancing statement which combines the two incomes.

If there is a wide difference between the two incomes it is possible that the PAYE system will result in too much tax being collected during the year. But it will be refunded at the end of the year, when the balancing statement is made out. The refunds are now allocated between the spouses in proportion to the tax paid by each.

Balancing statements are not prepared automatically so two income families, in particular should do a rough calculation each year to see that they are not being overtaxed. If they are, tax returns should be speedily prepared and a balancing statement asked for.

That is true for other taxpayers too. Many taxpayers lose out on the extra allowances they can claim — such as VHI and BUPA contributions; medical expenses etc.

Two income families should check their tax each year. The PAYE system can get things wrong.

Separate assessment

This is only a variation on the joint assessment option. Either spouse can opt for it provided they notify the tax office before July 6 in the year of assessment. Separate assessment then continues until the tax office is told otherwise by the spouse who first opted for it.

The total tax liability of the couple is not reduced in any way by separate assessment but most allowances are evenly split between them. Personal allowances, age allowances and blind persons' allowances are evenly divided while other allowances may be granted to the individual bearing the cost — allowance for medical insurance, for example, would be given to the person paying them.

The important point is that any allowances unused by one person can be passed back to the other. And the same is true for unused tax bands. So if the husband has moved into the 44p tax band while the wife still has not used up all of her 22p band, there is no loss. At the very latest the overtaxing will be sorted out when a balancing statement is prepared. It should be possible to prevent that problem arising, however, by dividing the allowances up broadly in proportion to each person's income.

Separate assessment is possibly the ideal option since it allows the couple to split the tax allowances fairly between them. Under ordinary joint assessment, the wife can very often find her income very heavily taxed since her husband is getting the benefit of most of the tax allowances. Separate assessment will not reduce their joint tax bill but it does give a better incentive for the wife to work.

Single assessment

This is where the couple decide to be treated exactly as if they were two single people for tax purposes. Their tax liabilities are kept entirely separate. If their incomes are about equal, a couple opting for single assessment may pay no more tax between them than they would if they opted for joint or separate assessment. But if their incomes are not equal or close to it they could end up with a higher tax bill.

The reason is that one spouse cannot pass on the benefit of unused allowances or rate bands to the other. Either spouse can serve notice on the tax man for single assessment at any time during the tax year. Once served the notice is applied to that year and all subsequent years until it is withdrawn. Only the person who served the notice in the first case can withdraw it.

There may be the odd freak situation where single assessment can reduce a tax bill. Such a situation might arise where one spouse is on a very low income — just below the income tax exemption limit. But, in general, there is no financial advantage to a couple in opting for single assessment.

Separated couples

If a separated couple
can agree on their tax
affairs they can
arrange matters to
their advantage.

A couple who have separated can get more tax relief than a couple living together although that does not mean that they will end up paying less tax. They may pay more despite the extra reliefs. Separated couples have more options on the income tax front and they can be jointly better off by picking the right one. That is if they can agree to do so.

Money problems may be a contributory factor to many a marriage break-up, but they do not end with the break-up of the marriage. The Revenue Commissioners are practical enough to recognise the reality of a situation but so long as the couple are married — whether separated or not — their tax affairs remain tied together. What the Revenue Commissioners have joined together let no man pull asunder. Mind you this can work to the benefit of the couple — it certainly need not work against them. And the Revenue Commissioners would seem to have little other alternative. But to make the best of the situation the couple need to work together — which seems rather ironic in the circumstances.

What follows only deals with spouses whose marriages have not been dissolved or annulled or who haven't got a divorce — couples who are, in fact, still married although separated. They have a range of options from which to choose.

Unfortunately there can be no hard and fast rule as to which is best. It depends on their particular circumstances. It can also depend on the couple jointly opting for the best alternative — both must choose some of the options — it is not enough for one of them to do so.

But let's look at the options in turn. It is important to realise that there can be no global rule of thumb on what is best. What is best for one couple may not be for someone in different circumstances. Each person needs to do their own sums.

Option one is to remain taxed as a couple without letting the tax man know anything about the separation. Even if there are maintenance payments being made, there is no problem so long as the principal earner is willing to meet the tax bills. Normally that is the husband and he would remain responsible for the tax liabilities of his wife — but tax would be stopped under PAYE on her income.

Couples and income tax — options compared

The couple Val and Pat	Single assessment		Jointly assessed	Separated with child	
	Val	Pat	Val/ Pat	Val	Pat
Gross income	£19,000	£12,000	£31,000	£19,000	£12,000
First £17,000 @ 22p	£3,740	£2,640	—	—	—
First £34,000 @ 22p	—	—	£6,820	—	—
First £20,150 @ 22p[1]	—	—	—	£4,180	£2,640
Remainder @ 44p	£880	nil	nil	nil	nil
Deduction for standard rates allowances[2]	£1,254	£1,254	£2,504	£2,288	£2,288
Total tax	**£3,336**	**£1,386**	**£4,312**	**£1,892**	**£352**
Income after tax	£15,634	£10,614	£26,688	£17,108	£11,648
Combined after tax	**£26,248**		**£26,688**	**£28,756**	

Notes: 1. Single parents have a special wide band to compensate for the standard rating of the single parents tax allowance. 2. Standard rated allowances (personal, PAYE and part of the single parent's) at 22p in the £ — the figures are based on bands and allowances for 2000/2001.

The table above shows three ways in which a married couple might be taxed. Their combined tax bill is different in each case. Most married couple are jointly assessed. But they can opt to be taxed as two single individuals. The difference that can make to the combined tax bill is shown in the first three columns of figures above.

If Val and Pat opt to be taxed as two single individuals, the lower earner Pat cannot transfer the benefit of unused 22p tax band to the higher earner, Val. So they end up paying more tax than if they were jointly assessed — a combined £4,722 compared with £4,312 giving them a combined take-home pay of only £26,248 whereas if they were jointly assessed it would be £26,688.

The third example assumes that Val and Pat are separated and have a child. Provided the child is under 16 or permanently incapacitated and lives with each at some time during the year both can claim the single parent's tax allowance. Their combined tax bill, in this case, is lower than it would be if they were jointly assessed because of the benefit of the extra tax allowance for single parents.

That could work to the detriment of the wife who would normally have very minimal tax allowances and would be paying heavy tax. They could, however, agree to split the allowances more equally between them — by opting for separate assessment — more about that below.

The do-nothing approach may be alright where the wife is not going to work and the husband has agreed to support her but it can pose problems otherwise.

Maintenance payments from husband to wife (or vice-versa) can cause difficulties from a tax point of view. A spouse making such payments is entitled to deduct them from his or her income for tax purposes. In which case the payments become taxable in the hands of the recipient. But in this case both spouses are treated as if they were single individuals — each with only single person's allowances.

Of course, opting for single assessment is an option for all married couples but in the case of couples living together there can be no tax saving as a result and there may be a tax loss. That's because a low earner cannot pass unused standard rate tax band — at 22p in the pound — over to the high earner who may be paying tax at 44p in the pound.

A separated couple may, in some instances, get better tax allowance after separation than they did before because they may both be entitled to single parent's allowance.

That may also be the case with separated spouses but there is a difference. If there is a child or children for which children's allowances are being paid, the spouse looking after the child or children can claim a single parent's allowance. It is sufficient to have looked after the children at some time during the tax year so, in fact, both spouses can get this allowance. It is not available to a couple opting for joint assessment so it can make opting for single assessment worthwhile.

But where there is single assessment, maintenance payments may be subject to tax in the hands of the recipient. They are taxable if the recipient has sufficient income to put her or him into the tax net. This only applies to maintenance payments which are legally enforceable and only to those in respect of a spouse. Payments in respect of children are different. The person making the payment gets no tax relief on the money but it is not taxable in the hands of the recipient.

Unlike the situation of married couples living together it is possible for the joint tax bill of a separated couple to be less under single assessment than it would be under joint assessment.

But that is not always the case. Joint assessment is the option automatically applied to married couples who are living together just as the single assessment option is automatically applied to separated couples who wish to transfer tax liability for maintenance payments. But a separated couple can opt for joint assessment, if they wish.

A husband making maintenance payments may work out that he would be better off foregoing the tax relief on the maintenance payments and getting the full married allowances instead although if he does claim that allowance, it is likely that his wife would lose. But she may not. She would no longer be taxed on the maintenance payment — a gain — although she would lose a single parent allowance if she was getting it.

Whether the gains outweigh the losses depend on each individual case.

But where both spouses are resident in the State and both decide to opt for joint assessment they may do so. The tax allowances are split equally between them, but if one spouse has spare allowances or spare low tax rate bands, they can be transferred to the other spouse. They can, indeed, opt to split allowances in any way they like — and agree between them.

Spouses may split their joint tax allowances between them whatever way they like.

The possibilities are practically endless. But in all cases the joint tax bill of the couple remains the same — all that differs is the split of income between them.

Share incentives

Tax-free profit sharing

It is possible to get up to £10,000 of your income tax free each year through an approved profit sharing scheme.

PAYE workers have few opportunities of getting tax-free income. Wages are automatically taxed and the tax definition of wages is wide. It includes practically all monies paid by an employer to an employee. Most non-cash benefits are taxable too. They are treated as benefits-in-kind and their cash value is liable to income tax. Examples are company cars and loans at preferential interest rates.

But there are some benefits that can be provided tax free by an employer. They include subsidised canteen meals and sporting facilities that are available to all employees, childcare facilities, and certain bonus payments paid under an approved profits sharing scheme. Most of those need to be negotiated by the work-force as a whole — the benefit is not confined to any one individual. But that is not the case with profit-sharing schemes.

Profit sharing is often advocated as a means of improving industrial relations in a firm. Workers who are going to benefit directly from the increased profitability of a company are likely to be more productive than those who are not.

Incomes can be linked to profits by way of straight forward cash bonuses. But cash bonuses are liable for tax in the same way as wages and that reduces the incentive somewhat.

But if the bonuses are given in the form of company shares and the value does not exceed £10,000 a year no tax liability arises provided certain other conditions are met. This is a benefit-in-kind which is not taxable.

To be attractive, of course, the company should be quoted on the stock exchange so that the shares can be readily sold at some stage in the future. But they do have to be held for three years and for at least two years of that they must be held by trustees. After the two years they can be passed on to individual workers and may be sold although there is some claw back of the tax concession.

The rules of the scheme must apply equally to all workers. The level of bonuses may be related to salary or years of service or both but those are the only criteria which can be used. Blue-eyed boys or green-eyed girls cannot get special treatment.

Whatever benefit employers get from operating profit sharing schemes must be doubled when the bonus comes in the form of shares. The total amount to be given out in shares may be linked in some way to profitability or productivity in the same way as any other bonus scheme. A worker may by preference take the bonus in the form of cash. But in that case it is taxable. Those who take it in the form of shares get it tax free so long as they hold the shares for three years.

During those three years, and subsequently if they hold onto the shares, the workers have a direct interest in the performance of those shares on the stock exchange. So the employer has built in an initial incentive of a bonus scheme and an ongoing incentive in the form of share ownership.

Obviously this type of profit sharing scheme is of particular interest in companies whose shares are listed on the stock exchange although many of those schemes are, in fact, operated by firms whose shares are quoted abroad rather than in Dublin. Even before the ending of exchange controls on investment abroad, the Central Bank granted exemptions to such schemes.

Unfortunately this profit sharing tax concession really requires the company's shares to be marketable.

More popular of course, than the profit sharing scheme, are share option schemes that are usually associated with top executives although the 1999 Finance Act provides some incentives for their extension to all employees in companies with marketable shares.

SAYE

Save As You Earn (SAYE) schemes have been operated in Ireland for some years mainly by British companies. The 1999 Finance Act provided a formal framework for their operations providing some tax concessions where workers are given options to buy shares at a discounted price and the money needed to eventually exercise the options is saved over a three or five year period.

That may sound a bit complicated but it isn't. It works like this. The workers are given options to buy shares in the company at a fixed price. That price can be up to 25 per cent below the current value of the shares. Those options can be exercised in three, five, or seven years time when, hopefully, the shares will be worth a lot more than the price fixed at the time that the option was given. If the shares haven't risen in price, then there is no need to exercise the option. So there is no chance of incurring a loss.

As an adjunct to the share options the workers involved agree to save a fixed amount each week or month out of their pay packages. That money comes out of their net pay i.e. after tax, and goes into a special fund. The only tax concession on the savings part of the deal is that the money in the fund grows tax-free – any interest or bonus earned is free of income tax and DIRT.

Similar schemes have been in operation in Britain since 1972. They got an extra boost there in 1980 when new legislation was introduced as part of Margaret Thatcher's policy of spreading share ownership as widely as possible.

SAYE schemes are obviously less attractive to workers than the bonus type scheme where up to £10,000 worth of shares a year can be given tax-free. Under the SAYE scheme the shares have to be paid for albeit at what may be a bargain basement price. But they are likely to be more favoured by employers for the very reason that the shares aren't entirely free. The company should also benefit from a more motivated and involved workforce. To get Revenue approval schemes must comply with a number of requirements.

- All workers with more than a minimum service must be invited to participate. Workers with more than three years service can't be excluded.

- The same rules must apply to all but they may provide for the level of share option granted to vary according to pay levels and/or length of service.

- The workers must contract to save at least £10 and at most £250 a month over a three or five-year period. The actual amount saved should be geared to provide about the right amount to pay for the shares when the options are exercised.

No income tax is payable either when the option is granted or when the shares are actually purchased. That might not seem like a concession at all but remember that the worker will be getting shares worth more than the price paid. That's a benefit he's getting from his employer. Normally the difference between the price paid for the shares and their actual value would be treated as a benefit in kind and taxed as such.

Let's take an example.

Suppose the worker has an option to buy 1,000 shares at 200p each. That was the price fixed at the time the options were granted. It is now three or five years later and the shares have trebled in value to 600p. In exercising his option the worker will be paying £2,000 for the 1,000 shares that are now worth £6,000 on the stock market. He'll be making £4,000 on the deal. And that's tax free since it is not considered to be a benefit-in-kind.

But although there is no income tax liability the worker may be liable for Capital Gains tax when the shares are sold. The gain is calculated as the difference between the price the shares are sold for and the price actually paid. The first £1,000 of gain in any tax year is exemption and there is also an inflation adjustment. For details of Capital Gains Tax see page 259.

If this worker sold his shares immediately after buying them he would be liable for tax on £3,000. The standard rate of Capital Gains tax is 20 per cent so the tax payable would be £600. Of course if the sale was spread over a number of years the tax could be avoided entirely.

But tax or no tax Save As You Earn schemes effectively allow workers to share in any growth in their company's fortunes without taking any risk themselves. They have to save a regular amount but the savings are kept in a risk-free account and the option to buy the shares doesn't have to be exercised if the share price has gone down.

The Revenue has prepared specimen rules and forms for use in these schemes. Copies can be obtained from your local tax office.

Relief on loans to buy shares

Tax relief can be obtained on loan interest used to buy shares in the company you work for.

There are other ways of getting tax relief on buying shares. Tax relief can be claimed on the interest on loans raised to fund the purchase of shares in the company you work for. You need to be a full time director or employee. In the case of a private company you need only be a part-time director or employee.

But the company cannot be quoted on the stock exchange so the shares cannot be very marketable and that reduces the attractions somewhat. There are also restrictions relating to non-trading companies. But in the case of a private trading company there is no upper limit on the relief which may be obtained on loans used to buy shares in it. In the case of a non-private company, there is an upper limit of £3,000 in tax relief per individual. This limit is in addition to any tax relief on mortgage interest.

Business Expansion Scheme

There is another share incentive scheme — the Business Expansion Scheme — which allows tax relief on up to £25,000 used to buy shares in certain qualified companies. In general such companies are those manufacturing, and internationally traded service companies, which are entitled to the concessionary 10 per cent Corporation Tax.

The concession is also available on money invested in certain tourism ventures aimed at bringing tourists from abroad. While investments in hotels, guest-houses, and self-catering accommodation are excluded, that still leaves a wide range of possibilities.

The concession was extended to the music industry in 1996 for projects involving the production, marketing and promotion of new artist's studio recordings and associated videos.

It is a generous tax concession but you do need to take care. You have three options. You can:

- Invest in a fund which will in turn invest your money in a number of BES projects thereby spreading the risk;

- Invest in a single project at arms length;

- Invest in your own project in which you will take a management interest.

The second option is obviously the most risky. The shares you buy, either directly or through an investment fund, cannot be quoted on any stock exchange. So you have no easy way of judging exactly what they are worth. There is no market price. Neither will you have any great idea of the ventures' future prospects. And, most importantly, you may have no guarantee that you will be able to dispose of the shares in the future.

You may get some basic accounts, or you may not. Either way you will not be able to do the type of detailed analysis necessary to really value the shares or to evaluate the prospects of the venture during the five years for which you have to hold the shares if the tax relief is not to be clawed back.

But the tax concession is generous. The trick is to reduce the risk as much as possible. The ideal way is to opt for one of the

There is a wiser way to invest in shares.

We all want to make the most of our money. And wiser investors will know that shares have out performed all other long term investments.

The only problem is knowing just which shares to invest in. That's where Scope comes in. Scope is a new product for anyone who wants to invest in shares.

Scope is a package of five easy to understand investment options. We help you choose which option is right for you, and we do all the rest.

To find out more about Scope, talk to your broker, ask your Irish Life Financial Adviser, call into any Irish Permanent branch or freephone 1800 400 500 for a copy of our brochure.

It's the wiser way to make your money work harder.

Shares made simple
Tel: 1850-30-60-90

Irish Life

BES funds which allow for the investment to be spread over a number of different ventures and relying on reliable fund managers to value the initial shares that they buy.

But remember that promoters usually charge a 3 per cent fee up front and may have a conflict of interest in so far as they may also collect fees from the companies in which they invest. Also not all funds have guaranteed exit mechanisms. Be wary of any fund that doesn't.

Let's have a look at the detail.

The BES concession is aimed at encouraging risk investment in small to medium sized ventures in manufacturing, traded services, and certain tourism and music projects. Traded services are ventures which have to compete in the international market place.

The investor buys shares in the venture and gets full tax relief on that investment. So for every £1 put in, a top tax payer gets a tax rebate of 44p. But the shares have to be held for at least five years. Normally there is an exit mechanism put in place to guarantee that there is someone there to buy the shares at the end of the five years. There should also be some agreed process for valuing the shares at that stage.

Guarantees are no longer allowed. Investors have to accept a risk. But provided the shares are really worth whatever is paid for them initially, the tax relief provides a sizeable cushion against loss.

Someone buying shares worth £10,000 at a real cost, after tax relief, of £5,600 will be doing alright if he or she can sell those shares at the initial £10,000 at the end of the five years. A real initial investment of £5,600 will have grown to £10,000 over five years. That is a compound return of just over 11.5 per cent a year after allowing for an initial set-up commission of 3 per cent.

As well as the initial commission there is another initial cost in that it may take up to a year to get the tax rebate. The investor in our example has to put up the £10,000 and has to wait to get the £4,400 rebate or reduction in his or her tax bill. So there is a loss of interest on that money.

In any arms length BES investment make sure there is an exit mechanism and that you are getting initial value.

Rest on our laurels.

We don't use them.

In a recent independent survey carried out on behalf of the Irish Times, New Ireland's Unit-Linked Personal Pension Funds handsomely outperformed the field over 10, 15 and 20 years. For example, over 20 years our Personal Pension outperformed the nearest competitor by 29%. However, despite our recent success we are resisting the temptation to feel smug. Because at New Ireland all feelings of comfort and satisfaction are strictly reserved for our customers. It's their pension, after all.

NEW IRELAND
ASSURANCE

It's a New Ireland, alright.

For more information talk to your pensions adviser or call us on 01 617 2000.

Source: Irish Times Personal Pension Fund Survey 1999.

Note: Past performance is not necessarily a guide to the future. Unit values can fall as well as rise

You can get five years income tax back

Did you ever get that urge to quit your secure job and go out on your own, be your own boss, build your own business. It's a big step, not to be lightly taken, but if you've been working in Ireland there's a little extra incentive to help tip the decision. Leave the job, set up the business and the State will give you an income tax rebate of up to £60,000 to help finance your new venture. But you do have to take up full time work with the new company. It may sound too good to be true but it's not. The incentive is known as the Seed Capital Scheme. How does it work? Let's look at an example.

Tim is in his mid-thirties, a production manager with a multinational company. He's on a very good income and his future is secure enough. Indeed one of the problems is that its a bit too secure, predictable and certain. Tim's need for achievement is not being fully satisfied. He has identified a business opportunity in manufacturing and is confident that he has the skills to make it work. He has access to some capital but could do with a bit more. So how can the Seed Capital Scheme help him.

Basically it can provide him with some capital. The more he can put up himself the easier it is to borrow the rest. He can make a back-claim for tax relief extending over the past five years on up to a maximum of £125,000 invested in the new business. In essence that means that he can get back all of the tax he paid on up to £25,000 of income in each of those years. He has been paying tax at the old top rate of 46p in the pound on the top slice of his income and that top slice has been bigger than £25,000 a year. So his claim is for a rebate of £11,500 (46 per cent of £25,000) for each year — a total of £57,500.

Had he been earning less his rebate might be less. But he's entitled to the maximum of £60,000 provided he invests £125,000 in the business. The income tax rebate doesn't exclude him from benefiting from other State incentives such as grants and employment incentives. Tim's venture is in manufacturing but it could equally well be in a service open to international competition; tourism; a trading operation selling Irish goods abroad; certain shipping ventures; some research and development activities; and even the cultivation of crops in greenhouses.

The basic requirement is that the would-be entrepreneur is setting up a new business having been employed. The incentive isn't available to an existing businessmen moving into a new venture. To ensure that this requirement is met, the condition is that at least three-quarters of the claimant's income has to have come from paid employment and no more than £15,000 of their annual income should have come from other sources. There is nothing to stop a number of people getting together to establish a business and claim tax rebates. The only requirement is that each claimant owns at least 15 per cent of the shares in the venture.

a pension, like most things, gets better

You don't just wake up one morning at the age of thirty and discover you're a number one sports champion. (Some of the most successful pros started playing as toddlers, for goodness sake!) So what? Well, it goes to show that if you give something enough time you'll be surprised at what is possible. The same theory applies with a pension – you won't just wake up at the age of 65 with money for your retirement. Not unless you invest time – and money – in it now. So take a moment out: **call 1850 237 237** or drop in to any of our branches and ask for a copy of our free **Planning Your Pension Guide**.

the earlier you begin

You can reclaim the tax you paid in the last five years to invest in a new venture.

Ideally the investor should spread the risk among a number of ventures by investing in a fund. The shares bought have, by the nature of the scheme, to be in relatively small enterprises. While they have the potential to grow rapidly, they also have the potential to fail miserably. A spread of risk is advisable and that is best secured by investing in a fund. Picking a good fund manager is also important.

If things go well and the return is big enough there may be a liability for Capital Gains Tax but it is the full investment, before tax relief, which is taken into account as the purchase price of the shares. So in our example the purchase price is £10,000 i.e. not the actual post tax relief cost of £5,600. The first £500 of capital gains realised by an individual in any one year is tax-free so providing the net return on the investment does not exceed £10,500 on the initial real investment of £5,600 there would be no liability for Capital Gains Tax on present rules. Indeed a larger tax free gain would be possible given that the initial purchase price is adjusted upwards in line with inflation.

There is an even better use for the BES concession. That is to start your own venture. This is possibly easier in the tourism area than any other. The investment cannot just be in accommodation — that loophole which allowed people to set up tourism ventures comprising houses in Dublin 4 has been closed off. But it still leaves a lot of opportunities, particularly for people in rural areas.

Remember an investment of £100,000 in a venture will only cost £56,000 after tax relief. Spread that over say four investors and the sums involved need not be prohibitive. It is possible to start with a relatively small project. The possibilities are legion. They include the following:

- Caravan and camping sites
- Holiday hostels
- Holiday camps
- Pleasure boat hire
- Horse drawn caravan hire
- Equestrian centre services
- Sailing, yachting, marina services
- Sub-aqua centre services

- Heritage houses, castles, gardens
- Game fishing services
- Chauffeur-drive for tourists
- Outdoor activity centres
- Tourism guide agencies
- Tour coach services

The project must be aimed at attracting tourists from abroad and must have a three year marketing plan approved by Bord Failte. There are upper limits on the amount of the total investment which goes on land and buildings. It is up to 75 per cent in the case of hostels, holiday camps etc.; 70 per cent in the case of caravan and camping sites and equestrian centres; 65 per cent in the case of marina services; and 50 per cent for most other projects.

Further information can be obtained from Bord Failte, Baggot Street Bridge, Dublin, 4. The scheme is ideally suited to individuals or groups who are already paying high amounts of income tax. They can get the project up and running while retaining their jobs but reducing their tax bills.

A variant of the BES scheme, known as the Seed Capital Scheme, allows for tax relief on up to £125,000 invested in a new project. Under this scheme the relief comes by way of a refund of tax previously paid. Someone who has left a job and takes up full-time employment with the new company can claim back the tax they paid over the previous five years. The maximum relief for each year is £ 25,000. See page 294 for details.

Investment in music and films

Tax relief similar to BES relief is available on money invested in certain film projects and music projects. They tend to be relatively high risk and are best suited to those who are actually getting involved in the management of such ventures rather than outside investors. The incentive has been extended for five years from 1999.

In the case of films the project should, at the very least, have an advance sales agreement with the distributor and, of course, have the right people involved — director and performers.

Real independent choice and advice on investing money

If you've money to invest, we have a wide range of options including **PIPS, PEPS, WITH PROFIT BONDS, MANAGED FUNDS and SAVINGS AND INVESTMENT ACCOUNTS.** ACCBank is not a tied agent of any other financial institution. We can offer real choice and helpful advice so that you can make the most of your money.

For your free copy of our 'Savings Matters' brochure call your local ACCBank branch or call us on 1850 721 722

www.accbank.ie   e-mail info@accbank.ie

Covenants and medical expenses

With lengthening life expectancy a growing number of elderly people require nursing care in their later years. It can be costly and the means-tested state subvention is, at best, small enough. But tax relief can ease the burden.

An elderly parent paying for his or her own nursing care in a registered nursing home can claim tax relief on the expense involved. In this context nursing care is considered by the Revenue Commissioners to be a medical expense eligible for tax relief (see page 234). The concession can significantly reduce the real cost of nursing home care. In the case of an individual claim the first £100 each year is disallowed but given the overall cost involved that is small enough.

Tax efficient covenants

That's straight forward enough for an elderly person who has adequate income to pay the costs involved and against which to claim the tax relief. But tax relief is useless to someone not liable for tax and that's often the case with elderly people in this situation. Very often at least some of the cost is borne by family members, usually children. They don't automatically get tax relief but there are ways to successfully claim it.

The easiest is to have the elderly person defined as a dependent relative. That way he or she is considered to be a member of the family for tax purposes. It is then possible to include the nursing home costs and other medical expenses in a family claim for relief. This will only work, however, if the parent's income is no more than £220 above the maximum social welfare pension rate — currently about £5,512.

Provided the parent's income is below that level the child claims him or her as a dependent relative for tax purposes. A number of children can claim the same parent as a dependent. They can each then claim tax relief for any medical expenses they pay for — subject to the first £200 of each family's claim being disallowed.

The other way for children to get tax relief on contributions made to a parent's health care is by making the payments under covenant. The tax relief given on money covenanted to chil-

For most people, their mortgage is the largest and longest lasting financial commitment they will make. It deserves professional protection.

That's where **MortgageMinder** from Hibernian comes in.

MortgageMinder offers you the security of heavyweight mortgage protection and repayment cover at a price that won't leave you flat on your back.

For more information call your broker, contact your local Hibernian branch or phone Hibernian on (01) 607 8715.

You're safe in the hands of

HIBERNIAN

www.hibernian.ie

Sample wording for a covenant

I ....(name) of ....(address) covenant to pay my father/mother ....(name) of ....(address) an amount which after the deduction of standard rate tax amounts to £...........(sum) each year for seven years or during our joint lives or until (name of third party) says the covenant should end the first payment to be made during March 2000.

Signed, sealed and delivered by ....(name) in the present of ....(witness's name, address and occupation)

...............(Date)

dren over eighteen years of age was finally phased out in April of last year. But there is still tax relief on covenants in favour of permanently incapacitated people or in favour of anyone over 65 years of age.

A covenant is simply a legal undertaking to make payments to someone else. In order to qualify for tax relief the payments must be capable of lasting for at least six years. It is usual to make a covenant for seven years. The giver must be a taxpayer and the recipient should ideally not be liable for income tax at all. There can be some benefit where the giver pays tax at 44p and the recipient pays tax at 22p but it is limited.

In the case we're considering the recipient is a parent who is incurring heavy medical or nursing home costs. The parent can claim tax relief on such costs – in effect they provide an additional tax allowance which can very easily push him or her out

In a society that's genuinely mutual, everyone gains.

Like many animals the gazelle truly appreciate the notion of safety in numbers. The sheer number of the herd and speed of the group in flight, ensure that they thrive.

EBS works on similar principles. EBS is owned by its customers, and run for their benefit. This means a higher return on savings and lower mortgage rates, particularly over the long term. That's what being a member of a mutual building society is all about.

Passing value back to the customer - and only the customer. Like the gazelle, we work as a group. So, whether you're saving, investing or buying a home, you're better off in the long run with EBS.

To find out more about how you can benefit by doing business with EBS, drop into your local EBS office or call <<EBS*DIRECT*>> on **1850 654321.**

EBS
BUILDING SOCIETY

You're better off in the long run.

Chief Office: P.O. Box 76, 30/34 Westmoreland Street, Dublin 2. www.ebs.ie

of the tax net. So the parent has unused tax allowances while the child is paying tax, let us suppose, at 44p in the pound.

Let's see how a covenant might work. The child is restricted to covenanting no more than 5 per cent of annual income. Let's take the case of a son wanting to contribute £1,000 a year towards the cost of nursing home care for his mother. Other brothers and sisters could, of course, do the same thing.

The son makes out a covenant – a sample wording is given on the previous page — and pays £780 to the parent. The parent gets the other £220 by way of a tax rebate while the son also gets an additional tax relief of £220. The cost to the son is only £560 while his mother gets the benefit of £1,000 towards the nursing home costs.

The logic behind this is relatively simple although you do not have to understand it to benefit. Because the son has entered into a legal undertaking to pass the money to his mother, the taxman considers the £1,000 to be hers rather than his. But he has already paid £440 tax on the £1,000. That tax is returned. The mechanics of the process dictate that £220 goes back to the son and £220 to the mother.

Points to watch:

Covenants may provide no saving if a parent is in receipt of some means-tested benefit since the covenanted income will be treated as means.

The covenant should include a clause allowing it to be ended on the say so of a third party e.g. a trusted friend. This is just a precaution. A covenant can always be ended by the mutual consent of the parties but circumstances could arise where it is desirable to end it for one reason or another and the mutual consent cannot be obtained. For instance the covenant could, in some circumstances, prevent the parent from claiming some means tested benefit.

How to go about it

The covenant can be drawn up using the wording in the accompanying panel. You don't need a solicitor. You can get the wording typed out or even write it out filling in the blanks as appropriate.

The person making the covenant should also get a tax form R185 from his or her local tax office. It is a single page requir-

Current Account ✚

DO YOU KNOW EXACTLY WHAT YOU'RE GETTING?

WITH CURRENT ACCOUNT PLUS YOU DO.

Sometimes things aren't always what they're cracked up to be. That's where new Current Account Plus from TSB Bank is different. Because Current Account Plus is a complete banking package that gives you everything you need. This is exactly what you get:

- A Cheque Book
- A '3 in 1' card - that's a Cashcard, a Laser Card and a Cheque Guarantee Card all in one, and, for added security, your photograph and signature is laser-etched onto your card
- Access to over 1,500 ATMs
- Very competitive charges that are easy to understand and when you avail of other TSB Bank services you may qualify for discounts!
- Written notification of any charges and interest sent to you before they are applied to your account
- Overdraft facilities
- Standing Order & Direct Debit facilities

So go on call into TSB Bank today and open a new Current Account Plus - it's the easier way to manage your money. For further information phone 1850 21 11 11 or see our website at www.tsb.ie.

TSB BANK

We want what's best for you.

ing very little information such as RSI number and place of employment or source of income. That completed form together with the signed covenant and, of course, the money is given to the parent.

The parent can get a tax reclaim form from a local tax office or by phoning the special Revenue Commissioner's 24 hour phone number at (01) 8780100. The claim form together with copies of the covenant, form R185 and some evidence of the payment being made (a photocopy of the cheque or of the bankbook into which the money went) is returned to the tax office.

Appendices

Appendix 1: Tax rates

INCOME TAX

Rates

SINGLE			MARRIED		
1995/96					
First £8,900	27%		First £17,800	27%	
Balance	48%		Balance	48%	
1996/97					
First £9,400	27%		First £18,800	27%	
Balance	48%		Balance	48%	
1997/98					
First £9,900	26%		First £19,800	26%	
Balance	48%		Balance	48%	
1998/99					
First £10,000	24%		First £20,000	24%	
Balance	46%		Balance	46%	
1999/2000					
First £14,000	24%		First £28,000	24%	
Balance	46%		Balance	46%	

2000/2001

SINGLE		MARRIED (one income)	
First £17,000	22%	First £28,000	22%
Balance	44%	Balance	44%
SINGLE PARENT		**MARRIED (two income)**	
First £20,150	22%	First £34,000	22%
Balance	44%	Balance	44%

WALL
DRILLED WITH
LASER

Those of you with a penchant for DIY will appreciate the importance of having the right tools. Laser is so simple to use that it's bang on for every job. Laser also cuts down on the need to carry cash. Which is particularly handy if you can't find a hole in the wall.

Your Bank or Building Society has all the details.

The better way to pay.

Basic allowances –

all standard rated in 2000/2001 except where noted

	1996/97	1997/98	1998/99	1999/00	2000/2001
Personal:					
— Single	£2,650	£2,900	£3,150	£4,200[1]	£4,700
— Married	£5,300	£5,800	£6,300	£8,400[1]	£9,400
Widowed allowance	£3,150	£3,400	£3,650	£3,150)	£4,700
Widowed additional allowance	—	—	—	+£500[1])	£1,000
PAYE	£800	£800	£800	£1000[1]	£1,000
Home working spouse's allowance:	—	—	—	—	£3,000
Age allowance:					
— Single	£200	£400	£400	£400	£800
— Married	£400	£800	£800	£800	£1,600
Incapacitated Child	£700	£700	£800	£800	£1,600
Dependent Relative	£110	£110	£110	£110	£220
Blind Person	£700	£700	£1,000	£1,500	£3,000
Employee caring for incapacitated person	£7,500	£7,500	£8,500	£8,500	£8,500[4]
Single Parent					
—Widowed	£2,150	£2,400	£2,650	£2,650)	£4,700
	—	—	—	+ £1,050[1])	
—Other	£2,650	£2,900	£3,150	£3,150)	£4,700
	—	—	—	+£1,050[1])	
Widow/'er in year after bereavement	£1,500[2]	£1,500[2]	£5,000[3]	£5,000[3]	£10,000[5]

[1] Standard rated. [2] £1,000 in second year and £500 in third year. [3] £4,000 in second year, £3,000 in third year, £2,000 in fourth year, and finally £1,000 in fifth year. [4] Not standard rated. [5] £8,000 in second year, £6,000 in third year, £4,000 in fourth year and £2,000 in fifth year.

an agent of TSB Bank

Fresh thinking — New banking

Call our Telephone Banking now
1850 200 808

Note that other than acting as a deposit agent, it is not within any terms of authorisation as defined in the Investment Intermediaries Act 1995, to accept cash, other funds or securities on behalf of clients or to act on a discretionary basis in the management of client funds.

Open now in Superquinn

Exemption limits

Persons with low incomes are granted complete exemption from income tax. The limits are as follows:

	1996/97	1997/98	1998/99	1999/2000	2000/2001
Single or widowed	£3,900	£4,000	£4,100	£4,100	£4,100
Married	£7,800	£8,000	£8,200	£8,200	£8,200
Single/w'ed over 65	£4,500	£4,600	£5,000	£6,500	£7,500
Married over 65	£9,000	£9,200	£10,000	£13,000	£15,000
Single/w'ed over 75	£5,100	£5,200	£5,500	£6,500	£7,500
Married over 75	£10,200	£10,400	£11,000	£13,000	£15,000

Since 1994/95 the limits are increased by £450 for the first and second child and by £650 for each subsequent child. So for a married couple under 65 with two dependent children the threshold is £9,100 i.e. the basic £8,200 plus twice £450. Persons earning more than these exemption limits are entitled to marginal relief paying tax on the amount over the threshold at 40p in the pound.

PRSI and levy

PRSI rates (including the health levy) for 2000/2001 for most private sector and State employees are as follows:

	Private Sector	State Sector	Self Employed
First £26,500 (£25,400 in 99/00)	6.5%	3.15%	7%
Remainder	2%	2%	2%

No PRSI is payable on the first £100 weekly for the private sector; £20 weekly for the public sector; and on an annual £1,040 for the self-employed. Those earning less than £226 in any week are exempt from the 2 per cent health levies. Also exempt from the levy are self-employed people with incomes under £11,752.

Loans for a lot more...for a lot less.

Pulling together funds for those certain extras can sometimes be a bit of a struggle. So it's nice to know you can join a movement renowned for lending a helping hand - a movement owned by its members, for the benefit of its members. We're your credit union. If you need a loan for a car... for home improvements... help with education costs... or simply a well-deserved break - we can help make it happen.

Likewise, if you want a most attractive return on your savings, it's at hand.

Savings & loans

As a member, you could be entitled to low cost loans[†] - not more than 1% per month on the reducing balance. That's just 12.6% APR. You'll also find our loans often have built in life assurance[*] for extra peace of mind.

CREDIT UNION

What's more, you'll be happy to hear that individual extras - such as transaction charges - simply don't exist when you save or borrow with us. So talk to us today. And put some of your finances in much friendlier hands.

Many hands working together

Irish League of Credit Unions, 33-41 Lower Mount Street, Dublin, 2 Tel: (01) 6146700 Fax (01)6146701

CAPITAL ACQUISITIONS TAX
Threshold Levels

Relationship to donor	1997	1998	1999	From 1/12/99
Child, or the minor child of a deceased child. Also from child to parent but only for inheritance tax	£185,550	£188,400	£192,900	£300,000
Brother, sister, child of brother or sister or lineal descendant other than a child, or the minor child of a deceased child	£24,740	£25,120	£25,720	£30,000
If none of the above	£12,370	£12,560	£12,860	£15,000

From December 1, 1999 there is a single tax rate of 20 per cent. The distinction between gifts and inheritances was also removed from that date. Prior to that the rates were as follows:

Amount	Rate
Up to threshold	nil
Next £10,000	20%
Next £30,000	30%
Balance	40%

There are major concessions for agriculture land passing to a farmer; for business assets, and for businesses or farms passing to a nephew or niece who has worked on the farm or in the business for at least five years. Since December 1999 family homes are exempt from the tax subject to certain conditions— see page 276.

Probate Tax

A probate tax of 2% is levied on the estates of individuals who died after June 18, 1993. Where the deceased was domiciled in the State the tax applies to the net assets i.e. assets less debts, both inside and outside the State subject to certain exemptions. Where the deceased was domiciled outside the State, only the net assets situated in the State are liable for the tax. Estates worth less than £40,000 are exempt since December 1, 1999. Previously the threshold was £10,980. Transfers between spouses are exempt. The valuation of farm land is reduced by 30% of its market value. Property held jointly at the time of death is exempt from the tax if it automatically passes to the survivor without the need for probate. Superannuation benefits are also exempt as is certain heritage property and property passing to charities. Tax not paid within nine months of the death is liable to interest at 1 per cent per month.

A Permanent Answer To All
Your Financial Needs...

Irish Permanent can help you with many aspects of your finances thanks to a wide range of mortgage, investment and banking products:

- **Mortgages** with no application fee and no legal fee payable to Irish Permanent.*

- **Bureau de Change** with very competitive rates.

- **Interest paying Current Accounts**.

- **ATM Accounts** for instant access.

- **Visa Card** with up to 56 days free credit.†

- **Savings and Investments** - a range of competitive products to choose from.

- **Car Finance** designed to put you in the driving seat.◆

- **Personal Loans** for just about everything you need.◆

- **Life and Pension** products for a more secure future.

- **Commercial Property Loans** designed to get you up and running faster.*

*To find out how we can help you,
call to your local Irish Permanent branch.*

www.irishpermanent.ie

CAPITAL GAINS TAX

The first £1,000 of gains made by an individual (£2,000 for a married couple) in any one tax year are exempt from the tax. The exemption was double that prior to April 1992. The indexation relief (see below) does not apply to development land. Inflation is taken into account in calculating taxable gains. For tax purposes the acquisition price of the asset is multiplied by an index number which adjusts it for inflation in the intervening period. The index numbers are as follows:

Assets bought in	And sold during						
	1993/94	1994/95	1995/96	1996/97	1997/98	1998/99	1999/00
1974/75	5.656	5.754	5.899	6.017	6.112	6.215	6.313
1975/76	4.568	4.647	4.764	4.860	4.936	5.020	5.099
1976/77	3.935	4.003	4.104	4.187	4.253	4.325	4.393
1977/78	3.373	3.432	3.518	3.589	3.646	3.707	3.766
1978/79	3.117	3.171	3.250	3.316	3.368	3.425	3.479
1979/80	2.812	2.861	2.933	2.992	3.039	3.090	3.139
1980/81	2.434	2.477	2.539	2.590	2.631	2.675	2.718
1981/82	2.012	2.047	2.099	2.141	2.174	2.211	2.246
1982/83	1.693	1.722	1.765	1.801	1.829	1.860	1.890
1983/84	1.505	1.531	1.570	1.601	1.627	1.654	1.680
1984/85	1.366	1.390	1.425	1.454	1.477	1.502	1.525
1985/86	1.287	1.309	1.342	1.369	1.390	1.414	1.436
1986/87	1.230	1.252	1.283	1.309	1.330	1.352	1.373
1987/88	1.190	1.210	1.241	1.266	1.285	1.307	1.328
1988/89	1.167	1.187	1.217	1.242	1.261	1.282	1.303
1989/90	1.130	1.149	1.178	1.202	1.221	1.241	1.261
1990/91	1.084	1.102	1.130	1.153	1.171	1.191	1.210
1991/92	1.056	1.075	1.102	1.124	1.142	1.161	1.179
1992/93	1.019	1.037	1.063	1.084	1.101	1.120	1.138
1993/94	—	1.018	1.043	1.064	1.081	1.099	1.117
1994/95	—	—	1.026	1.046	1.063	1.081	1.098
1995/96	—	—	—	1.021	1.037	1.054	1.071
1996/97	—	—	—	—	1.016	1.033	1.050
1997/98	—	—	—	—	—	1.017	1.033
1998/99	—	—	—	—	—	—	1.016

TAKE CARE OF THE THINGS YOU VALUE

Appendix 2: Motoring

Civil Service Milage

Milage allowances applicable to civil servants.

Official annual milage	Under 1138cc	1139cc to 1387cc	1388cc and over
Up to 2,000	49.87p	57.70p	66.50p
2,001 to 4,000	54.98p	62.98p	72.50p
4,001 to 6,000	29.44p	33.38p	38.04p
6,001 to 8,000	27.74p	31.35p	35.69p
8,001 to 12,000	24.33p	27.30p	30.98p
Over 12,001	20.92p	23.25p	26.27p

The Revenue will accept the following simplified schedule of milage rates based on the above:

Official annual milage	Under 1138cc	1139cc to 1387cc	1388cc and over
Up to 12,000	36p	40p	47p
Over 12,000	21p	24p	27p

Motoring Benefit-in-kind

The value of the benefit-in-kind assessed for tax is reduced as follows as the business milage in the tax year increases. The percentage of the full charge assessed is as follows. From 1996 a 20 per cent reduction is granted where the person supplied with the car spends at least 70 per cent of his or her time away from the place of work and does at least 5,000 business miles in a year.

Business miles

15,001 to 16,000	97.5%	16,001 to 17,000	95%
17,001 to 18,000	90%	18,001 to 19,000	85%
19,001 to 20,000	80%	20,001 to 21,000	75%
21,001 to 22,000	70%	22,001 to 23,000	65%
23,001 to 24,000	60%	24,001 to 25,000	55%
25,001 to 26,000	50%	26,001 to 27,000	45%
27,001 to 28,000	40%	28,001 to 29,000	35%
29,001 to 30,000	30%	over 31,000	5%

THERE'S SURPRISINGLY LITTLE INTEREST IN OUR CREDIT CARD.
12.9% TO BE PRECISE.

If you pay interest regularly on your credit card or use your credit card in the same way as an overdraft then the AIB Low Interest MasterCard should be of considerable interest to you.

It has a low APR of only 12.9% which is not just a short-term introductory offer.

Plus, there's no annual fee on this card in the first year or thereafter if you use your card 50 times or more in the preceding year.

Why pay more than you have to on your credit card? To pay less simply call our 24-hour AIB Credit Card Hotline on (01) 6685500. e-mail: credcard@aib.ie or visit any AIB branch.

There is no interest free credit period on this card. All credit cards are subject to an annual £15 government tax.

Road Tax On Private Cars

Category (engine cc)	Annual	Half year	Quarterly
Up to 1,000cc	£98	£55	£28
1,001 to 1,100cc	**£146**	**£82**	**£42**
1,101 to 1,200cc	£160	£90	£46
1,201 to 1,300cc	**£173**	**£97**	**£50**
1,301 to 1,400cc	£186	£105	£54
1,401 to 1,500cc	**£200**	**£112**	**£57**
1,501 to 1,600cc	£247	£139	£71
1,601 to 1,700cc	**£262**	**£147**	**£75**
1,701 to 1,800cc	£306	£172	£88
1,801 to 1,900cc	**£323**	**£181**	**£93**
1,901 to 2,000cc	£340	£191	£97
2,001 to 2,100cc	**£435**	**£244**	**£124**
2,101 to 2,200cc	£456	£256	£130
2,201 to 2,300cc	**£477**	**£268**	**£136**
2,301 to 2,400cc	£497	£279	£142
2,401 to 2,500cc	**£518**	**£291**	**£148**
2,501 to 2,600cc	£607	£341	£173
2,601 to 2,700cc	**£631**	**£354**	**£180**
2,701 to 2,800cc	£654	£367	£186
2,801 to 2,900cc	**£677**	**£380**	**£193**
2,901 to 3,000cc	£701	£393	£200
3,001cc or over	**£849**	**£477**	**£242**

Road Tax On Tractors

Agriculture	£45
General haulage	£128

Road Tax On Motorcycles

All motorcycles	£22

Veteran & Vintage

Motorcycles	£12
All other vehicles	£27

First Registration Charges

Motorcycles	£22
Private cars	
—not exceeding 2000cc	£20
—exceeding 2000cc	£40
Other	£40

Taxis and Hackneys — same as private cars

"Flexible savings and investments give us great freedom."

Lump Sum Investments

Regular Savings Accounts

Prize Bonds

Choose from the range
of Savings and Investment
options from your
local Post Office.

Helping you do more

FreeFone 1800 30 50 60
or call into your Post Office

Appendix 3:

SOCIAL INSURANCE
Maximum rates of benefit

	PRESENT RATE	NEW June '00
Retirement/Old Age Contributory Pension		
Under 80		
—Personal rate	£89.00	£96.00
—Person with qualified adult under 66	£144.50	£156.20
—Person with adult over 66	£148.90	£160.60
80 or over		
—Personal rate	£94.00	£101.00
—Person with qualified adult under 66	£149.50	£161.20
—Person with qualified adult over 66	£153.90	£165.60
Widow's/Widower's Contributory Pension		
—Under 66	£77.10	£81.10
—66 and under 80	£82.10	£89.10
—80 or over	£87.10	£94.10
Invalidity Pension		
Personal rate under 65	£75.20	£79.20
Personal rate 65 to 80	£89.00	£96.00
Personal rate 80 or over	£94.00	£101.00
Person under 65 with qualified adult	£124.70	£132.50
Person 65 to 80 with qualified adult	£138.50	£149.30
Person over 80 with qualified adult	£143.50	£154.30
Unemployment/Sickness Benefit		
Personal rate	£73.50	£77.50
Person with qualified adult	£116.70	£124.50
Orphan's Contributory Allowance	£51.60	£55.60
Payments for child dependants **widow's/widower's**		
—each qualified child	£17.00	£17.00
Old age and retirement pensioners		
—Each child	£15.20	£15.20
Disability pensioners		
—Each child	£15.20	£15.20
Unemployment/sickness benefit		
—Each qualified child	£13.20	£13.20

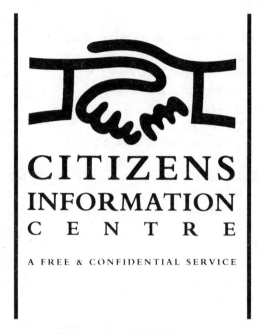

CITIZENS
INFORMATION
C E N T R E

A FREE & CONFIDENTIAL SERVICE

What do *YOU* know?

About Income Tax? Social Insurance?
Health Entitlements?
Farm Grants and Subsidies?
Education? Social Welfare Pensions?
E.C. Entitlements?
etc.

What you don't know, you can find out.
Use your Local Citizens Information Centre
(see Golden Pages and Independent Directory for details)

There is a network of over 80 Citizens Information centres operating
nationwide, offering a free and confidential information service.
They are supported by the National Social Services Board.

SOCIAL ASSISTANCE

Maximum weekly rates of social assistance

BENEFIT	PRESENT RATE	NEW June '00
Old Age Non-Contributory Pension		
Under 80		
—Personal rate	£78.50	£85.50
—Person with qualified adult	£122.70	£137.20
80 or over		
—Personal rate	£83.50	£90.50
—Person with qualified adult	£127.70	£142.20
Widow's/Widower's non-contributory pension		
—Under 66	£73.50	£77.50
—66 and under 80	£78.50	£85.50
—80 or over	£83.50	£90.50
Disability allowance		
Personal rate	£73.50	£77.50
Person with qualified adult	£116.70	£124.50
Unemployment Assistance (short-term)		
Personal rate	£72.00	£76.00
Person with qualified adult	£115.20	£123.00
Unemployment Assistance (long-term)		
Personal rate	£73.50	£77.50
Person with qualified adult	£116.70	£124.50
One-parent family payment (*including one child*)		
–under 66	£88.70	£92.70
–66 years and over	£93.70	£100.70
Carer's Allowance		
Under 66	£76.50	£80.50
66 years and over	£81.50	£88.50
Increases for child dependents		
Lone Parents	£15.20	£15.20
Others	£13.20	£13.20

Child Benefit

	PRESENT RATE	NEW June '00
For first and second child	£34.50	£42.50[1]
For third child onwards	£46.00	£56.00

[1.] *From September 2000*

Applying for a Social Welfare Payment?

Don't lose out

A P P L Y   O N   T I M E

Don't get left behind...!

If you become **unemployed...**

You don't need to have your P45 straight away. You can call to your Social Welfare Local Office and apply for an unemployment payment on the first day that you become unemployed.

If you become **ill...**

Don't delay! You can pick up a claim form for Disability Benefit from your doctor.

If you are **retiring from work...**

at age 65 you should claim a Retirement Pension 3 months before your 65th birthday

or

at age 66 you should claim an Old Age (Contributory) Pension 3 months before your 66th birthday so that your claim can be decided on time. (You may if you wish continue to work and get Old Age (Contributory) Pension at the same time.)

If you have ever worked abroad you should apply for your pension at least six months in advance to avoid delays.

N E E D   M O R E   I N F O R M A T I O N ?

Call to your Social Welfare Local Office or contact the information Service, Department of Social, Community & Family Affairs, Store St., Dublin 1. Ph: 01 874 8444

Information is also available on the internet at **www.dscfa.ie** and on AERTEL.

The Department of Social, Community and Family Affairs

Index